The Open Source Alternative

The Open Source Alternative:

Understanding Risks and Leveraging Opportunities

HEATHER J. MEEKER

WILEY

John Wiley & Sons, Inc.

For general information on our other products and services, or technical support, please contact our Customer Care Department within the United States at 800-762-2974, outside the United States at 317-572-3993 or fax 317-572-4002.

Wiley also publishes its books in a variety of electronic formats. Some content that appears in print may not be available in electronic books.

For more information about Wiley products, visit our web site at http://www.wiley.com.

Library of Congress Cataloging-in-Publication Data:

Meeker, Heather J., 1959-
    The open source alternative : understanding risks and leveraging opportunities / Heather J. Meeker.
       p.   cm.
  Includes index.
       ISBN 978-0-470-19495-9 (cloth)
       1. Open source software—Law and legislation.   2. Computer programs—Patents.   3. Copyright—Computer programs.   4. Computer software industry—Licenses.   5. Free computer software—Law and legislation.   I. Title.
    K1519.C6M44   2008
    346.04'8—dc22

                                                                                        2007034466

Printed in the United States of America

10 9 8 7 6 5 4 3 2 1

Contents

Preface

In the late 1990s, working as a lawyer in a technology licensing practice, I found more and more of my clients using software provided under a very unusual license. My colleagues at the time advised clients to avoid this kind of software, because although this software was free of charge, it was likely to infringe intellectual property rights and so the risk of using it was too high. Clients, however, presented with tempting morsels of ready-to-use, tested, free software, and pressed by product release deadlines, do not tend to follow that kind of advice. So, by necessity, I began learning about this kind of free software. I had to advise clients about how to use that software, while managing rather than eliminating the risks. This is how I was thrown into the swimming pool of open source.

This book is the result of some 10 years working on open source legal issues. It is intended to be a practical guide for lawyers and businesspersons who wish to understand the legal issues surrounding open source software licensing. The law of open source is complex and constantly changing. Those called upon to make decisions about open source will find little to guide them in traditional legal materials. There is virtually no case law on many crucial open source legal issues, and the relevant copyright statutes have barely begun to account for computer software itself, much less open source.

Because this book is intended to inform both lawyers and businesspersons, it goes into only moderate detail about both legal and technical principles. There is plenty of in-depth material available on legal principles and software technology, and I have included some references to them for those who want to investigate further. The explanations of legal and technical principles in this book are intended to provide a quick summary for those readers who are not familiar with them, and a refresher for those who are.

I have often heard advocates claim that open source will kill proprietary software, or vice versa, yet it is now plain that neither will annihilate the other any time soon. Open source and proprietary software are likely to coexist for decades to come. My hope is that this book will help you better understand the legal principles at work in the heterogeneous software landscape of today.

How to Use this Book

This book is for businesspeople, technicians, and lawyers who want to understand more about the risks and rewards of open source. The first part of this book is for everyone. The second part is for lawyers, or for others who want to find out more about the legal intricacies of open source. At the end there is a glossary, an index, and a collection of documents and forms to help you in your business.

I encourage those readers who are not lawyers to read the section for lawyers, if only to understand the complexity of the legal issues involved. That section contains more legal terminology and assumes more understanding about legal principles, but it should be accessible to non-lawyers as well.

A Note on Terminology

There is a glossary at the end of this book, but a few terms must be noted at the outset. Taxonomy is always one of the gating items in writing about open source. I have chosen terms that I hope will preserve a neutral point of view. So, in this book, the following terms have the following meanings:

"Hereditary" describes a license with so-called "viral" or "copyleft" terms, sometimes called a "free software" license. It refers to licenses such as GPL, LGPL, MPL, and CDDL. This term is not in common usage.

"Permissive" describes a so-called "non-viral" license, like BSD, MIT, or Apache. This term is in relatively common usage.

"Open source" describes any license that fits the Open Source Definition. It includes both permissive and hereditary licenses. This term is in nearly ubiquitous usage.

"Proprietary" describes a license that restricts distribution or use to object code. This term is in nearly ubiquitous usage in the open source community, and so I bow to convention in using it, even though I consider it misleading. Of course, open source is just as proprietary as "proprietary" software, because neither's copyright interests have been abandoned. The only truly nonproprietary software, in the copyright sense, is that dedicated to the public domain.

The views expressed herein are personal to the author in her individual capacity, and should not be attributed to Greenberg Traurig, LLP or any client of that firm or the author.

Heather J. Meeker
January, 2008

PART ONE

Leveraging Opportunities

It is tempting to approach using open source as a risk. But open source is first and primarily a powerful technological opportunity. Even so, participating in the open source movement is a step better taken with foresight and understanding. To many businesspeople or lawyers today, learning about open source can seem a daunting task. This part focuses on the basis and theory of open source licensing, and how it can be used in commercial businesses. It is intended to help you learn the basics of how to use open source intelligently in business.

CHAPTER 1

Introduction: How UNIX Gave Birth to Linux, and a New Software Paradigm

L awyers and businesspeople who are first learning about open source tend to think of it as an entirely new paradigm, or a disruptive technology. But open source is easier to understand within its historical context. It is true that open source software licensing is the biggest sea change in technology licensing since software licensing began. But the more things change, the more they stay the same. This chapter outlines the historical background for the free software movement and the later open source movement, and explains why and how they arose.

IN THE BEGINNING WAS THE WORD, AND THE WORD WAS UNIX

The term "open source" refers primarily to a type of outbound licensing paradigm, but also to a method of software development. Although media attention to both of these aspects of open source has burgeoned in the last decade, both the licensing paradigm and the development method have been in use ever since modern software was developed.

Although there are many software applications and utilities licensed under open source schemes, the "killer app" of open source is the Linux operating system.[1] Understanding the free software movement of the 1990s without understanding UNIX is a little like trying to understand Martin Luther without knowing who the pope is—you may learn the doctrines of Protestantism, but they will seem arbitrary if you do not know their historical context. The philosophical tenets of open source can seem arbitrary out of context, and many lawyers and businesspeople struggle with them for this reason: Those who grew up in the age of Windows do not know much about an operating system, like UNIX, that they have never used.

The company that came up with the first modern computer operating system was not a software company but a telephone company. UNIX was developed by AT&T Bell Laboratories back when AT&T was a much-feared corporate monopoly. As a result, the company was operating under a consent decree from the Department of Justice that required AT&T not to engage in commercial activities outside the field of telephone service. AT&T had enormous research and development resources, and boasted among its ranks some of the best and brightest computer engineers of the day. AT&T set its engineers loose to develop technology within the corporate context of a not-for-profit subsidiary called AT&T Bell Laboratories.

In the 1970s, two scientists at Bell Labs, Ken Thompson and Dennis Ritchie, not only came up with UNIX, but invented a computer programming language in which to write it. That language was called C. The origin of the name UNIX may be apocryphal, but it was allegedly a pun on the word "eunuchs"; it is a quasi-acronym for Uniplexed Information and Computing System, and a successor to the earlier Multiplexed Information and Computing Service (MULTICS), but with more focused functionality. UNIX and C were tremendously innovative. UNIX was written to operate the computers of the day: large mainframes whose use was limited to huge corporations, such as banks and utilities, government, and academia. C was an extraordinarily flexible and powerful programming language. Many of the languages today, C++ and Java, for instance, are heavily based on the syntax of C.

---

[1]This is more completely called the GNU/Linux operating system, a distinction to be explained later in this chapter.

Because of the consent decree, AT&T was not allowed to exploit UNIX as a commercial product. So it licensed copies of UNIX to universities and others all over the world for one dollar. It soon became common practice for computer scientists to share their improvements and innovations for UNIX freely—no one tried to exploit the modifications, because there was no serious market for the product. Computers were still in use by relatively few organizations, all software was custom-written and had to be configured and installed individually, and there was no consumer computer industry.

Eventually, the consent decree was lifted. By this time, UNIX was in wide use by academics who were accustomed to treating it like a scholarly research project, not as a commercial product. UNIX was being used in at least two ways: to run computers to support other academic projects, such as statistical analyses and scientific calculations, and as a device for teaching students the nuts and bolts of operating system design. After the decree was lifted, AT&T started granting commercial licenses for UNIX, under original equipment manufacture (OEM)–type commercial licensing terms.[2] Once this happened, the many UNIX licensees no longer shared their modifications, which caused what is called *forking:* the development of many incompatible versions. Each vendor—IBM, Sun, and even Microsoft—developed its own "flavor" of UNIX licensed in object code form only.

The free software movement was a direct reaction to the privatization of UNIX. Computer scientists, particularly academics, thought operating systems needed to be freely available in source code form. Thus, "free software" refers to free availability of source code, not price. (As the Free Software Foundation pithily says, "Think free speech, not free beer.") This free availability was important because an operating system is a fundamental tool, and if it works improperly, slowly, or badly, all users suffer. Thus, free software became a political movement, based on a normative idea that the forking and inaccessibility of UNIX should never happen again. It is no accident that the computer science luminaries who

---

[2]This term is not used consistently in the industry; here I use it to mean a source code license allowing the OEM to make modifications but to distribute object code only, where the source code is designated a trade secret.

initiated the movement were men who started their careers using UNIX and struggled with the problems that its privatization engendered.

ALONG COMES LINUX

Now, a few factors dovetailed to make Linux the vehicle of the free software movement.

In the late 1980s, computer science was undergoing a revolution. UNIX was no longer the most common operating system. This period saw the rise and fall of the first microcomputers: the Apple II, the TRS-80, and, of course, the personal computer. UNIX did not run on those boxes. There was no UNIX-like operating system for the new, cheap, Intel-type processors that were beginning to dominate the desktop market. These processors ran on DOS and later the Windows operating system, both products of Microsoft.

Several people tried to write smaller, more nimble operating systems that would be useful alternatives to UNIX. Such systems had to be compatible with UNIX programs, but free of the intellectual property rights of AT&T. Most notably, systems emerged based on the then-current UNIX interface specification. UNIX compatibility was essential so UNIX applications could run on those systems. One was a scholarly project called MINIX, written by Andrew Tanenbaum to help him teach operating systems and software at Vrije University in Amsterdam; it filled the academic void that the privatization of UNIX left behind. The other, to become far more famous, was Linux, the first version of which was written by a teenage computer programmer in Helsinki named Linus Torvalds. Torvalds released the first version of Linux in 1991.

Meanwhile, the GNU Project had developed into a major project to build a free alternative to UNIX. (GNU is a recursive acronym for "GNU's not UNIX.") By the early 1990s, this project had been in operation for many years. The mission of the GNU Project was to build an entire operating system, whereas Linux was only a kernel. An operating system includes not only a kernel, but development tools like compilers, debuggers, text editors, user interfaces, and administrative tools. The GNU Project was struggling with kernel development, and Linux arrived in time to provide the final piece of the puzzle. In tandem with the GNU Project, Richard Stallman of the GNU Project pioneered free software by developing the GNU

General Public License. The Free Software Foundation (FSF), a not-for-profit organization that supports the GNU Project, became the publisher and steward of that license. The FSF convinced Torvalds to make his kernel available under free software licensing terms, and the rest is history. The GNU/Linux operating system is what most people call Linux.

Finally, the last element of serendipity occurred: the economic recession of the early 2000s. A nosediving technology industry was desperate to cut costs and keep innovation alive, and lots of programmers were out of work and looking for something to do to keep embarrassing gaps out of their resumes. This was the perfect environment for open source to blossom. Blossom it did. Statistics on adoption of Linux are hard to come by, but most agree that it is gaining exponentially in popularity, particularly outside the United States.

Now, What Is Open Source?

To understand open source, you must understand what source code is and why access to it is important. Most computer users today use desktop computers with Windows operating systems. When you run a program on your desktop computer, such as a word processing program or an e-mail program, the file on your computer that contains the program is called, for instance, myprogram.exe. The "exe" stands for "executable." The file you are accessing is an executable file, or a file containing instructions that the computer can read and perform.

Programmers do not write executable code, they write source code. Programmers and corporate lawyers are a lot alike, in that they rarely write anything from scratch. When we write a contract, we rarely sit down to a blank page to begin. We use a model or form agreement, and add provisions from our libraries of provisions, which we have developed or collected over the years. Programmers work in exactly this way. If a programmer were writing a word processing program, he or she would need to include a way to save a file to a disk drive. But it would not be efficient—or even advisable—for the programmer to write it from scratch. Rather, he or she would use a prewritten component, or "library routine," to accomplish this. By using a prewritten routine, programmers make their coding more efficient, and they have more assurance that the code will be free of bugs and interoperable with the platform on which the program will run.

Lawyers writing contracts reuse provisions informally and idiosyncratically, but in programming, this process is highly formal. If you are writing a program and want to use a routine to write a file to disk, for example, the development language you are using will include a library routine called something like "writefile." That routine will need some information, such as where the file will be written, the name of the file, the information to be written, and how many bytes will be required. The documentation for the "writefile" routine will specify what information needs to be communicated to the routine when it is executed. Lawyers should think of this as similar to conforming an arbitration provision in a contract with the rest of the agreement: Definitions of "parties" and "business days" should not conflict. When writing contracts, lawyers do this by making global changes to the text. Those who have never written a contract might consider instead the example of writing a slew of thank-you letters. The letter might say: "Dear_____. Thank you for the lovely_____." Part of the letter is the same every time, and other parts vary. The parts that are the same are dictated by custom and manners.

In programming, this reuse is done formally and systematically. Programmers write their program in a text processor (or development environment). The code looks like cryptic English, and comprises a series of instructions telling the computer's processor what to do. Any skilled programmer can read this code, which is called source code. But the computer cannot execute this code as it is written. Once programmers have all the code written, and have included references to the library routines they need in that code, they run a large, complex program called a compiler. The compiler translates the source code into object code—a set of binary instructions that the computer's processor can execute. A related program, called a linker, then links the resulting object code to the referenced library routines, making sure information will be passed properly between the components, and produces a program that can be executed by the computer: an "executable" file, which usually contains many object code files. It is important to understand that programmers do not necessarily need access to the source code for the library routines. They only need to know what information to send to the routines and what information they will send back. The routines are usually "black boxes" to programmers: They do not need to know what is inside the box, just what goes in and what comes out.

To use another example that lawyers and businesspeople may recognize, a compiler is a lot like a redlining program. It runs in "batch" mode; in other words, once you enter some information (such as identifying the current and prior version and how you want the deletions to look) and press "go," the program runs without user interaction. The end product is a file that you do not edit. If you discover a mistake in the redline, you must go back to fix the document, then rerun the redlining program. Similarly, if there is a bug in a computer program, you do not edit the object or executable file. You must correct the source code and recompile the program. This is why access to source code is crucial. Without source code, you cannot fix errors, and must rely on the program vendor to do so.

AND THIS IS JUST THE BEGINNING

Open source, then, is not exactly new. Many of its tenets and practices are almost as old as the software industry. However, open source has come to be a focus of legal discussion as a result of having transformed from a set of informal industry practices to a political movement, with attendant intellectual property licensing practices.

Open source software licensing is a very complex topic. Some legal issues related to it are quite thorny and undecided. Also, formulating best practices in open source development requires familiarity with a complex set of facts and industry practices as well as the political, business, and legal principles at work. Best practices in this area change quickly and sometimes unexpectedly. This book, therefore, is not intended to give you all the answers. Instead, it is intended to provide you with the background and tools to understand this area of law and develop your own conclusions and best practices, to better leverage opportunities and manage risk.

CHAPTER 2

Free Software and Open Source

VIRUSES AND FREEDOMS

The first thing any lawyer learns about open source is that there are two kinds of open source licenses: "viral" and "nonviral."

When lawyers use the term "viral," they are referring to a license condition that requires the licensee to redistribute source code in outbound licenses only on the same terms as the inbound license. Although many find this a difficult concept, it is not fundamentally different from licensing conditions common in proprietary software licensing—a paradigm with which most licensing lawyers and businesspeople are quite familiar.

Consider, for example, the typical original equipment manufacturer (OEM) source code software distribution agreement. Such an agreement typically grants the OEM licensee the right to redistribute copies of software, subject to certain flow-down provisions that restrict the terms on which the OEM may grant end user licenses. Exhibit 2.1 shows some similarities and differences between a viral license agreement and an OEM source code license agreement.

Thus, the flow-down provisions of the GNU General Public License (GPL), in scope and structure, are not unlike those of OEM contracts that have been used in the software business for many years.

Terminology in this area is fraught with peril. The term "viral" is a pejorative term that is not well received by software developers. In addition, the term "viral" is imprecise, because sometimes it is used to refer only to the GNU General Public License and sometimes it refers to all

GPL AND OEM LICENSES: NOTHING NEW UNDER THE SUN?

Typical OEM Source Code Software Distribution Agreement	Free Software License (e.g., GPL)
License grant to copy, modify, and distribute	Same
Distribution by licensee in object code format only	Distribution by licensee must be in source code format
Flow-down provisions designate the source code as trade secret and prohibit distribution	Flow-down provisions designate the source code as open and require distribution

software licenses with "viral" terms. The imprecision arises because the GPL is considered "more viral" than other licenses (for reasons explained further in Chapter 14).

Advocates of this licensing scheme call it free software. But this term requires immediate explanation, because of the ambiguity of the word "free," which can mean either free of charge or free of restriction. It is also a term generally associated with free software advocates—those who prefer free software from a normative perspective. For those wishing to use a more neutral term, there are several alternatives, none of which is in universal parlance. The word "reciprocal" is also commonly used to describe free software licenses. Free software licenses are reciprocal in the sense that they require any licensee to "contribute back" to the community any changes the licensee distributes—though this can be misleading, for two reasons. First, this class of licenses may or may not require the source code to be made publicly available; it generally requires the programmer to make modifications available in source code form to all licensees to whom a copy of the binary form of the software is distributed. Only a few free software licenses actually require that modifications be contributed back to the original source code tree, and those licenses are not used frequently. This ambiguity is glossed over because the reciprocity is required in effect; under a free software license, the licensee cannot prevent any of its sublicensees from distributing the software—thus the software is effectively within the reach of the community. However, lawyers use the word "reciprocal" to describe provisions in agreements that place the same obligations on both parties. Free software licenses do not do this at all; most of the conditions apply only to the licensee.

For a more accurate term, I recommend "hereditary," because the terms of the license initially applied to the software are "inherited" by all subsequent licensees of the same code, subsets of it, or variations of it. This parallels a concept in object-oriented programming that allows objects or data structures to inherit the characteristics of the parent sets to which they belong.

Regardless of the terminology, "viral" and "nonviral" software licensing regimes are quite different. Nonviral (i.e., permissive) software licenses are mostly unremarkable in the sense that they do not require any complex compliance procedures. The hereditary software licenses are what cause open source to be a topic of continuing controversy in the law and in the software industry.

PHILOSOPHY OF FREE SOFTWARE

Chapter 1 described the technical antecedents to free software. This chapter describes the political positioning of free software in somewhat more depth. This book is a practical guide and thus treats the subject only briefly, but there is ample discussion on the Web available for those who wish to learn more.

Advocates of free software are quick to note that the use of the word "free" refers to freedom rather than price—in other words, *libre,* not *gratis.* As the Free Software Foundation (FSF) says, "Think free speech, not free beer." Most free software licenses do not prohibit the distribution of the software for a fee; however, they do prohibit the placing of restrictions on exercise of a sublicense. Thus, in practical terms, it is impossible to charge license fees for free software, for at least two reasons.

1. As an economic matter, this prohibition on restrictions makes it impossible for the initial licensor to exclude anyone from receiving a copy of the software, and therefore the licensor will not be able to extract economic rents from licensees in the form of license fees.
2. As a licensing matter, charging license fees for use of the work is generally prohibited by the actual terms of hereditary software licenses—either by expressly excluding the ability to charge license fees or by implication because charging license fees would be considered a prohibited restriction.

However, it is possible, and in fact common, to charge maintenance, customization, and other services fees for access to and modification of free software. Open source business models are based on this idea, and are discussed in greater detail in Chapter 11. Nevertheless, many feel that the rhetoric of the free software movement is antibusiness, although it is probably more accurate to describe it as anti–private property.

To understand the context for legal issues in open source, it is essential to understand the political landscape of the free software movement. By now, many people and companies have taken public positions along the political and rhetorical spectrum. A frequent complaint of those learning about open source is that what is written is usually not written from an objective point of view. (This is a particular complaint of attorneys, who are accustomed to reading treatises and outlines that state the law neutrally.) It is therefore important to understand who the leading commentators on the topic are and their position on open source.

The best-known philosophers of the free software movement are Richard Stallman, Eric Raymond, Bruce Perens, and Eben Moglen. Stallman, one of the original organizers of the GNU Project, has generally been the lightning rod for the free software movement and its most pithy and outspoken advocate. He is the author of the GPL, and remains a significant contributor to the GNU Project. Stallman believes that software should all be free and that programmers should be motivated by enhanced reputation and community good, rather than remuneration or profit. The structure of the GPL is intended to bring all software into the free software model. The hereditary nature of the license is Stallman's intentional—and ingenious—method of doing this.

For instance, Richard Stallman writes:

> Given a system of software copyright, software development is usually linked with the existence of an owner who controls the software's use. As long as this linkage exists, we are often faced with the choice of proprietary software or none. However, this linkage is not inherent or inevitable; it is a consequence of the specific social/legal policy decision that we are questioning: the decision to have owners.[1]

---

[1] Richard Stallman, "Why Software Should Be Free," www.gnu.org/philosophy/shouldbefree.html.

The essence of Stallman's philosophy is that access to software is expedient, and also a normative good.

> Software development used to be an evolutionary process, where a person would take an existing program and rewrite parts of it for one new feature, and then another person would rewrite parts to add another feature; in some cases, this continued over a period of twenty years. Meanwhile, parts of the program would be "cannibalized" to form the beginnings of other programs. The existence of owners prevents this kind of evolution, making it necessary to start from scratch when developing a program. It also prevents new practitioners from studying existing programs to learn useful techniques or even how large programs can be structured.[2]

Stallman also posits that ownership is not necessary to create incentives for people to develop software, because (1) some people will develop software for the interest and satisfaction of it with no external incentive, (2) some companies will develop software because it helps them create and use other products, such as computer hardware, and (3) software programmers can earn their livelihood providing services.[3]

Stallman is also a proponent of other political goals, some closely related to free software (such as his opposition to software patents) and some not related (such as his opposition to antidrug laws, his opposition to the Iraq war—and his exhortation to boycott Harry Potter books, due to objections about the misuse of copyright to protect them).[4] Stallman states that "intellectual property" is a propaganda term and objects to its use.[5]

Eben Moglen, who was until 2007 the General Counsel of the Free Software Foundation, is a Columbia University law professor and has been a frequent advocate, lecturer, and commentator on free software issues since his affiliation with the FSF in the early 2000s. Moglen is critical of the commercial software industry, and claims that free software will vanquish—or already has vanquished—the proprietary software industry

---

[2]Ibid.
[3]Ibid.
[4]www.stallman.org.
[5]Ibid.

due to its superior quality and robustness.[6] Moglen recently announced his departure from the board of directors and General Counsel position at the FSF to focus on his academic activities, but he will undoubtedly continue to be involved in the free software movement.[7]

Eric Raymond is a prominent software engineer, prolific writer, and open source advocate. He coined the phrase "With enough eyeballs, all bugs are shallow," which expresses the benefit of community mainte-nance and support that flows from the open source development model.[8] He authored the seminal article on open source development, entitled "The Cathedral and the Bazaar." In this article, Raymond explains that the development of proprietary software is like the building of a cathedral—designed by few, and built with resources provided and controlled by private means. Open source development, however, follows the model of the bazaar. In an open source development model, the best features and functionality evolve into popular use much as good ideas evolve into popular use in the marketplace of ideas. Development is a collaborative process, resources are not scarce, and no one person or organization directs the project.

Raymond has publicly aired his disagreements with Richard Stallman, including in a 1999 article entitled "Shut Up and Show Them the Code." Raymond holds libertarian political views, and his advocacy of market-driven assessment of software development models is consistent with those views. In other words, while Stallman and Moglen believe free software is a normative goal, Raymond believes it is a practical goal and means to an end—the end being better software. Eric Raymond is one of the original organizers of the Open Source Initiative (OSI). His political views on off-topic issues (such as his support of firearms)[9] have sometimes made him a

---

[6]For an example of this recurring theme in his speeches and articles, see Eben Moglen, "Anarchism Triumphant: Free Software and the Death of Copyright," http://emoglen.law.columbia.edu/my_pubs/anarchism.html.

[7]K. C. Jones, "Eben Moglen Steps Down from Free Software Foundation," *Information Week,* April 25, 2007, www.informationweek.com/software/showArticle.jhtml?articleID=199201489.

[8]This statement is generally attributed to Raymond but is also called "Linus' Law." Quoted in Moglen, "Anarchism Triumphant."

[9]www.catb.org/~esr/guns/.

figure of controversy.[10] Notably he opposes government regulation of the Internet and campaigned against the Communications Decency Act.[11]

Bruce Perens is a software engineer and a frequent writer and speaker on open source topics. He is the primary author of the Debian Free Software Guidelines and the Open Source Definition and cofounder of OSI. Perens left OSI shortly after cofounding it, due to philosophical differences with Eric Raymond and the OSI's direction. Of this action, he wrote, "[A]lthough some disapprove of Richard Stallman's rhetoric and disagree with his belief that all software should be free, the Open Source Definition is entirely compatible with the Free Software Foundation's goals, and a schism between the two groups should never have been allowed to develop."[12] Perens is generally viewed as a strong free software advocate, but is less inclined to incendiary rhetoric than Stallman, Moglen, or Raymond.

These are the principal open source proponents. There are also those who take public stands against open source. These include Bill Gates, founder of Microsoft, who famously (and allegedly) called open source advocates "communists,"[13] prompting a reply by Richard Stallman on his personal web page calling intellectual property communist and a later accusation that Gates himself was a communist.[14] Chief executive officer (CEO) Steve Ballmer has generally been Microsoft's public advocate against open source, famously (and allegedly) calling it a "cancer."[15] Finally, Daryl McBride, the CEO of

---

[10]See http://en.wikipedia.org/wiki/Eric_S._Raymond#_note-11. Wikipedia may overstate the case. For instance, its references to Raymond's views on IQ and race actually point to a posting more about IQ than race.

[11]www.catb.org/~esr/netfreedom/.

[12]See "It's Time to Talk about Free Software Again," http://lists.debian.org/debian-devel/1999/02/msg01641.html.

[13]The actual quotation is illusive but has occurred in many responses. See, e.g., J. S. Kelly, "Opinion: Is Free Software Communist?" CNN.com, February 11, 2000, http://archives.cnn.com/2000/TECH/computing/02/11/free.software.idg/.

[14]http://mailman.fsfeurope.org/pipermail/fsfe-ie/2005-February/001830.html.

[15]Once again, the actual quotation source is illusive (because it is not available via search on the *Sun-Times* web site) but is attributed widely to an interview in the *Chicago Sun-Times* dated June 1, 2001.

SCO, made various public statements against open source in the course of the litigation of the *SCO v. IBM* case, including arguing that the GPL violated the constitution.[16] Those who speak out against open source are relatively few, and tend to do so as spokespersons for corporate interests; it is not clear whether they do so as a matter of personal philosophy. In any case, no well-known advocate against open source lecturesor writes in the philosophical manner of Stallman, Moglen, Raymond, or Perens.

For additional context, the novice to open source politics should understand a few other players in the open source world.

Open Source Initiative

The Open Source Initiative was formed in 1998 with a mission to harmonize the workings of the free software movement and commercial software development. The purpose of the OSI was to "build bridges among different constituencies in the open-source community."[17] The OSI promulgates the Open Source Definition, and maintains the certification trademark Open Source—although most would argue that the term is generic in the trademark sense.[18] The OSI is the organization responsible for certifying software licenses as open source licenses. Its web site (www.opensource.org) lists all the certified licenses in existence. OSI previously certified almost any license agreement that fit the open source definition. However, recently it announced a change in policy that requires any newly certified license agreement not only to fit the open source definition but also to be substantially different from existing certified licenses. This is a part of the "nonproliferation" movement in open source. (See the discussion of proliferation in Chapter 4.)

Mozilla Foundation

The Mozilla Foundation is a not-for-profit foundation formed to steward the Mozilla Public License (MPL) and run various open source projects,

---

[16]Open Letter on Copyrights from Daryl McBride, President and CEO, The SCO Group, Inc., December 4, 2003, www.sco.com/copyright.

[17]http://opensource.org/.

[18]Perens apparently tried unsuccessfully to register the mark. http://en.wikipedia.org/wiki/Open_source_software.

most notably including the project for the Firefox browser. The Firefox code base was derived originally from the code for the Netscape browser; Netscape created the Mozilla project in 1998 and provided the code for that purpose—an end run around the "browser wars" of the late 1990s. Mozilla was the code name for the project before it was used to publicly denominate the project—a pun on "Mosaic killer."[19] Mozilla was run under the aegis of Netscape for some time and formed an independent entity in 2003.[20] Mozilla generally has been viewed as a business-friendly open source project that promulgates the Mozilla Public License as an alternative to the GPL. Mozilla has been run since inception by Mitchell Baker, an advocate for open source and personal digital empowerment.[21]

Linus Torvalds

Linus Torvalds is a famous figure in open source, but his focus appears to be more practical than political. Torvalds wrote the original Linux kernel while he was still a student, for a 1996 master's thesis project at the University of Helsinki. The GNU Project had been seeking a kernel, and decided to use Linux as its kernel core. (See Chapter 1 for more details.) Torvalds is one of the principal maintainers of the Linux kernel, through his position at Open Source Development Laboratories (OSDL). Some observe that Torvalds and Stallman were strange bedfellows in the GNU/Linux projects. Torvalds is a free software advocate, and some would argue that he has done more to advance the cause of free software than any other person, because he provided the original "killer app" for the movement: the Linux operating system kernel. However, Torvalds does not engage in antibusiness rhetoric and in fact has been associated with at least one technology startup, Transmeta Corporation. The Linux kernel now consists in very small part of Torvalds's initial contribution, but his ongoing involvement with the Linux project means he remains a key figure in open source.

There has been some serious discussion of whether calling free software philosophy "communist" is accurate or merely pejorative.[22] Certainly the

---

[19]http://en.wikipedia.org/wiki/Mozilla.

[20]www.mozilla.org/foundation/.

[21]See her blog at http://weblogs.mozillazine.org/mitchell/.

[22]Over the years, various thoughtful articles have appeared on this topic, such as www.freesoftwaremagazine.com/node/1707.

free software movement embraces values that place the good of the community over personal enrichment. However, it has a decidedly anarchist character—which makes it a different model from that of a strong centralized government that sets economic policy. The marketplace of ideas model is fundamentally a libertarian one. Eric Raymond has described the free software model as a "gift economy." In this model, all agree that the reward for creating quality software is reputation rather than profit.

Proponents of free software are almost all universally opposed to software patents, an issue discussed in detail in Chapter 7. However, at this point, I merely pause to note that the political posture of the free software movement often crosses over into matters of patent policy. Other issues espoused by leaders of the free software movement include those surrounding musical and audiovisual digital file sharing, the Digital Millennium Copyright Act, and data privacy issues.[23]

As the discussion demonstrates, thought leaders in the free software movement are not always aligned in their thinking. The FSF generally represents the end of the spectrum that most fervently advocates free software at the expense of commercial software. However, other members of the movement have taken a more moderate, and some would say more practical, view that free software and proprietary software should and must coexist.

The rhetoric of the free software movement probably discouraged business participation in open source in the 1990s. At this point, however, many of those who use and support open source either disregard or try to dispel the rhetoric;[24] today the open source movement is stronger and far more complex than the rhetoric that created it. As time goes on, the very success of the free software movement is eroding the power base of its most vehement advocates. While participants in the movement have grown exponentially over the more than 15 years since free software entered the software industry consciousness, the participants' demographics have inverted: Whereas in 1990 there were virtually no commercial participants, today they make up the vast majority. Corporate participants pay less attention to the

---

[23]See, e.g., Moglen, "Anarchism Triumphant," and Richard Stallman's personal page at www.stallman.org/.
[24]For an amusing (and rare) critique, see Ryan Paul, "Why I Dislike RMS," *LXer,* February 18, 2005, http://lxer.com/module/newswire/view/31994/index.html.

political goals of the movement and more to its results in terms of lines of useful code.[25]

DEFINITIONS: FREE SOFTWARE AND OPEN SOURCE

Lawyers love definitions, and many look for definitions of free software and open source. There are two competing definitions. The free software definition was authored by Richard Stallman and is more normative in nature. The open source software definition was authored by Eric Raymond and is more descriptive in nature.

Free Software Definition

Four freedoms:

0. The freedom to run the program, for any purpose.
1. The freedom to study how the program works, and adapt it to your needs.
2. The freedom to redistribute copies so you can help your neighbor.
3. The freedom to improve the program, and release your improvements to the public, so that the whole community benefits.[26]

Items 1 and 3 require access to source code.

The other definition is the open source definition promulgated by OSI.[27] This broader definition includes permissive software licenses. The elements are:

1. Free redistribution
2. Source code available
3. Derivative works permitted
4. Integrity of the author's source

---

[25]Jane K. Winn, "Legitimate Authority over Free and Open Source Software," manuscript on file with author. These figures are estimated, but few observers would be likely to disagree that the sheer number of corporate participants today has outstripped the original hacker community base.

[26]www.gnu.org/philosophy/free-sw.html.

[27]http://opensource.org/docs/definition.php. The Debian Social Contract states that the Open Source Definition was based on the Debian definition at www.debian.org/social_contract.

5. No discrimination against persons or groups
6. No discrimination against fields of endeavor
7. Distribution of license with derivative works
8. License must not be specific to a product
9. License must not restrict use of other software
10. No provision of license may be predicated on any individual technology or style of interface

Some attorneys have commented, and not without reason, that the GNU General Public License does not strictly fit item 9 of the open source definition, because it seeks to control code not covered by the license (i.e., code written by licensees and integrated with GPL code). The OSI anticipates this commentary and explicitly states, on the web page where it displays the open source definition, that the GPL complies with the definition.[28] In any case, these conflicting definitions demonstrate the differences in viewpoint between advocates of free software and the OSI. The FSF's mission is to promote free software to the exclusion of proprietary software. The OSI's mission is to make open source software available to all, including the business community.

WHAT'S IN A NAME? THE VIRAL AND THE NONVIRAL

As noted in Chapter 1, the nomenclature for licensing paradigms for free software and open source varies and is inconsistent. Choosing one can be treacherous because of the political implications. Here are some of the categories in common use.

- **Proprietary.** This is the term of art typically applied by members of the open source movement to software that is not open source. In a legal sense, it is a misnomer. The licensing paradigm of free software depends for its enforceability only on copyright law—it "lives

---

[28]To understand the motivation for this comment and the answer to it, see the in-depth discussion of the derivative works issue and GPL compliance later in this book.

or dies on copyright law."[29] Thus, free software is just as "proprietary" as proprietary software in the sense that it is governed by proprietary rights; however, this term is used almost universally in the open source community, and then unambiguously refers to software that is licensed in object code form only (or more precisely, software licensed in object code form as a matter of course, with source code sometimes delivered within the context of a source code escrow).

- **Copyleft.** This pun is a term used by the FSF to apply to the licensing paradigm of the GPL—so called because the GPL turns conventional licensing on its head by requiring source code to be freely available rather than kept as a trade secret. It also refers more specifically to the conditions in a hereditary license that require any redistribution of code to be on the terms of that license.

- **Viral and nonviral.** The term "viral" is used primarily by lawyers and open source opponents to describe the hereditary licensing paradigm. It is used in two different senses: one to describe all hereditary licensing and one to describe GPL. The first sense may be thought of as vertical: Once a set of licensing terms is applied to particular software code, it is always applied to that code, despite licensing from one licensee to the next in a vertical channel. The second may be thought of as horizontal: The GPL requires neighboring code to be covered by GPL as well. (See the discussion in Chapter 14.) It is not advisable to use the term "viral" in discussions with free software advocates; in other words, it is politically incorrect. "Nonviral" merely means open source or permissive licenses that are not hereditary.

- **Permissive.** This term is used to describe licenses like BSD, MIT, and Apache, which do not require relicensing on particular terms. This term is in fairly common use and is both neutral and accurately descriptive.

- **Hereditary.** This is my term of choice for the copyleft or free software class of open source licenses. It is also a term from C++ and Java programming, used to describe sets of data and procedure

---

[29]This pithy statement has been variously attributed but seems to come originally from Larry Wall in *Open Sources: Voices from the Open Source Revolution* (O'Reilly, 1999).

called "classes") that inherit characteristics from other classes. It is
not in common use, but it is neutral and reasonably descriptive.

- **Open source.** This term is used to describe both hereditary and
  permissive licensing paradigms. It is in ubiquitous use.

Here are some terms that do not apply to open source, but are sometimes confused with those that do.

- **Freeware.** This term does not have a universally consistent meaning.
  Its most frequent meaning is software released in binary-only form (i.e.,
  "proprietary" software) but licensed for redistribution free of charge.
- **Shareware.** This term usually means software released in binary-
  only form (i.e., "proprietary" software) but licensed free of charge,
  sometimes with a payment required on the honor system for continued use, or with a code key disallowing use beyond a certain initial
  evaluation date.
- **Public domain.** Ten years ago, many people confused open source
  with public domain, but few do today. It is possible for an author to
  designate a work of authorship to the public domain by making an
  unambiguous statement to that effect.[30] This means that the author
  has no further copyright interest in the work. No copyright licensing
  terms need be applied to the work, and no copyright notices should
  be applied to it. Confusion about this point has led to software being
  released with copyright notices and designated as "public domain."
- **Shared source.** This is a term used by Microsoft to describe a
  licensing program it devised as an answer to the publicity and popularity of the open source movement.[31] This licensing paradigm, as
  originally formatted, did not fit either the open source or free software definition.
- **Scripting languages.** Scripting or high-level interpreted languages
  such as PERL, PHP, and HTML are often confused with open
  source. These languages are executed in source code form and thus
  have no compiled form. Therefore, they are always freely available in

---

[30]*National Comics Pub. v. Fawcett Pub.*, 191 F.2d 594, 598 (2d Cir., 1951).

[31]The Microsoft explanation of its shared source licenses appears at www.microsoft
.com/resources/sharedsource/licensingbasics/sharedsourcelicenses.mspx. Microsoft has since formatted open source licenses as part of this shared source
program.

source code form, although they can be licensed under either open source or limited (such as end user license) terms.

OPEN SOURCE DEVELOPMENT MODEL

There is much discussion of whether the open source business model or the proprietary model is a better model for development of software. A detailed discussion of this topic is beyond the scope of this book. Much discussion of this issue is available in business journals and the reports of technology consultants. The open source development model applies to code covered by both hereditary and nonhereditary licenses.

The open source development model is a collaborative model. It anticipates the participation of many developers in the development of a single product or module. Theoretically, any open source project can have hundreds or thousands of contributors. In practice, however, this is rarely the case. Most open source projects are relatively small, involving the work of one contributor or a small number of contributors. Some open source projects, such as Linux or Apache, are very large development projects. Nevertheless, although they may have many contributors, these projects have a small number of gatekeepers, or "committers," who decide what contributions will be checked in to the official source tree.

In this sense, the model is not a pure model of the bazaar. It is more like a free market with a specialist's desk. In well-known open source projects, these gatekeepers include some of the most respected computer scientists in the world. The gatekeeper decides which modifications are included in the source tree, based on technical considerations, including security and stability of the code and compatibility with other technology, and the desires of the community at large on issues such as features and functionality. This works if and only if the gatekeeper is a respected member of the community who shepherds the project for community good. Otherwise the project will fork.

Theoretically, any open source project can fork into many different versions, because all open source licenses grant unfettered rights to modify code. However, in practice, there has been little forking in open source developments. Open source advocates argue this is because the best ideas are accepted into the open source tree. There is no proprietary developer to arbitrarily avoid new product features that are not by a proprietary developer, and thus there is no need to fork.

From a technical point of view, gatekeeping is accomplished via a code management utility called a *revision control system*. The most popular open source utility of this type is the Concurrent Versioning System (CVS), which is licensed under GPL. Nonprogrammers who want to understand open source would be well served to learn how the process of adding source code to a product source tree is accomplished—to help them understand the reality of open source development and how software engineers accomplish ongoing due diligence (see Chapter 4). A revision control system allows only designated persons to check code into the source tree. It also keeps track of published versions, what was added, changed, or deleted and when, and who made the change; it further helps reconcile conflicting changes. However, it is a technical tool that follows the policy set by the project. Project management decides who is a committer, not the revision control system. Project management for open source ranges from full-fledged not-for-profit foundations with advisory boards to ad hoc groups of programmers who have never met face to face.

Proponents of the open source development model posit that it produces better software than the proprietary model. In truth, the jury is probably still out on the question of which model produces better products, and the answer may change with time or context. On the side of open source, all licensees can contribute bug fixes (instead of just reporting problems, which is all they can do with proprietary software), the availability of source code means competitors can offer maintenance (resulting in better service because competition fosters quality), and the model is thought to result in better security (because "back doors" and other security issues are obvious to anyone examining the code, and thus they can be quickly addressed). On the side of proprietary software, commercial software vendors are better funded, decision-making authority about the code base is executive rather than consensual, and the coders are actually getting paid for their work.[32]

---

[32]The question of what motivates programmers in open source is the subject of much discussion, with the open source side mostly taking the view that publicity, professional acknowledgment, and altruism are better motivators. However, the change in demographics of open source contributors over time means that many open source programmers are now paid to contribute by the companies that employ them. See Winn, "Legitimate Authority over Free and Open Source Software."

CHAPTER 3

Common Open Source Licenses and Their Structure

A ll open source licenses, by definition, freely allow the licensee to exercise all of the rights of copyright with respect to the licensed software. The difference between hereditary software licenses and permissive software licenses is that hereditary software licenses place significant conditions on the exercise of certain rights—generally the distribution right.[1] Some open source software licenses contain explicit license grants, and some contain implicit ones. As a drafting matter, conventional software licenses almost always contain a license grant in a form similar to this: "Licensor hereby grants to Licensee the right to. . . ." However, many open source software licenses are drafted in an informal style and contain "license grants" stating "Permission is granted . . ." or a "You have the right to. . . ."[2]

---

[1]In GPL version 3, the trigger for copyleft restrictions is referred to as the act of "propagating," however, this word is defined self-referentially to the scope of applicable copyright law, to distribution in the United States. Other open source licenses simply refer to distribution, or (as in the MIT license) "dealing in" the software.

[2]Generally this is considered poor drafting, because the passive voice does not identify the actor. Thus, "Licensor hereby grants to Licensee" precisely identifies the actor (Licensor); "permission is granted" does not. As an interpretational matter the grantor may be obvious, but the lack of clarity in the passive voice can cause confusion—for instance, when the reader must determine whether the grant is directly from the ultimate licensor, or a sublicense through a series of licensors. The passive voice in open source licenses was probably intended to emphasize the direct licensing paradigm, rather than sublicensing.

In addition, many open source licenses contain significant implicit license grants ranging from implicit grants of copyright interests to implicit grants of patent interests and other intellectual property interests. Thus, the Berkeley Software Distribution (BSD) license states: "Redistribution and use in source and binary forms, with or without modification, are permitted." There is no express grant of the right to copy, prepare derivative works, or publicly perform or display, but these rights are universally understood to be granted under this license.

More controversial is the implicit patent license grant in the GNU General Public License (GPL) version 2 and GNU Lesser General Public License (LGPL) version 2.1.[3] Neither of these documents contains an express patent license. The only mention of patents in either document is a statement that software patents threaten software freedom (in the preamble) and the so-called liberty-or-death provision in section 9 of the GPL: negation of the license grant in the event that the license grant cannot be made free of restrictions born of patent interests. However, most free software advocates take the position that these licenses include an implicit grant of all patent rights necessary to practice the grants of copyright license that are expressed in each document. Most permissive licenses also lack express patent license grants, and the same analysis presumably applies. This subject is treated in detail in Chapter 7.

All hereditary software licenses also contain terms that require one of two things:

1. All distribution by the licensee is effectuated on the exact terms of the same license (see, e.g., GPL), or
2. The license allows distribution on other terms so long as the source code for the software is also available on the exact terms of the same license (see, e.g., the Mozilla Public License).

All open source licenses contain broad warranty disclaimers and limitations of liability. Most also include disclaimers of any license grant under any trademark of the licensor—not that any such grant would necessarily be implied in the first place.

---

[3]Version 3 of the GPL (and the corresponding version of LGPL) switched to an express patent license grant.

Many open source licenses also contain instructions on how to apply the license to new code. Generally, these instructions are intended to be included explicitly in the header or notice file of source code to which the license will pertain.

Most open source licenses contain few or no terms regarding governing law, venue, integration, and severability. In general, the absence of these terms is an attempt to avoid focus on U.S. law. Governing law and venue provisions in open source licenses are actually quite controversial—a fact that always surprises lawyers, who tend to feel that any choice is usually better than none.

DIRECT LICENSING

Once of the most difficult concepts in open source—particularly for lawyers or businesspeople who are accustomed to proprietary license agreements—is that open source licenses are direct licensing models. In other words, a licensee that accepts software under the terms of the GPL and distributes it to another does not sublicense the rights in the software. Most open source licenses are direct grants from the author to anyone who wishes to take the software under that license. If licensees contribute their own code to the software, they, too, license directly on those terms. Therefore, in given software modules, the rights to some portions may come from one licensor and the rights to other portions may come from other licensors. (See Exhibit 3.1.) The practical effect of simultaneous grants from multiple licensors will be discussed in more detail later in this book (with regard to patent license grants and open source enforcement); however, this concept is critical, so those learning about open source need to use it as a baseline for all understanding of the open source licensing model.

Exhibits 3.2 and 3.3 list many of the licenses approved by Open Source Initiative (OSI) as well as a few others that are in common use.

GPL

The GPL is the most widely used open source license.[4] The license is stewarded by the Free Software Foundation (FSF), which is responsible

---

[4]For instance, see http://freshmeat.net/stats/. Over 60 percent of the software projects use GPL.

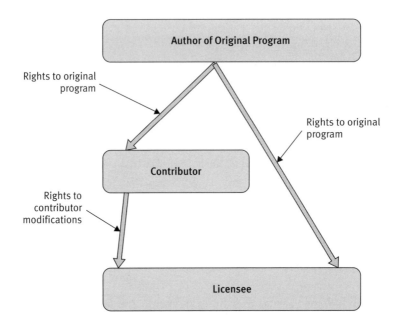

Rights to original program

Rights to original program

Rights to contributor modifications

EXHIBIT 3.1   **DIRECT LICENSING MODEL OF OPEN SOURCE**

for issuing new versions. Version 1.0 is no longer in use. Version 2.0 was released in 1991, and version 3.0 was released on June 29, 2007.

The versioning structure for the GPL has been adopted by many other licenses. First, the license itself states the text of the license itself cannot be modified. What this means in legal terms is unclear, as legal documents usually are not considered subject to copyright protection.[5] The hereditary terms of the license require relicensing on the terms of the GPL, so in that sense the license cannot be modified by licensees who are bound to it. The statement that the license cannot be modified is likely intended not so much as an assertion of copyright ownership as a way to discourage

---

[5]It is possible that they could be. See *Nimmer on Copyright,* Section 2.18[E]: "There appear to be no valid grounds why legal forms such as contracts, insurance policies, pleadings and other legal documents should not be protected under the law of copyright." However, as a practical matter, rights in contract language are almost never enforced and are generally thought to be so functional as to have little or no copyright protection.

EXHIBIT 3.2 **COMMON OPEN SOURCE LICENSES**

License	Hereditary?	Steward/Author[a]	Projects[b]	Comments
Academic Free License	No	Lawrence Rosen		Allows licensor to "adapt" license to different requirements.
Adaptive Public License	See comments			
Affero GPL (1.0)	Yes	Affero, Inc./FSF	Affero Project	Generally considered the "most viral" license. See Section 2.d. of the license.
Apache Software License (1.1)	No	Apache Foundation	Apache (superseded by version 2.0)	Apache 1.0 is largely no longer in use; version 1.1 removed the "advertising" clause.
Apache License (2.0)	No	Apache Foundation	Ant, tomcat, Xerces	Permissive license, but far more detailed terms than BSD or MIT, or Apache 1.0 or 1.1.
Apple Public Source License		Apple	Darwin	Corporate-style license, many provisions specific to Apple.
Artistic License	No (though the point has been debated[c])	Larry Wall	PERL, CPAN	Nonhereditary, but more restrictions than most permissive licenses. Many projects under this license are dual licensed under GPL
Attribution Assurance Licenses	No	Edwin A. Suominen		Based on BSD, with expanded attribution provisions.
New BSD License	No	FreeBSD		Template license—many variants in use. Major variants are the "3-clause" and "2-clause" variants. Earlier versions contained an advertising clause.

(continued)

EXHIBIT 3.2 (CONTINUED)

License	Hereditary?	Steward/Author[a]	Projects[b]	Comments
Computer Associates Trusted Open Source License 1.1	Yes	Computer Associates	Ingres	Corporate-style license, CPL derivative.
Common Development and Distribution License	Yes	Sun	OpenSolaris Netbeans	Recent addition to OSI list, based on MPL. Successor to Sun Public License.
Common Public License 1.0	Yes	IBM		Successor to IBM Public License. See also Eclipse license.
Eclipse Public License	Yes	Eclipse Foundation	Eclipse Project	Variant of CPL.
Educational Community License	No			
Frameworx Open License	Yes	Frameworx Company		
GNU General Public License (GPL)	Yes	FSF	Linux, GNU	Most commonly used license.
"GPL plus exception"	Yes	FSF	GNU Classpath	Variant of GPL that allows linking (dynamic or static) to proprietary code. This can be hard to distinguish from GPL—look for the "exception" notice, usually at the end of the license text file that identifies the code as covered by GPL.
GNU Library or "Lesser" General Public License (LGPL)	Yes	FSF		Variant of GPL that allows dynamic linking to proprietary code.

License	OSI Approved	Author/Owner	Used by	Notes
Historical Permission Notice and Disclaimer	No		BSD kernel	BSD Variant. Voluntarily repudiated by its author.
IBM Public License	Yes	IBM		Similar to GPL generally, but drafted conventionally. Uses derivative works scope calculus similar to that of GPL. Largely superseded by CPL and Eclipse.
Intel Open Source License	No	Intel		BSD with an export provision. Intel has disavowed its use.
MIT license	No		X Window System, PuTTY	Most popular permissive license, after BSD. Also called X or X11 license.
Mozilla Public License 1.0 (MPL)	Yes	Mozilla Foundation		Original corporate-style hereditary license, based on Netscape Public License. Note broad patent license termination provisions.
Mozilla Public License 1.1 (MPL)	Yes	Mozilla Foundation	Firefox, Thunderbird	For major differences between version 1.0 and 1.1, see Chapter 7.
MySQL (GPL + FLOSS Exception)	Yes	MySQL	MySQL	Like GPL, but allows linking to open source code.
Netscape Public License		Netscape	Netscape browser	Original basis of Mozilla Public License. Not an open source approved license. Contains specific rights for Netscape.
Open Software License	Yes	Lawrence Rosen		Copyleft requirements are triggered by online use. Contains limited warranties regarding originality of code.

(continued)

EXHIBIT 3.2 (CONTINUED)

License	Hereditary?	Steward/ Author[a]	Projects[b]	Comments
OpenSSL	No		OpenSSL	See discussion on "miscellaneous licenses" later in this chapter.
PHP License	No	PHP Group	PHP programming language	
Python Software Foundation License	No	Python Foundation	Python programming language	Permissive license drafted in a more conventional style than BSD or MIT. Earlier versions of this license contained a governing law provision. There is a good explanation of the change at www.python.org/download/releases/2.4.2/license/.
Qt Public License (QPL)	Yes	Trolltech	QT Toolkit	GPL variant.
Reciprocal Public License	Yes	Technical Pursuit		Stronger restrictions than GPL.
Ricoh Source Code Public License	Yes	Ricoh		Based on Netscape Public License.
Sleepycat License	Yes	Sleepycat	Berkeley DB	Similar in form and style to BSD, but contains strong distribution restrictions. Sleepycat's products are dual licensed under commercial terms.

License name	Steward[a]	Organization	Example projects[b]	Notes
Sun Industry Standards Source License (SISSL)	Yes	Sun	OpenOffice (now under LGPL)	Now largely superseded by CDDL. For more information, see www.openoffice.org/FAQs/license-change.html.
Sun Public License	Yes	Sun	Older versions of Netbeans	Now largely superseded by CDDL.
University of Illinois/NCSA Open Source License	No	University of Illinois		Combination of BSD and MIT licenses.
Vovida Software License v. 1.0	No	Vovida Networks (part of Cisco Systems)	VOCAL	
W3C License	No	World Wide Web Consortium (W3C)		Permissive. Note that W3C is a standards organization; this license covers copyrightable material, and standards can cover other types of intellectual property.
Zope Public License	No		Zope	BSD-like.
zlib/libpng license	No		Zlib, libpng	Permissive license.

[a]Some licenses have stewards that promulgate new versions that can be chosen by licensees. Some licenses are promulgated by authors or projects who claim copyright in them but have no formal system for stewardship. Others are dedicated to the public domain.

[b]This information is not included here for all of the licenses. A blank in this column does not mean the license is not used.

[c]http://en.wikipedia.org/wiki/Artistic_License.

EXHIBIT 3.3 POPULAR OPEN SOURCE LICENSES—QUICK COMPARISON TABLE

License	Hereditary?	Patent Grant?	Scope (Hereditary only)
Affero GPL (not OSI approved)	Yes		Same as GPL, but copyleft requirements are triggered by acts other than distribution: 2 d) If the Program . . . is intended to interact with users through a computer network and if . . . any user interacting with the Program was given the opportunity to request transmission to that user of the Program's complete source code, you must not remove that facility from your modified version of the Program or work based on the Program, and must offer an equivalent opportunity for all users interacting with your Program through a computer network to request immediate transmission by HTTP of the complete source code of your modified version or other derivative work.
Apache Software License (1.1)	No	No	
Apache Software License (2.0)	No	Yes	
Artistic license	No (debated[a])	No	
BSD license	No	No	
Common Development and Distribution License	Yes	Yes	1.9 A. Any file that results from an addition to, deletion from or modification of the contents of a file containing Original Software or previous Modifications B. Any new file that contains any part of the Original Software or previous Modification
Common Public License 1.0	Yes	Yes	"Contribution" definition: i) changes to the Program, and ii) additions to the Program;

License			
Eclipse Public License	Yes	Yes	Same as CPL.
GNU General Public License (GPL)	Yes	No (version three will have one)	"Works based on the Program." FSF's basic position is that this includes all derivative works, including all code linked in the same executable.
"GPL plus exception" (also MySQL FLOSS exception license)	Yes	No	Same as GPL, but code under this variant can be linked to code under non-GPL FLOSS (i.e., open source) licenses.
GNU Library or "Lesser" General Public License (LGPL)	Yes	No (version released with GPL3 will have one)	Same as GPL, but code under LGPL can be used as a dynamically linked library for code under proprietary licenses.
IBM Public License	Yes	Yes	Same as CPL.
MIT license	No	No	
Mozilla Public License 1.0 (MPL)	Yes	Yes	1.9. "Modifications" means any addition to or deletion from the substance or structure of either the Original Code or any previous Modifications. . . . A. Any addition to or deletion from the contents of a file containing Original Code or previous Modifications. B. Any new file that contains any part of the Original Code or previous Modifications.
Mozilla Public License 1.1 (MPL)	Yes	Yes	See MPL 1.0.
Sleepycat License	Yes	No	For an executable file, "complete source code" means the source code for all modules it contains.

The first row (Eclipse Public License, top-left region) also carries the note: ". . . Contributions do not include additions to the Program which: (i) are separate modules of software distributed in conjunction with the Program under their own license agreement, and (ii) are not derivative works of the Program."

[a]http://en.wikipedia.org/wiki/Artistic_License.

others from creating alternate versions of the license or, at least, using the name of the GPL for any such alternate versions.[6]

The GPL states that a licensee taking code under that license has the option to use the code under the current version of the license or any subsequent version. This clause can be quite confusing for novices. It means that a licensor adopting the GPL must ultimately accept the terms of any subsequent version. However, in effect, this may be true for the licensee as well. For instance, if the licensor adopts the GPL for its code version 1.0 and subsequently releases an update version 1.1, most licensees will choose to use the updated version. Thus, any changes in the license that take place between the release of version 1.0 and 1.1 generally will be applied to most licensees. However, the versioning rubric of the GPL prevents the licensor from sticking to an earlier version if the subsequent version issued by the steward is not acceptable. Thus, if the steward issues a subsequent version that is less favorable to a licensor, the licensor may be at the mercy of the license steward.

Those unfamiliar with GPL version 2.0 would to do well to read it through; however, I advise not spending too much time analyzing the language of the document for legal purposes until after you read Chapter 14. The "preamble" of the agreement is generally thought to be the equivalent of recitals in a traditionally drafted license agreement. However, the document is not written in the style characteristic of most license agreements.

Some readers are confused by the use of the number 0 to designate the first paragraph of the GPL. In computer programming, ordinal counting often begins with 0 rather than 1. Thus, the first element of an array in the C language is element 0 rather than element 1. This is a convention in low-level computer languages—the kind generally used by programmers of the caliber and experience of those who organized the GNU Project. Other, higher-level languages (like BASIC), designed for less experienced programmers, sometimes do not follow this convention.

---

[6]This does not mean alternate versions do not exist. The most common are GPL plus exception, used for library routines such as the standard C library, and GPL plus FLOSS exception, used for dual-licensing structures such as that of MySQL.

Several provisions of GPL2 are known by colloquial names or have notable features:

- Section 3 (Object Code Distribution Requirements) does not actually require a licensor to distribute source code. It requires that the licensor that is distributing code in binary form accompany the object code with complete corresponding source code, or make a written offer for three years to give any third party a copy of corresponding source code at a nominal fee.
- Section 5 states that the GPL is a license and not a contract. See Chapter 15 for a discussion of this point.
- Section 7, often known as the liberty-or-death provision, states that if the licensor cannot distribute under the terms of the license without patent-related restrictions, it cannot distribute at all.

Note that the GPL does not have a governing law provision. This means that background law will dictate what state or country's law will be used to interpret it.

GPL + Exception (or Special Exception)

GPL + Exception contains a "special exception" that allows other, proprietary code to be combined into the same executable file (or to link, dynamically or statically) to code covered by this version of the license. This version most notably applies to the standard C library that is associated with the GNU C compiler. Because languages such as C implement most functionality in standard libraries, a compiler for such a language will cause library code to be compiled into the executable program that the compiler produces. If these libraries are covered by a restrictive license, such as the GPL, all code generated using the compiler would be covered by GPL as well. (For more on how this works, see Chapter 12.)

The GPL + Exception license is less restrictive than the Lesser General Public License (LGPL). The LGPL explicitly allows code covered by it to be linked to proprietary code as a dynamically linked library, but does not allow static linking. In addition, it contains restrictions on the amount of in-line code and large macros that can be used from LGPL code. The GPL + Exception license allows any kind of linking. However, it is not clear whether it allows the use of code covered by that license as in-line functions or macros.[7]

GPL + FLOSS EXCEPTION

The GPL + FLOSS Exception, a variation of GPL + Exception, is used most notably by MySQL AB with its dual-licensing model. The exception allows linking to software covered by certain non-GPL open source licenses but not proprietary code.

LGPL

LGPL sometimes has been called the "Library" GPL but is properly known as the "Lesser" GPL. Code covered by LGPL can be used as a dynamically linked library by code covered by any other license (including a proprietary license). LGPL has two features that are often overlooked. First, it places a 10-line limitation on the use by proprietary code of macros or in-line functions extracted from LGPL code. Many argue that this restriction is nearly impossible to police, because modern compilers compile functions in-line automatically when it is efficient to do so. (For a discussion of in-line functions, see Chapter 12.) The second feature is the reverse engineering prohibition limitation in Section 6:

> [Y]ou may also combine or link a "work that uses the Library" with the Library to produce a work containing portions of the Library, and distribute that work under terms of your choice, provided that the terms permit modification of the work for the customer's own use and reverse engineering for debugging such modifications.

This is not consistent with the terms of many end user licenses, which restrict reverse engineering entirely, so care must be taken when integrating LGPL libraries with proprietary programs.

The preamble to the license says: "We use this license for certain libraries in order to permit linking those libraries into non-free programs." The FSF explicitly discourages the use of LGPL, because "it does [l]ess to protect the user's freedom than the ordinary General Public License." "For example,

---

[7]See the prohibition on in-line functions or macros of more than 10 lines in the LGPL, Section 5.

permission to use the GNU C Library in non-free programs enables many more people to use the whole GNU operating system, as well as its variant, the GNU/Linux operating system." The FSF therefore uses either LGPL or GPL + Exception to cover code libraries commonly used by development utilities like the GNU C Compiler so that proprietary application programs can be developed using those development utilities. As a corollary, GPL programs that consist of libraries intended for dynamic linking are purposely licensed to require only GPL applications to use them.

CORPORATE HEREDITARY SOFTWARE LICENSES

Corporate hereditary software licenses were an attempt to capture the basic software licensing paradigm of the GPL, but in a license drafted in conventional legal language. Each such license requires either relicensing on identical terms or relicensing on proprietary terms only if the licensor also make available source code under the terms of the license.

The first of these licenses was the Mozilla Public License (sometimes called MPL). This license was drafted in connection with the licensing of Netscape's browser, which was made an open source project in 2002[8] and became the basis of the open source Firefox browser. The Mozilla Public License, however, is drafted in such a fashion that it cannot be applied to other code without modification, because it contains express provisions regarding the Mozilla trademark and makes explicit references to Mozilla code. While other free software projects have adopted this license in essence, they have made minor modifications to apply it to their own code. A recent example is the Sugar CRM License, which is essentially the Mozilla Public License with the names changed and the addition of an advertising clause. The Mozilla Public License has been criticized for its lack of adaptability to other code bases. However, several later corporate hereditary licenses heralded as improvements to the MPL are substantially the same as the Mozilla Public License in all ways save the scope of patent licenses and patent termination clauses.

---

[8]Most of the code, that is. http://en.wikipedia.org/wiki/Mozilla. The code for the browser was originally released under the Netscape Public License.

Chronologically, the next corporate free software license was the IBM Public License. However, this license was soon replaced by the Common Public License (CPL), which was in turn partly superseded by the Eclipse Public License.

Another branch of the corporate hereditary license family was started by Sun Microsystems. This included the Sun Industry Standards Source License, which was replaced[9] by the Common Development and Distribution License (CDDL), authored by Sun Microsystems and approved by the Open Source Initiative in early 2005. The CDDL, like the CPL, is a template license.

These licenses are all written in the typical style of license agreements. They differ with respect to their patent licenses and patent license termination (sometimes called "patent peace") provisions. CDDL segregates the patent license grants by the original author and later contributors. CPL and Eclipse use the same grant for both. All of these licenses have similar capture clauses—they limit the grant to patents covering the contribution or combinations with the original work. MPL and CDDL clarify that the patent grant applies only to the version to which the contributor contributed (as opposed to prior or later versions of the project, or downstream changes) and that no patent license is granted for code the contributor deletes from the software.

Each of these licenses has a patent license termination clause intended to discourage patent litigation. The CDDL has the broadest such clause, fashioned after the Mozilla Public License equivalent, which terminates all rights—copyright and patent—that the contributor received under the license. CPL and Eclipse only terminate the patent licenses and leave the copyright license intact. The Eclipse patent license termination provision is the narrower of the two, triggered only by claims relating to the project itself, whereas termination in the CPL is triggered for a given recipient by any claim against that particular recipient, whether related to the project or not. There are some variations on what triggers the termination—whether the trigger includes filing a declaratory judgment action (excluded by MPL and CDDL) or counterclaim (included by CPL). MPL is the only license where the patent license termination is retroactive in some cases.

---

[9]http://blogs.sun.com/webmink/entry/addressing_proliferation_deeds_not_just.

OTHER HEREDITARY SOFTWARE LICENSES

A number of other hereditary software licenses are not based on these licenses but are in frequent use.

SleepyCat Software promulgates a slightly different type of hereditary software license. Its drafting style is different from both GPL and the corporate hereditary licenses. Its hereditary provisions do not require licensing on identical terms but require licensing on free software terms generally. Thus, a licensee taking a license under the SleepyCat license agreement has the choice of relicensing under those identical terms or another free software license, such as GPL, LGPL, or the Mozilla Public License.

The Open Software License was written by lawyer and open source advocate Lawrence Rosen, and is currently in version 3.0. It is a hereditary license. Its hereditary provisions are triggered by "External Deployment"— a defined term that includes, according to Section 5:

> use, distribution, or communication of the Original Work or Derivative Works in any way such that the Original Work or Derivative Works may be used by anyone other than You, whether those works are distributed or communicated to those persons or made available as an application intended for use over a network.

This is a lower threshold than the distribution threshold used in GPL. This license also contains a limited provenance warranty (Section 7), whereas most open source licenses disclaim all warranties. It also contains a disclaimer of implied licenses (Section 4); not only does GPL not include this, version 3.0 expressly does not limit implied licenses that might exist in addition to the express ones in its terms.

PERMISSIVE LICENSES

There are essentially three types of permissive licenses: BSD, MIT, and Apache. The BSD (or Berkeley Software Distribution) license is the most widely used permissive open source license. It consists of a license grant (or, more accurately, a permission statement), a notice requirement, and a disclaimer. There are many variations of this license in common use. Its text reads:

* Copyright (c) <year>, <copyright holder>

* All rights reserved.

* Redistribution and use in source and binary forms, with or without modification, are permitted provided that the following conditions are met:

* Redistributions of source code must retain the above copyright notice, this list of conditions and the following disclaimer.

* Redistributions in binary form must reproduce the above copyright notice, this list of conditions and the following disclaimer in the documentation and/or other materials provided with the distribution.

* Neither the name of the University of California, Berkeley nor the names of its contributors may be used to endorse or promote products derived from this software without specific prior written permission.

* THIS SOFTWARE IS PROVIDED BY THE REGENTS AND CONTRIBUTORS "AS IS" AND ANY EXPRESS OR IMPLIED WARRANTIES, INCLUDING, BUT NOT LIMITED TO, THE IMPLIED WARRANTIES OF MERCHANTABILITY AND FITNESS FOR A PARTICULAR PURPOSE ARE DISCLAIMED.

* IN NO EVENT SHALL THE REGENTS AND CONTRIBUTORS BE LIABLE FOR ANY DIRECT, INDIRECT, INCIDENTAL, SPECIAL, EXEMPLARY, OR CONSEQUENTIAL DAMAGES

* (INCLUDING, BUT NOT LIMITED TO, PROCUREMENT OF SUBSTITUTE GOODS OR SERVICES;

* LOSS OF USE, DATA, OR PROFITS; OR BUSINESS INTERRUPTION) HOWEVER CAUSED AND

* ON ANY THEORY OF LIABILITY, WHETHER IN CONTRACT, STRICT LIABILITY, OR TORT

* (INCLUDING NEGLIGENCE OR OTHERWISE) ARISING IN ANY WAY OUT OF THE USE OF THIS

* SOFTWARE, EVEN IF ADVISED OF THE POSSIBILITY OF SUCH DAMAGE.

While the permission to use software in "source code *and* binary forms" suggests that distribution must take place in both forms—and thus the license requires disclosure of source code—the BSD license is universally understood to be a permissive license. In addition, some lawyers are concerned that the "permission" is not a license, or is not an irrevocable license. However, this issue rarely comes up as a serious concern given the context; the BSD license is simply not enforced in practice.

Nonprogrammers may wonder about the asterisks that precede each line. In some computer languages, asterisks are one way to indicate that the text that follows is commentary rather than programming language statements that are meant to be compiled and executed by the computer. This format reflects that the text of the license often is placed directly into the source code for the software it covers.

The Massachusetts Institute of Technology (MIT) license reads:

Copyright (c) <year><copyright holders>

Permission is hereby granted, free of charge, to any person obtaining a copy of this software and associated documentation files (the "Software"), to deal in the Software without restriction, including without limitation the rights to use, copy, modify, merge, publish, distribute, sublicense, and/or sell copies of the Software, and to permit persons to whom the Software is furnished to do so, subject to the following conditions:

The above copyright notice and this permission notice shall be included in all copies or substantial portions of the Software.

THE SOFTWARE IS PROVIDED "AS IS", WITHOUT WARRANTY OF ANY KIND, EXPRESS OR IMPLIED, INCLUDING BUT NOT LIMITED TO THE WARRANTIES OF MERCHANTABILITY, FITNESS FOR A PARTICULAR PURPOSE AND NONINFRINGEMENT. IN NO EVENT SHALL THE AUTHORS OR COPYRIGHT HOLDERS BE LIABLE FOR ANY CLAIM, DAMAGES OR OTHER LIABILITY, WHETHER IN AN ACTION OF CONTRACT, TORT OR OTHERWISE, ARISING FROM, OUT OF OR IN CONNECTION WITH THE SOFTWARE OR THE USE OR OTHER DEALINGS IN THE SOFTWARE.

This license does list the rights granted and grants at least one of the rights under patent law (the right to sell).

Note that while both licenses require the entire license to be reproduced, this does not imply that the license is hereditary; the license text acts as a notice rather than an active set of licensing terms, when code received under one of these licenses is distributed under other terms.

Apache 1.0

The Apache 1.0 version was repudiated due to complaints about its advertising requirements, which stated:

> 3. All advertising materials mentioning features or use of this software must display the following acknowledgement: This product includes software developed by the University of California, Berkeley and its contributors.[10]

Apache 1.1

Apache 1.1 version was released in 2000. It removed the advertising clause.[11]

Apache 2.0

Apache 2.0 version was released in 2004. Although substantially longer and more formal than the earlier versions, it remains a permissive license with easy compliance requirements. This version turned the license into a template license (see the discussion of license proliferation in Chapter 4) and added an express patent license and corresponding patent license termination provisions.[12]

Artistic License

The Artistic License is an early open source license, written by Larry Wall to cover the PERL interpreter. PERL is a high-level scripting language that is now available under either the Artistic License or the GPL. The Artistic License is essentially a permissive license but contains provisions pertinent to attribution, such as the requirements in Section 3 to include

---

[10]www.apache.org/licenses/LICENSE-1.0.

[11]www.apache.org/licenses/LICENSE-1.1.

[12]www.apache.org/licenses/LICENSE-2.0.

notices in each changed file stating how and when the file was changed and to "rename any non-standard executables so the names do not conflict with standard executables." The Artistic License is not in wide use, but has recently been revised and clarified by the PERL Foundation and will be applied to future versions of PERL. This new version 2.0 allows relicensing under the terms of other hereditary licenses.[13]

MISCELLANEOUS LICENSES

True to the iconoclastic spirit of open source, there are some amusing and idiosyncratic forms of "open source" licenses—none of which, by the way, is an approved open source license.

One example is the "beer-ware" license:[14]

 # 'The Beer-Ware License' (Revision 42)

<tobez@tobez.org> wrote this file. As long as you retain this notice you

can do whatever you want with this stuff. If we meet some day, and you think

this stuff is worth it, you can buy me a beer in return.

—Anton Berezin

A variant of it requests tacos instead of beer:[15]

The BarCamp License (Revision 1):

<tyler@bleepsoft.com> wrote this code. As long as you retain this notice you can do whatever you want with this stuff. If we ever meet at a BarCamp, and you think this code is worth it, you can buy me some tacos in return.

—R. Tyler Ballance

---

[13]www.perlfoundation.org/artistic_license_2_0.

[14]www.tobez.org/download/port-tools/port-idea. Thanks to Daniel Berlin for the citation.

[15]http://tyler.geekisp.com/code/BarCampLicense.txt. Thanks to Daniel Berlin for the citation.

And another promotes the petting of cats:

> This program is catware. If you find it useful in any way, pay for this program by spending one hour petting one or several cats.[16]

Anyone interested in more "otherware" trivia should visit the Wikipedia page devoted to it.[17] Some have described these licenses as social commentary on the length and complexity of the GPL.

For an interesting variant of GPL dealing with hardware design, there is a MIThril license:

> The purpose of this document is to disambiguate the application of the GNU General Public License to licensing hardware design. It is the intent of the authors to make clear how the language of the GPL is to be interpreted in the specific case of hardware design documents that are licensed under the GPL as construed by the MIThril Hardware Design GPL Interpretation.[18]

The tendency of developers unfamiliar with licensing practice to write their own licenses has resulted in some legal conundrums. One example—fortunately rarely seen at this point—is the so-called public domain license. This is an internally inconsistent "license" that simultaneously states that code is in the public domain and requires certain protections of copyright, such as copyright notices or license conditions. However, these licenses are increasingly difficult to find; they have fallen into disuse as understanding of open source licensing and the distinction between open source and public domain has improved.

One additional license worth mentioning is the license for OpenSSL, an extremely popular open source secure socket layer toolkit. The licenses for this toolkit are described in this way:

> The OpenSSL toolkit stays under a dual license, i.e. both the conditions of the OpenSSL License and the original SSLeay license apply to the toolkit. . . . Actually both licenses are BSD-style Open Source licenses.[19]

---

[16]http://lists.debian.org/debian-devel/1999/01/msg01921.html. Note the query whether this qualifies as a "free" software license.

[17]http://en.wikipedia.org/wiki/Otherware.

[18]www.media.mit.edu/wearables/mithril/hardware/MHDGPLI.txt. Thanks to Peter Moldave for the citation.

[19]www.openssl.org/source/license.html.

This literally says the code is covered by the two licenses simultaneously, which is unusual; often open source packages with multiple licenses are covered in part by one license and in part by another. Most business users would be relatively unconcerned by the use of software under any BSD-style permissive license, even several of them at once. However, many users are concerned by language at the end of the Original SSLeay License, the second of the two licenses:

> The license and distribution terms for any publicly available version or derivative of this code cannot be changed; i.e., this code cannot simply be copied and put under another distribution license (including the GNU [General] Public License).[20]

This statement appears to say that this license is a hereditary one. However, the industry generally treats this as a permissive license, probably primarily because the project has characterized this license as a "BSD-style" license. This is an example of a case in which the software industry struggles to interpret nonstandard open source licenses. Many open source licenses are written in a manner that is vague or difficult to interpret, but the less the authors say about them, the more uncertain the questions of interpretation are.

NON-SOFTWARE LICENSES

One category of licenses based on the concept of open source licenses does not cover software code. These licenses may incorporate "copyleft" concepts but are primarily intended to cover non-software copyrightable works, such as music, artwork, or text. The most commonly used of these licenses are the GNU Free Documentation License[21] and the Creative Commons licenses.[22]

The GNU Free Documentation License is a copyleft-style license for a "manual, textbook, or other functional and useful document." It is for "any textual work, regardless of subject matter or whether it is published as a printed book . . . principally for works whose purpose is instruction

---

[20]Spelling and punctuation conformed to U.S. usage.
[21]www.gnu.org/licenses/fdl.html.
[22]http://creativecommons.org/.

or reference." This license is promulgated by the FSF under the theory that free software requires free documentation or it cannot be properly used or modified. Some of the definitions in this license are fairly specific to informational works and do not apply well to other kinds of textual works. This license also discusses the format in which free documentation must be provided, to ensure that the format is editable without resort to a proprietary editor. It also contains certain attribution requirements with respect to the original work and modifications.

The Creative Commons licenses were written as part of the Creative Commons project. These are formal licenses written by attorneys that allow sharing of various copyrightable works using a menu approach. For instance, you may choose versions of the Creative Commons licenses that allow modification ("derivatives"), require attribution ("by"), or contain copyleft-type provisions ("sharealike"). The Creative Commons web site contains a license selector that allows you to choose attributes such as these and recommends a license containing those attributes. In addition, each license comes with a summary that describes the attributes of the license in simple terms as well as its full set of legal terms and conditions. The licenses generally disclaim warranties on behalf of the licensor. While some grant only limited rights, Creative Commons licenses are fairly well accepted by the open source community. Those releasing copyrightable works to the public who do not wish to choose a copyleft license such as GPL or a permissive license such as BSD should consider a Creative Commons license as a more flexible alternative. While these are not strictly open source licenses and a full discussion of them is beyond the scope of this book, they are an interesting alternative to the lay drafting style of licenses such as GPL and a nod to the discretion of authors to choose terms under which they will make their works available. The licenses were written to provide a recognizable standard for certain types of licensing while also providing a set of traditionally drafted terms. The Creative Commons also acts as a web portal to make certain copyrightable works available under the terms of its licenses.

The difficulty with these types of licenses arises when they are applied improperly to software code. For instance, authors who choose to apply a Creative Commons license to software may find that there is little guidance on what scope of modifications must be covered by the license. This is because the "sharealike" versions of these licenses rely on background copyright principles to determine the meaning of the "Adaptations" that must be covered by the license.[23] The more difficult problem, though, is the converse. When open source licenses are applied to non-software textual works, many of the provisions in the open source licenses are nonsensical. For instance, the requirement to make a "source code" available for a book or song makes little sense. Licensees sometimes struggle a great deal with this, and in such cases the interpretation of the license is extremely uncertain.

---

[23]For the definition of Adaptations in a sharealike Creative Commons license, see, e.g., http://creativecommons.org/licenses/by-sa/3.0/legalcode.

CHAPTER 4

Due Diligence, License Proliferation, and Compatibility

Today's software development takes place overwhelmingly in a heterogeneous landscape. Most software code bases today include all kinds of software—open source software, free software, and proprietary software—or any other categories of license one cares to name.

WHAT IS THE PROBLEM WITH COMBINING SOFTWARE?

Putting different kinds of software together is like holding a dinner party for my relatives. Maybe, if I go to a lot of work, I can serve food everyone will eat: My middle-age uncle on his low-carb diet wants meat and fish; my sister the vegan wants only locally grown vegetables; and my teenage nephew will eat anything as long as it comes from McDonald's. But what if all the dinner guests have not only their own preferences, but a vehement, polemical disgust for the foods the others eat? It is hard to bring everyone to the same table. That is what the software world can be like today.

Like many problems in the world, the difficulty in the software world comes not from the participants being different but from participants being unable to coexist with the others. Software licenses, like people who are certain that they are right, place restrictions on the others with whom they coexist. With enough restrictions, and when those restrictions are mutually exclusive, coexistence is difficult or impossible.

Avoiding this incompatibility in the software world can be a difficult job. Developers using software in a code base need to make sure they are not combining it in ways that will violate the licensing terms that apply to each piece. The process of making sure is called *due diligence*.

WHAT IS DUE DILIGENCE?

The process of due diligence, or housekeeping, for a software code base is familiar to most professional software developers. If you provide software to others, and you do so under a specific set of licensing terms, it is essential that you actually have the right to provide that software under those terms. If you do not, you have both infringed the copyrights of your licensors and caused your licensees to do the same. To ensure that this does not happen, you, as licensor, must ensure that your "inbound" rights—the rights granted from others to you—are as broad as your "outbound" rights—the rights you have exercised, or granted to others.

In Exhibit 4.1, the product's code base consists of two elements: (1) code written by the provider of the code base (you), and (2) code written by others. The code written by others can be open source or not, as long as the "outbound" rights granted to the licensee are no greater than the "inbound" rights granted to you. Keep in mind that any rights granted to you that you intend to pass on to your licensees must be either sublicensable, or granted directly to your licensees as well as you.

In Exhibit 4.1, there is no problem, because the inbound grant (license to distribute, copy, prepare derivative works) is equal to the outbound grant (license to distribute, copy, prepare derivative works) and the inbound grant is sublicensable. However, Exhibit 4.2 shows a problem.

For instance, if your inbound license grants to you only the right to distribute and copy, but not to modify (such as with the Creative Commons Attribution, No Derivatives license), and you put material you received under that license into a code base that is licensed outbound to others under a broader license to distribute, copy, and prepare derivative works (such as Creative Commons Attribution, Share-Alike license), you are in violation of your inbound license, and your licensees are unwittingly infringing your licensor's intellectual property rights.

Fortunately, in a project that consists entirely of open source code, this is never the case, because all open source licenses, by definition, grant all of the rights of copyright. The difficulty with open source is reconciling

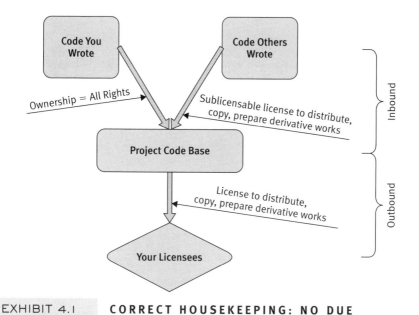

EXHIBIT 4.1 **CORRECT HOUSEKEEPING: NO DUE DILIGENCE PROBLEM**

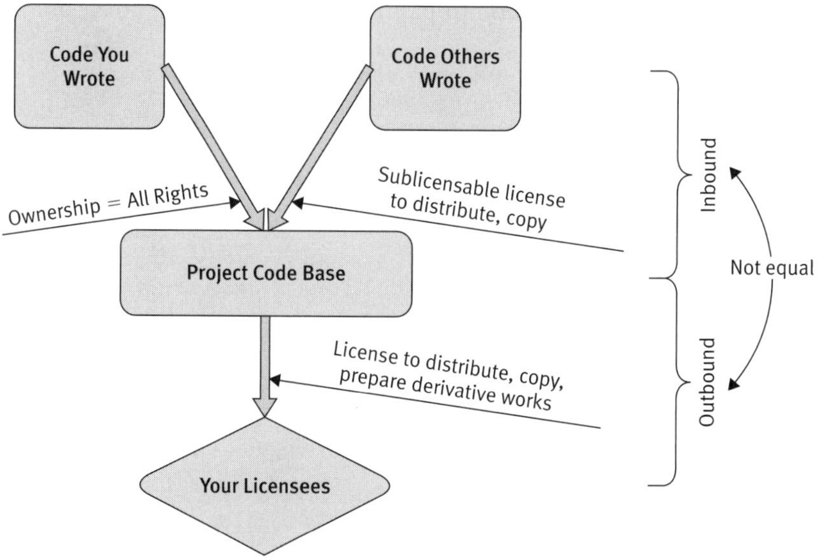

EXHIBIT 4.2 **DUE DILIGENCE PROBLEM: LICENSE SCOPE**

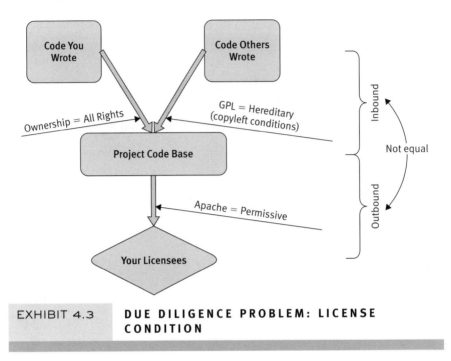

EXHIBIT 4.3 **DUE DILIGENCE PROBLEM: LICENSE CONDITION**

the conditions attached to the licenses, not the scope of the licenses themselves. So, as Exhibit 4.3 shows, the picture changes.

Exhibit 4.3 shows a due diligence problem. The code base includes a module whose inbound rights are covered by the GNU General Public License (GPL). This means the "copyleft" requirements of the GPL will attach when you distribute code to your licensees, requiring you to distribute that code under GPL. However, your outbound license is Apache. Thus, you have failed to attach appropriate conditions to your outbound license, and you have a diligence problem. You—and your licensees, if they distribute code—are violating the GPL and the copyright of the author of the GPL code. Here, in contrast to the situation in Exhibit 4.2, the problem arises not from inadequate scope of inbound rights but inadequate scope of outbound license conditions.

The more inbound licenses apply to your code base, the more complicated the due diligence task. This process, and the complications engendered by it, is not specific to open source. This process receives so much attention in the open source world because the rise of open source has caused developers to have better, and less expensive, access to code—and to combine code from many different sources. Also, managers of open source code bases sometimes mistakenly assume that open source obviates the need for due diligence. The only thing that has changed due to open source is the volume of diligence to be conducted, not the basic nature of it.

To provide your software to customers so that they can actually use it, rather than inheriting infringement issues, you need to make sure you do your housekeeping—your due diligence.

LICENSE CONDITIONS AND DILIGENCE PROBLEMS

When we speak of license conditions, we are talking about the so-called copyleft provisions of hereditary licenses. All of these hereditary licenses are like the different guests at my dinner party: Their diets are mutually exclusive. The defining feature of hereditary licenses is that the code covered by the licenses, and any modifications, always must be made available under the same licensing terms. Thus, once code is released under GPL, all licensees who accept it under GPL must provide it to others only under GPL, and no other license.

The GPL says:

> 6. Each time you redistribute the Program (or any work based on the Program), the recipient automatically receives a license from the original licensor to copy, distribute or modify the Program subject to these terms and conditions. You may not impose any further restrictions on the recipients' exercise of the rights granted herein.

Note the "further restrictions" prohibition. This is what causes the code released under this license not to be licensable on any other terms. The terms of any other license would likely be considered "restrictions" contrary to this requirement of the GPL.

Other hereditary licenses work the same way, each applying its own terms, with a couple of notable exceptions. For example, the Lesser General

Public License (LGPL) specifically allows relicensing under GPL, and some of the corporate-style hereditary licenses allow relicensing under binary commercial licenses, so long as the original code is simultaneously made available under the hereditary terms. See, for instance, these provisions:

From the LGPL version 2.1:

> 3. You may opt to apply the terms of the ordinary GNU General Public License instead of this License to a given copy of the Library. . . . Once this change is made in a given copy, it is irreversible for that copy, so the ordinary GNU General Public License applies to all subsequent copies and derivative works made from that copy. This option is useful when you wish to copy part of the code of the Library into a program that is not a library.[1]

From the MPL:

> **3.6. Distribution of Executable Versions.**
>
> You may distribute Covered Code in Executable form only if the requirements of Section 3.1–3.5 have been met for that Covered Code, and if You include a notice stating that the Source Code version of the Covered Code is available under the terms of this License, including a description of how and where You have fulfilled the obligations of Section 3.2. The notice must be conspicuously included in any notice in an Executable version, related documentation or collateral in which You describe recipients' rights relating to the Covered Code. You may distribute the Executable version of Covered Code or ownership rights under a license of Your choice, which may contain terms different from this License, provided that You are in compliance with the terms of this License and that the license for the Executable version does not attempt to limit or alter the recipient's rights in the Source Code version from the rights set forth in this License. If You distribute the Executable version under a different license You must make it absolutely clear that any terms which differ from this License are offered by You alone, not by the Initial Developer or any Contributor. You hereby agree to indemnify the Initial Developer and every Contributor for any liability

---

[1]http://opensource.org/licenses/lgpl-license.php.

incurred by the Initial Developer or such Contributor as a result of any such terms You offer.[2]

Other than scattered exceptions like this, code licensed under a hereditary license is forever covered by that license. In law, we say that the license "runs with" the rights to the software (like an easement or right-of-way that runs with the title to land).

This same problem exists in the proprietary software world. If your software product contains a library of code that is licensed to you by a developer or supplier, the agreement that licenses that library to you will inevitably contain so-called flow-down provisions that must be included in any of your downstream outbound licenses. These provisions typically include warranty disclaimers, limitations of liability, and reverse-engineering prohibitions. In the proprietary licensing context, for instance, most licenses limit the scope of downstream licenses and place restrictions on the use of code. But in open source licensing, the flow-down provisions work in reverse: Instead of keeping the source code confidential, the copyleft and "additional restrictions" prohibitions keep it from being kept confidential.

So, now we have established that the guests at the dinner party will not eat the same meal. But what causes them not to be able to sit at the same table?

LICENSE COMPATIBILITY

When people decry open source "compatibility" problems, they mean two very different things, which are almost never distinguished properly: relicensing and combination. You might think of relicensing as a vertical compatibility problem and combination as a horizontal one.

The relicensing problem is demonstrated by Exhibits 4.2 and 4.3. If the terms of the inbound license are not consistent with the terms of the outbound license, a due diligence problem results. As described, most hereditary licenses cannot be substituted for each other, so any hereditary license can cause a relicensing issue.

---

[2]http://opensource.org/licenses/mozilla1.1.php.

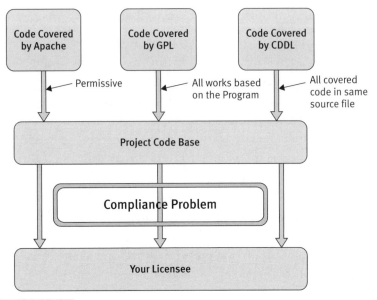

EXHIBIT 4.4   **DUE DILIGENCE PROBLEM: COMBINATION (HORIZONTAL COMPATIBILITY)**

The second set of compatibility problems has to do with combining code covered by different and irreconcilable hereditary licenses in the same code base. This is the problem of the dinner guests who cannot abide each other's presence at the table. See Exhibit 4.4.

In Exhibit 4.4, the code base contains code received under Apache, GPL, and the Common Development and Distribution License (CDDL). Neither Apache nor CDDL can be relicensed under GPL.[3] The developer solves this issue simply by passing the licenses for the code through to its licensees. In other words, the code base contains three parts, each licensed under its own terms. This is like the dinner table where no one eats the same meal.

---

[3]For Apache 2.0 and GPL 2.0, this represents a difference of opinion between the Free Software Foundation (FSF) and the Apache Foundation. FSF says that GPL and Apache are not compatible (i.e., Apache code cannot be relicensed under GPL) and Apache says, more or less, that they are. www.apache.org/licenses/GPL-compatibility.html. See Chapter 18 on GPL3 for compatibility of Apache 2.0 and GPL3.

But because one of the licenses is GPL, this solution does not work. The GPL is, essentially, the diner who cannot tolerate the presence of the others.[4] Of all the commonly used open source licenses, the GPL claims the broadest reach on neighboring code.[5] The GPL's exact reach is complicated, and is covered in Chapter 14. To understand the combination problem, it is necessary only to know the Free Software Foundation's (FSF) basic claim about the GPL's scope: It covers all code in the same executable as any GPL code. In other words, anything that is part of the same computer program—dynamically or statically linked code, plug-ins, libraries, and so forth—must all be covered by GPL. That is why Exhibit 4.4 is a combination problem. If the other code covered by CDDL and Apache is part of the same code base, and it is in the same executable, it must be covered by GPL if the developer is to comply with the requirements of GPL. However, as we already know, CDDL code cannot be relicensed under GPL.

In contrast, if you use code under LGPL and code under CDDL code in the same code base, you can, in fact, distribute the code of each of these modules, side by side, each under its own hereditary terms. (See Exhibit 4.5.) For instance, LGPL code can be combined with other code by using the LGPL code as a dynamically linked library (because the license expressly allows this). LGPL is in this sense horizontally compatible with CDDL, because CDDL allows its code to be combined with code in separate source files (such as a dynamically linked library). LGPL and CDDL are thus compatible for combination but not for relicensing.

In case it is not obvious already, it is worth observing that permissive licenses like Berkeley Software Distribution (BSD) are almost always "compatible" with other licenses, whether open source or not. In other words, code you receive under the BSD license can be licensed to others

---

[4]This is not unique to the GPL, of course. Proprietary licenses certainly have restrictions against combination. Some even have prohibitions against combining their software with GPL code. Others are aimed toward value-add requirements or not disclosing proprietary applications program interfaces.

[5]For the most part. Affero GPL is even more restrictive. However, given its limited use as of this writing, I have not focused on it. Please note that GPL3, which contains a provision expressly allowing combination with Affero GPL code, may result in the more frequent use of Affero GPL in the future.

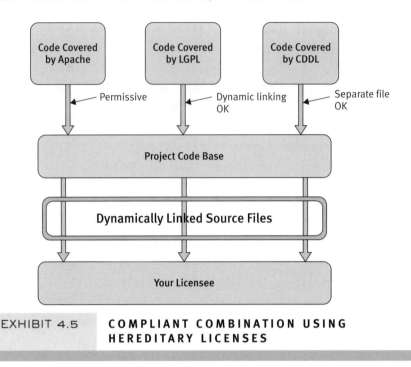

| EXHIBIT 4.5 | COMPLIANT COMBINATION USING HEREDITARY LICENSES |

under most any license: commercial, permissive, or hereditary. In licensing terms, this means (1) the scope of the grant of rights and conditions under the inbound license is broader than or equal to the scope of the grant of rights and conditions under the outbound license, and (2) the few conditions imposed in the inbound license are easy to carry forward to the outbound license.

CHOICES IN AN INCOMPATIBLE WORLD

To the uninitiated, this whole compatibility issue may seem surprising. After all, the open source definition explicitly requires:

9. License Must Not Restrict Other Software

The license must not place restrictions on other software that is distributed along with the licensed software. For example, the license must not insist that all other programs distributed on the same medium must be open-source software. . . . *Yes, the GPL is conformant with this requirement. Software linked with GPLed libraries only inherits the GPL if it forms a single work, not any software with which they are merely distributed.*

Note the italicized comment, which anticipates criticism of the GPL in light of this requirement. If all open source licenses were truly nonrestrictive with respect to combined code, all open source software could be combined with perfect horizontal compatibility. But that is not the way the open source world works.

While the preceding discussion analyzes problems of compatibility from the viewpoint of developers who integrate open source code into their products, this viewpoint should inform authors as well; authors are the ultimate arbiters of what licensing terms will apply to their code. The choice to apply one open source license or another to a work is both a philosophical and a practical one. When authors choose GPL, that choice is usually a philosophical one, or because it is the most popular open source license and thus much compatible code will be available to combine with it.[6] Other authors choose to align themselves with the political and technological missions of organizations like Apache or Mozilla, which take more permissive postures with respect to code combination.

However, some authors are more concerned about practical considerations, such as maximizing adoption of the code or promoting the use of the code in commercial products. If so, the authors who seek to release code under an open source license should be mindful of combination problems and ask what developers will need to do to comply with the license chosen. That choice should be based on the behavior incentives the authors wish to create.[7] Placing licensees in challenging compliance situations—such as releasing library code designed to be dynamically linked to other applications under GPL—will discourage all but those willing to place their entire code base under GPL. In a sense, authors who release code under GPL purposely seek to create compliance problems, to force all developers to adopt GPL to the exclusion of all else— and that is a philosophical choice. However, some authors create such problems unintentionally, and, not understanding the choice, lead their licensees into infringement or impossible compliance situations.

---

[6]See, e.g., David A. Wheeler, "Make Your Open Source Software GPL-Compatible. Or Else," June 5, 2002, revised March 21, 2006, at www.dwheeler.com/essays/gpl-compatible.html.
[7]For more on how to make such a choice, see Chapter 11.

A difference of opinion exists within the open source community over whether Apache 2.0 and GPL2 are compatible (i.e., whether Apache 2.0 works can be relicensed under GPL2). The Apache Foundation "considers this issue to be in legal limbo, at least until we get a definitive answer regarding the survivability of implied patent licenses."[8] Permissive licenses are generally considered compatible with any outbound license; at least this is the objective of a permissive license. However, the FSF made a public statement that Apache 2.0 was incompatible with GPL2 because of Apache's express patent license and patent termination provisions.

Here is the Apache Foundation's posting about the dispute:

> After spending a couple hours on the phone with the FSF, we have a better understanding of the particular interpretation of the GPL that might lead one to construe the following: granting an explicit patent license causes any implicit patent licenses to be null and void; revoking that explicit patent license causes the person who is claiming infringement of their patent to lose the patent rights that would otherwise have been attained via the GPL's implicit rights; loss of patent rights means loss of right to use; GPL section 7 allows a patent owner to claim infringement of a patent within a GPL'd work and continue to distribute that work as GPL up until a third party imposes a restriction on the rights of others to distribute (i.e., until a judgment or injunction is placed on the work).

> GPL section 6—"You may not impose any further restrictions on the recipients' exercise of the rights granted herein"—does not apply to patents because the "rights granted herein" are only copyright.[9]

> This is our current understanding of the position held by the FSF; whether our understanding is correct has not yet been confirmed.

> Note that this is contrary to our previously stated belief that the GPL forbids the continuing use of a GPL'd work by an entity that has claimed the work contains infringement of its own patented technology. Apparently, it is okay for the distribution and use to continue up until a judgment or injunction has been issued because the FSF does not believe a claim of patent infringement amounts to a restriction on the rights of others

---

[8]www.apache.org/licenses/GPL-compatibility.html.
[9]Ibid.

to redistribute, and the constraint on further restriction applies only to those rights listed within the GPL itself (copyright).

Aside from the substantive question here, this dispute is worth observing as a case study in the politics and legal positioning of the open source movement. First, the FSF's position on most patent issues—such as the existence and scope of implied patent licenses and the fact that explicit patent licenses void implicit ones—must be understood as advocacy rather than conventional legal analysis. Most lawyers would put the issue in more shades of gray, because that is the state of the law. (See the discussion on implied patent licenses in Chapter 7.) Most commercial intellectual property licenses contain statements such as "No licenses will be implied" or "Licensor hereby disclaims any implied licenses." Thus most intellectual property licensing lawyers would question whether any express license at all would have the same effect.

Second, this issue turns in part on the interpretation of the so-called liberty-or-death provision of the GPL:

> 7. If, as a consequence of a court judgment or allegation of patent infringement or for any other reason (not limited to patent issues), conditions are imposed on you (whether by court order, agreement or otherwise) that contradict the conditions of this License, they do not excuse you from the conditions of this License. If you cannot distribute so as to satisfy simultaneously your obligations under this License and any other pertinent obligations, then as a consequence you may not distribute the Program at all.

FSF's position is that the termination of the license in Apache 2.0 will happen in some instances where the liberty-or-death provision has not yet been invoked, and this difference is a "further restriction" prohibited by GPL. Of course, if FSF is incorrect and either (1) the express patent license does not void all implied licenses or (2) there is no implied patent license, this is not a reason for incompatibility.

Naturally, as the Apache Foundation points out,[10] this matters only if there actually are patents covering the work. The Apache Foundation has no patents,[11] and it seems likely that few of its contributors have valid patents

---

[10]Ibid.
[11]Ibid.

on their contributions.[12] Thus the problem may be far more theoretical than real.

In any case, the FSF pronounced GPL version 3.0 (GPL3) compatible with Apache 2.0,[13] ending the compatibility controversy, at least for GPL3.

An Embarrassment of Riches?

License proliferation, as a concept, is transparent in the proprietary licensing context. The concept of proliferation arises in open source licensing because of the limited number of licenses there are from which to choose. In the world of proprietary licensing, there is no finite set of choices, so proliferation has never been a topic of discussion. Every licensor writes his or her own license. Once the universe of licensing terms is reduced to a finite number of approved licenses, the desirability of multiple licenses comes into sharper focus.

The proliferation debate arises in part due to compatibility problems described earlier. In a sense, there is an inherent problem with the existence of many hereditary licenses, all of which are mutually exclusive. But the proliferation debate is also a product of the sheer number of licenses characterized as open source. Again, to those from the proprietary world, this complaint may seem an odd one. The administrative problem of confirming that all inbound licenses are consistent with outbound ones long predates open source. The rise of open source has actually made legal review of inbound licenses easier, not harder. Almost all open source software is licensed under about a dozen licenses or trivial variations of the same.[14] For anyone accustomed to the due diligence process, the task

---

[12]Those who care about their patents simply do not tend to contribute software covered by those patents to open source projects like Apache. The decision to do so is a decision to forgo substantial enforcement rights.

[13]gplv3.fsf.org/rationale. The explanation is less than clear, but given that many thought GPL2 and Apache 2.0 were compatible in the first place, following the rationale may be more work than it is worth.

[14]For instance, see http://freshmeat.net/stats/. Over 60 percent of the software projects use GPL, and LGPL and BSD account for about another 10 percent. However, these statistics only reflect projects on Freshmeat.net, and corporate projects, which may be more likely to use corporate licenses like CDDL and MPL, may be less likely to be listed on that site.

has not actually become harder—except perhaps in the sense that open source licenses may be more opaque and harder to review than proprietary licenses, or that the availability of open source has increased the amount of inbound licensed code. Currently there exist about 60 approved open source licenses.[15] However, many are variations on a theme (such as MIT and BSD), and many of them are rarely used.

The problem with license proliferation and the due diligence chores it engenders actually results from the natural evolution that has occurred in the way software is developed. Over time, more and more code is reused. In the twenty-first century, there are fewer and fewer compelling reasons to reinvent the software wheel. The tendency of the industry is now to focus on the margins rather than the basics. This is a result of the maturity of the industry, not open source. Open source is just part of the equation—a free and useful part.

One of the complaints about license proliferation is that laypersons choosing licenses for their own software are confused by the wealth of choices. However, the argument that restricting choice benefits those making the choice is a challenging one to support. Some have observed that the sentiment against drafting new licenses is intellectually or morally troubling. Obviously any copyright owner has the right—within limits on license enforceability—to draft whatever license he chooses. Their intellectual property rights give them this power. Freedom of contract with respect to one's property is a fundamental tenet of political freedom, some observe, and limiting that freedom is wrong. The normative position that all software should be licensed under a single license leaves the treacherous question of who chooses the license.

But in taking a position against license proliferation, the open source community is applying the same cultural norms to licenses that it does to software. In the open source world, everyone has the unfettered right to change and fork a code base, but people tend not to. Although they possess the right, they forgo it voluntarily. Lack of standardization has obvious practical problems. If there are 500 versions of Linux, no one will write applications for it. So there is at the same time a legal freedom to fork and a social pressure to avoid forking. Similarly, those in the open

---

[15]This discussion is based on the listing of licenses at www.opensource.org/licenses/.

source world concerned with license proliferation generally seek to discourage new licenses, not prohibit them.

Still others observe that the problem is not one of too many licenses but too many poorly drafted licenses. Well-drafted licenses make compliance easier, not harder. Most people—lawyers and businesspeople alike—find some open source licenses difficult to understand. While many open source licenses employ a lay person's drafting style in a well-intentioned attempt to increase readability and clarity, the result sometimes is the opposite, with many important matters left vague or ambiguous. Some have observed that the GPL reads more like a political manifesto than a license agreement.[16] It is one thing to have to read and know 100 licenses. It is quite another to have to research the cultural context for the use of 100 licenses to know what they mean.[17] This necessity is born of the licenses being written in nonstandard styles that require outside commentary to interpret them.

Whether you believe the proliferation debate to be worth its press or not, the debate has resulted in some interesting consequences that anyone navigating the waters of open source should understand. First, writing a new open source license—or even a variation on an old one—is a very unpopular thing to do. Because many open source code releases are intended to create goodwill in the development community, using a new license can backfire. Second, having a license approved by the Open Source Initiative (OSI) promises to become very difficult; OSI proposes to add a new requirement that new licenses "not be duplicative" as a criterion for approval, whereas the original criteria for approval are largely limited to compliance with the Open Source Definition.[18] Of course, not all licensors place great importance on the OSI's blessing. Some very popular projects seem unaffected by the lack of OSI certification.

---

[16]A search on Google for "GPL political manifesto" yields lots of hits; see, e.g., Bruce Perens's article, "The Open Source Definition," at http://perens.com/OSD.html.

[17]See the discussion of trade usage in interpreting open source licenses in Chapter 14.

[18]"Open-Source Referees Change the Rules,"*Eweek*, April 7, 2005, www.eweek.com/article2/0,1895,1783791,00.asp.

For instance, the original SugarCRM license was a variant of the Mozilla Public License that was not officially approved by OSI, but SugarCRM was universally understood to be an open source product.[19] Nevertheless, the OSI's shift in position reflects a growing reluctance in the community to support more licenses.

REUSABILITY

One criticism of some existing open source licenses that relates tangentially to the proliferation debate is the question of reusability. Licenses like the Mozilla Public License or the Apple Public Source License are not templates, in the sense that the name of the licensor is "hard-coded" into the license. In order for the license to be reused for works of others, there must be textual changes to the license terms as described in this provision of the MPL:

> **6.3. Derivative Works.**
>
> If you create or use a modified version of this License (which you may only do in order to apply it to code which is not already Covered Code governed by this License), You must (a) rename Your license so that the phrases "Mozilla," "MOZILLAPL," "MOZPL," "Netscape," "MPL," "NPL" or any confusingly similar phrase do not appear in your license (except to note that your license differs from this License) and (b) otherwise make it clear that Your version of the license contains terms which differ from the Mozilla Public License and Netscape Public License. (Filling in the name of the Initial Developer, Original Code or Contributor in the notice described in Exhibit A of Appendix A shall not of themselves be deemed to be modifications of this License.)[20]

Moreover, licenses like the Netscape Public License (NPL) are asymmetrical, reserving special rights for the licensor. Thus, paragraph V of the "Amendments" section of the NPL allows Netscape to license contributions on proprietary terms as well as the terms of the license, whereas other licensees do not have that choice and must abide by the hereditary

---

[19]Sugar CRM has since switched to GPL3. www.sugarcrm.com/crm/gplv3-faq.html.
[20]MPL version 1.1.

nature of the license.[21] These provisions make it unfeasible for any party other than Netscape to use the license.

The OSI has demonstrated a preference for template licenses like Common Development and Distribution License, the most recent corporate-style license approved by the organization. Although it was promulgated by Sun,[22] CDDL does not name a particular licensor and is intended to be adoptable by anyone without modification. The OSI has also taken steps to recommend against the continued use of certain licenses by asking their authors to disavow them—although the OSI also points out that it cannot prohibit the use of those licenses.[23] For instance, Intel repudiated its own variant of the BSD license in an announcement in 2005.[24]

Finally, as an added gloss on the proliferation debate, some observe that all the popular licenses are U.S. licenses, although the open source movement is intended to be an international one. The efforts of countries to write open source licenses particular to their jurisprudence have been discouraged due to the license proliferation debate, but that discouragement can easily sound like parochialism when it comes from the drafters and stewards of U.S. licenses. Concerns about U.S.-centric focus to open source have, in part, resulted in efforts to revise popular licenses like GPL to account for international concerns and make their language less dependent on U.S. copyright law terms and concepts.

---

[21]http://en.wikipedia.org/wiki/Netscape_Public_License.

[22]http://www.sun.com/cddl/.

[23]www.opensource.org/docs/policy/licenseproliferation.php.

[24]"Intel Withdraws Open Source License, Receives Applause,"*Newsforge*, March 29, 2005, http://software.newsforge.com/article.pl?sid=05/03/29/227206.

CHAPTER 5

Audits and Compliance Initiatives

Much legal activity in the open source area consists of compliance analysis—in other words, determining whether a company is complying with all the relevant license conditions of its inbound open source licenses. This activity is the process by which companies conduct due diligence (as described in Chapter 4). This activity has many names—due diligence, open source counseling, and auditing—depending on context. Sometimes compliance work is performed in anticipation of a transaction, such as a merger or investment, and in those cases it is usually called due diligence. In other cases it is an ongoing process—partially to ensure that when a transaction occurs, the due diligence process will be quick and accurate. Lately the requirements of the Sarbanes-Oxley Act have motivated public or pre-public companies to undertake audits to minimize the risk of corporate or director liability. Finally, some companies undertake diligence as an ongoing process, simply to ensure good legal housekeeping and maintain their intellectual property house in good order.

Compliance work has two steps: information gathering and legal analysis. The first step is by far the most costly and time-consuming. In the contemporary technology company, open source compliance work has become a complex administrative task, and few companies have undertaken it from the beginning of their operations in a systematic and thorough way. The larger the organization, and the more backtracking there is to do, the more difficult the task. Companies composed of multiple divisions that conduct independent development, or companies composed of several acquired entities that have previously operated as independent companies, find it particularly difficult to mount a consistent and coordinated open source compliance program.

PROVENANCE AND OBJECTIVE CHECKING

There are two overarching approaches to the compliance audit process—provenance checking and code scanning—although these two approaches are not mutually exclusive.

The provenance method consists in recording and following an audit trail, based on internal records, of what code is in the code base; determining what licenses cover each element (or in the case of code developed from scratch in house, determining that there is no license to consider); and discovering how the code is used in the code base (to assess whether the requirements of hereditary licenses have been properly followed). A significant part of this task is organizing the data that are collected, preferably into a form that is centralized and searchable. The process is similar to a title search.

The code scanning method consists of using automated tools to examine the actual code base to determine what third-party code is in the code base and what licenses cover it. The automated tools used to accomplish this task range from the very simple (tools that locate copyright notices and license language embedded in the comments of the source code) to the very complex (tools that perform matching algorithms to make an objective comparison between the code base and known third-party code, and referencing an independent database of information about the licenses known to cover that code).

The code scanning method is necessarily more objective and more accurate, but also usually comes with an out-of-pocket price tag.[1] Many large companies use their own internally developed tools for code scanning, but outside consultants are also available to perform this work with

---

[1]Whether provenance or code scanning is more expensive, taking into account internal costs, is an open question, the answer to which undoubtedly changes from one situation to the next, and will change over time as more code scanning technology is developed and more competitors enter the code scanning field.

their own tools. The most famous purveyors currently are Black Duck Software, Inc.[2] and Palamida, Inc.[3] Due to cost considerations, most companies begin with the provenance method. They move to a code scanning method if they decide it is worthwhile to further minimize risk with increased accuracy or because the state or quality of their internal record keeping does not allow for a satisfactory provenance search.

Using the provenance method may seem like relying on a fragile chain of records, which can be corrupted at every turn. There is virtually no way, by technical methods, to prevent engineers from using code without preserving the license terms that may be embedded in the code. But provenance approaches may be more accurate than they seem. Much open source code is used with little or no modification. As a consequence, when open source code is integrated into larger products, the file names for the modules are almost always not changed. Changing them would usually cause operational problems, because every update of the open source package would have to be similarly changed if the build instructions for the product are to work after the update. If the file names have been preserved, it is relatively easy to discover, through online research that is time-consuming rather than difficult, what license covers the code module.

The case is different, of course, when open source code has been heavily modified or when parts have been removed from the open source package and copied into other code modules. If so, code scanning may be the only way to trace the licenses attached to the code, as the trail of the provenance has been lost. Most companies that conduct a code scan find at least some of these snippets in the code base.

With either method, the final step is analyzing the information and identifying any problems and methods for resolution. This step involves legal analysis, and should be performed by lawyers or with lawyer supervision and review.

If you are planning to engage in an audit, there are some practical aspects to consider about the difficulties of the project. If your company does substantial software development, if your organization is a large or

---

[2] www.blackducksoftware.com.
[3] www.palamida.com.

compartmentalized one, or if your organization is likely to use the same functionality in multiple product lines, you should start with the assumption that audit is a significant, possibly multiyear, initiative. While, theoretically, audits can be conducted much more quickly, they usually are not.

Software engineers are unlikely to spend the time and attention on an audit that lawyers or businesspeople wish or expect. There are several reasons for this: Engineers are rewarded primarily for their ability to finish development projects and meet release deadlines, and not to engage in legal housekeeping; they dislike the legal process and dealing with lawyers; they hold ambivalent beliefs about open source and how much corporate organizations should benefit from it; or they hold mistaken beliefs about what coding practices are acceptable from a legal perspective and may not wish their beliefs to be challenged. Pressure from management to engage in an audit may be met with resistance (or in some cases, hostility) and will be perceived by engineers as another brick on their already heavy load. The best way to address this problem, though perhaps not solve it, is to integrate the audit process in an effort to participate responsibly in the open source movement and to honor the requirements of open source rather than simply to avoid liability for the company. Education is key: Your legal department should hold sessions to educate engineering leadership on your company's open source policies and, perhaps as important, to allow the engineers to express their views on open source. In such sessions, engineers and lawyers usually find much common ground, so such sessions can greatly speed or facilitate the audit process.

Applying Policy and Legal Review

The point of conducting an audit is to apply corporate policy to use of open source code, but first an organization must develop a policy. To do this, the organization must develop an internal consensus on what use of open source is acceptable. Most organizations approach this task by classifying open source licenses into three categories:

1. Always approved (usually including the permissive licenses such as BSD (Berkeley Software Distribution), MIT (Massachusetts Institute of Technology), and Apache)
2. Never approved (more on this later)

3. Requiring legal review (usually including the free software licenses such as the GNU General Public License (GPL) and GNU Lesser General Public License (LGPL))

In the case of most hereditary licenses, legal review may be limited to confirming that the means of use of the code within in the product is consistent with the requirements of the license (such as use in a dynamically linked library for LGPL). Some organizations require a legal approval on this issue; others rely on engineers to confirm this aspect of use and approve the use under such a license with no further legal review. The most complex review usually is reserved for GPL code, due to the ambiguities of GPL interpretation (discussed in Chapter 14).

Organizations can be idiosyncratic when they decide which licenses are unacceptable for use. Some organizations include GPL, because of the uncertainty about its language and interpretation. Some organizations refuse to use the Mozilla Public License version 1.1 (MPL), because they are concerned that the enforcement value of their patent portfolios will be compromised by MPL's patent license termination provisions, which allow retroactive termination of licenses.[4] One organization of which I am aware places only LGPL in this category, due to a decision made by in-house counsel that it was too vague—a view some might share, but which was very odd in light of the fact that GPL was approved for use by the same company. The bottom line is that every organization has its own calculus for this classification, based more on the characteristics of the organization than those of the licenses, the key factors being the extensiveness and value of the company's patent portfolio and its tolerance for risk.

An "audit" implies a review of existing or past uses; developing policies for forward-going use is similar but not identical. Because of the perceived limitation on contractual remedies for open source licenses, many companies choose to limit compliance efforts to future releases and expend minimal effort on compliance for products already in the marketplace, particularly products that are expected to be reengineered or discontinued or products with frequent release cycles. While this strategy is not without risk, it is not irrational. The stated philosophy of organizations

---

[4]See Section 8.2(b) of the Mozilla Public License, version 1.1.

such as the Free Software Foundation is to limit their enforcement efforts to compliance going forward. So far no product has ever been subject to an injunction or damages award for past lack of compliance with the GPL.

SOME NUTS AND BOLTS

If you are engaging in a provenance-based audit, you need to know how to find accurate license terms for a given list of code modules. The list of modules in a product should be relatively easy to provide; your engineers can generate this information based on the build instructions for the product. When you receive this list, it is likely to be in either one of two forms: a list of modules or a list of modules indicating the licenses that cover them. Unless you are certain of your source's understanding of how to identify licenses, you should not take the latter at face value. People can, and often do, misidentify licenses. This happens largely for two reasons: Either the reviewers have insufficient training in how to identify licenses, or they are relying on inaccurate sources to find this information. If the information you are given is inaccurate, and if you rely on it, your assessment of compliance may be in error.

If you want to check the license that applies to a particular module, the most reliable way is to download the code for the module from the original source, and check the license referenced or duplicated in the source file. Most open source projects make their code available for download to anyone, either through their own site or through a public repository, such as www.sourceforge.org. Keep in mind that the accuracy of this exercise depends on the original source for the code—usually the project that makes the code available—faithfully applying the correct license terms to the code it makes available. You will have little or no visibility into the rights associated with the code beyond this point, unless you abandon the provenance method and perform a code scan. If this process is too time-consuming, you can simply examine the project's web site for a statement about the code's licensing terms rather than examining the source code itself. However, be aware that open source projects, particularly smaller ones, sometimes present incorrect or, more often, incomplete information about the licensing terms actually included in their code.

The most dangerous case, of course, occurs when the web page for the project indicates one license (such as LGPL) while the license in the actual code is a more restrictive license (such as GPL), which leads the unwary into compliance errors. (This particular confusion sometimes arises because LGPL code may by definition be relicensed under GPL. The project offering LGPL code may not explicitly state that, when distributed with the GPL code in the project, the LGPL code is "converted" to GPL code. The licensee must therefore accept all code under GPL if it is to use the project code base as a whole.) Sometimes confusion arises because some code in a project is intended to be used as a development tool and is licensed under a restrictive license (because the user is unlikely to distribute the code and invoke its hereditary requirements), but other code is library or run-time code and thus covered under a less restrictive license. This scheme is perfectly sensible but may be confusing for the uninitiated. Finally, you should be aware that some projects describe licensing terms for some, but not necessarily all, of the modules they make available. Boost is a good example: It states that the Boost license (similar to BSD) is the preferred license for code included in the project.[5] But not all contributing authors must use this license. Thus, you must examine the actual modules you are using to determine the applicable license.

Open source projects occasionally change license terms from one code version to the next, so you should be sure your client has provided you not only with the module names, but also with the versions being used. Projects usually change terms only with significant revisions.[6] If your source has not provided you with version information, it should be available in the first few header comment lines for the code.

Once you have a process for verifying the license terms that apply to code, you should determine who in your organization will be responsible for executing the process, both for the purposes of your audit and on an ongoing basis. Most companies initially view this as a legal task, but many eventually spread the responsibility for the task to legal, engineering, and

---

[5] See www.boost.org.

[6] To do otherwise is probably nonsensical; see the discussion of code release licensing strategy in Chapter 11.

administrative staff. Information gathering can be a time-consuming and inefficient use of skilled personnel such as attorneys and engineers. Particularly for short-term projects, clerks and interns can be a useful resource. Students with academic software backgrounds can accomplish this task with little training, because they generally are familiar with how to find and download open source code. However, they will require training to identify and distinguish the different licenses. Law students without software experience generally require some training on the process of how to find license terms but may be able to identify and distinguish license terms more easily than others. Paralegals and clerical personnel are also good choices, with appropriate training.

However, you may find it more sensible to separate responsibility for ongoing compliance work from responsibility for episodic audits or due diligence. Lawyers should be available to review difficult cases, but the objective is to create policies that avoid legal review except in edge cases. Engineers should be aware of the license terms for code they are using, if only to enforce the notion that license terms matter to your organization. Some companies find it useful to create forms for engineers to fill out to request open source to be added to a product, such as the form in Exhibit 5.1.

This is an example of a form to be filled out by engineers submitting a request to use open source software in a corporate development project.

OPEN SOURCE SUBMISSION FORM

I. Identify the Software
  1. Name of free or open source software ("FOSS"):_____
  _____

  2. How was the FOSS obtained? _____
  _____
      If downloaded, please provided URL: _____
  _____

  3. Name(s) of licensor(s): _____
  _____

EXHIBIT 5.1   OPEN SOURCE CODE SUBMISSION FORM

Check all that apply:
  ☐ Individual
  ☐ Business
  ☐ University/nonprofit

4. Are you aware of any intellectual property issues (patents, disputed ownership) or any disputes involving the FOSS (Y/N)?

_____

If yes, please describe: _____

_____

_____

Please do not investigate potential patent infringement issues without first discussing with legal. You should only list any issues of which you are already aware.

II. FOSS License Background

1. Which open source license(s) apply to the FOSS? (Please include version numbers if applicable, e.g., Apache License 2.0, and whether the license allows election of use under later versions, e.g., GPL version 2 or any later version) _____

_____

_____

2. Is the FOSS also available under a commercial license (sometimes called a "dual license") (Y/N)?_____
If yes, please explain which license will be used and provide rationale:

_____

_____

_____

3. From where was the license obtained? (Check all that apply.)
    ☐ license.txt or readme.txt included in package
    ☐ Source code or header file
    ☐ Web site: _____
    ☐ Other: _____

4. Attach a copy of the license:

III. Use of FOSS

1. In lay terms, how will the FOSS be used? _____

_____

_____

_____

2. In engineering terms, how will the FOSS be used? _____

_____

_____

_____

EXHIBIT 5.1   **CONTINUED**

3. Which of the following characterizes how the FOSS will be used? Check all that apply:
   □ Company Internal Tool (tools used in development by the Company, such as compilers, converters, debuggers, or parsers). if this is a development tool, please indicate whether it inserts any run-time code into developed products (such as standard language routines or classes).
   □ Company Internal Use (software applications or services used by the Company for internal purposes, such as intranet web server software).
   □ ASP Use (used as part of a service, including web sites, that will be accessible outside of the Company).
   □ Product Use (used in a product that will be distributed outside of the Company).
   □ Other: _____

4. The FOSS (or a portion of the FOSS, including libraries or redistributable elements) will be distributed to or made accessible to (check all that apply):
   □ Employees of the Company
   □ Employees of affiliates (e.g., sister companies, subsidiaries)
   □ Subcontractors or consultants of the Company
   □ Subcontractors or consultants of affiliates (e.g., sister companies, subsidiaries)
   □ Other third parties

5. For each of the following questions, if the answer is "yes," please provide an explanation:
   a. Will the FOSS be modified in any way?
   b. Will any portion of the FOSS source code be used in any other code?
   c. Will the FOSS be linked (dynamically or statically) to any other code?
   d. Will the FOSS and any other code run linked together in a shared address space?
   e. Will the FOSS and any other code exchange complex internal data structures?
   f. Will the FOSS and any other code be combined so that they effectively become two parts of a single program?
   g. Will the FOSS and any other code communicate through mechanisms other than standard APIs, pipes, sockets, command-line arguments, and similar mechanisms?
   Explanation: _____
   _____
   _____
   _____

EXHIBIT 5.1   CONTINUED

IV. Compliance with FOSS License. *Please consult the Legal Department if you require assistance with interpreting the requirements contained in the FOSS license.*

1. If the FOSS license includes attribution or notice requirements, how would you propose to comply with those requirements? _____

    _____

    _____

    _____

    ☐ The FOSS license does not contain an attribution or notice requirement that would apply to the proposed use.

2. If the FOSS license requires source code to be offered upon request, how would you propose to comply with that requirement? _____

    _____

    _____

    _____

    _____

    ☐ The FOSS license does not contain a source code offer requirement that would apply to the proposed use.

3. If the FOSS license would require the distribution of source code, how would you propose to comply with that requirement? _____

    _____

    _____

    _____

    ☐ The FOSS license does not contain a source code distribution requirement that would apply to the proposed use.

EXHIBIT 5.1   CONTINUED

Some organizations involve purchasing personnel or contract administrators in the process. This is sensible, because failure to include open source in existing purchase procedures is what causes the problem in the first place. Licenses for proprietary code, which generally require a license fee, are funneled through the purchasing department, which requests legal review when appropriate. Open source (and freeware as well) tends to circumvent this process because no fee payment is required. However, in a global sense, the use of open source code is similar to the acquisition of any licensor technology, so it is sensible to handle its acquisition through the same channels that the organization generally uses. Also, purchasing personnel may be more likely to know alternative technology— and most important, they are likely to keep records that are centralized for the organization rather than segregated by development project.

Therefore, when a request to license an open source module is submitted, purchasing personnel—rather than legal and engineering—are more likely to find that the matter has already been reviewed and disposed of within the context of a parallel development project.

This brings us to the final objective of the compliance review, which is to avoid duplication of work. For instance, if you are a communications software company, with 10 different product lines, you are likely to be using open source secure socket layer (OpenSSL) routines in all of them. If you review the license terms for OpenSSL each time you use it, you have wasted most of your time. Thus, the final task of the compliance review is to ensure that record keeping on a forward-going basis is centralized as well as streamlined.

If you are a lawyer, a client may request that you write an opinion letter about the results of your audit. For outside counsel, of course, this is a serious decision. Some of the compliance rules for the use of open source code within commercial products can be not only complex but based on legal rules that are uncertain or even unknowable. (See Chapter 14.) Thus, most attorneys are unwilling to write a formal opinion letter for such a situation.

CHAPTER 6

Notice Requirements

A lmost every open source license contains notice requirements. These always include the obligation to place a copyright notice on distributions, although the placement of the notices, and what type of distributions must include them, vary from license to license.

Notice requirements are not complicated to interpret and are rarely the subject of litigation claims or disputes.[1] Thus, compliance with them is neither intellectually challenging nor a primary focus of risk management. However, meeting notice requirements is time-consuming and complying with the exact letter of all the notice provisions for a product that embeds many open source modules can be impossible.

For instance, the Massachusetts Institute of Technology (MIT) license contains this notice requirement:

> The above copyright notice and this permission notice shall be included in all copies or substantial portions of the Software.

The Berkeley Software Distribution (BSD) license contains this:

> Redistributions in binary form must reproduce the above copyright notice, this list of conditions and the following disclaimer in the documentation and/or other materials provided with the distribution.

---

[1]However, notice violations may be increasingly the subject of informal enforcement. See http://gpl-violations.org/.

Some licenses require not only copyright notices and attribution but identification of code modifications, such as the Zope license:

> 5. If any files are modified, you must cause the modified files to carry prominent notices stating that you changed the files and the date of any change.

This is from the Reciprocal Public License, a license not used often, but with significant notice requirements:

> 6.2 Description of Modifications. You must cause any Modifications that You create or to which You contribute, to update the file titled "CHANGES" distributed with Licensed Software documenting the additions, changes or deletions You made, the authors of such Modifications, and the dates of any such additions, changes or deletions. You must also cause a cross-reference to appear in the Source Code at the location of each change. You must include a prominent statement that the Modifications are derived, directly or indirectly, from the Licensed Software and include the names of the Licensor and any Contributor to the Licensed Software in (i) the Source Code and (ii) in any notice displayed by the Licensed Software You distribute or in related documentation in which You describe the origin or ownership of the Licensed Software. You may not modify or delete any pre-existing copyright notices, change notices or License text in the Licensed Software.

Here is the requirement from the Attribution Assurance License:

> 2. Redistributions of the Code in binary form must be accompanied by this GPG-signed text in any documentation and, each time the resulting executable program or a program dependent thereon is launched, a prominent display (e.g., splash screen or banner text) of the Author's attribution information, which includes:
>
> (a) Name ("AUTHOR"),
> (b) Professional identification ("PROFESSIONAL IDENTIFICATION"), and
> (c) URL ("URL").

The difficulty interpreting these provisions arises in part from the unanticipated nature of products that might include the covered code and methods of distribution. Keep in mind that most open source licenses are general templates, not written for the particular code they apply to. Also, even if the author of the license has the particular code in mind, the general tendency of software migration to more and more embedded and transparent implementations makes notice provisions more challenging to locate and record. Most notice provisions are written to be appropriate for application software and are harder to apply to embedded software in appliances or low-level computer routines whose existence is transparent to the user. In addition, notice routines for large programs with many components can be burdensome to update and maintain, particularly if the notices do not reside in a single location. For instance, if notices are included in product documentation or manuals, engineering changes that result in the use of different modules, requiring different notices, may not be properly communicated from the engineering team to the marketing or product packaging team.

While it is unfortunate that open source notices tend to be drafted impractically, notice provisions are certainly a reasonable requirement—common in all software licenses, whether open source or not. Notice requirements serve at least three purposes: (1) proprietary rights maintenance, (2) attribution, and (3) licensee education. In the United States, copyright notices are of relatively minor importance due to the changes in copyright law arising from the Berne Convention.[2] However, most open source authors consider copyright notices a substitute for a right of attribution. Because the motivation of open source authors is thought to be primarily reputational, attribution is an important incentive for authors to make their code available. However, it is unclear how well copyright notices serve to accomplish this. Some authors apparently agree, because they require additional attributive notices, as does Apache 1.1, which requires this:

> 3. The end-user documentation included with the redistribution, if any, must include the following acknowledgment: "This product includes software developed by the Apache Software Foundation (http://www.apache.org/)." Alternately, this acknowledgment may appear in the software itself, if and wherever such third-party acknowledgments normally appear.[3]

---

[2] For an explanation, see the Library of Congress informational Circular 3 at www.copyright.gov/circs/circ03.html.

[3] www.apache.org/licenses/LICENSE-1.1.

Finally, notices serve a purpose in open source software that does not apply to the proprietary software context. For licensees to know the extent of their rights in an open source component, the product must place licensees on notice that the component is being used. Then, if licensees wish to take maximum advantage of the existence of that component in the product, such as modifying it to be compatible with the licensees' own needs, licensees must be aware of the right to do this. This purpose works slightly differently for hereditary software and nonhereditary software. For permissive software, licensees may not have independent access to the module, because the licensor may have modified the component and not made the modifications available in source code form. However, because the overwhelming majority of open source components are used in development with no modification, most often licensees will effectively have separate access to the source code from the original project that offered it. For hereditary software, licensees must be made aware of the availability of the module in source code form from the licensor, the licensing terms, and how to obtain a copy. Copyright notices do not serve this purpose.

Some open source licenses address this problem by requiring the entire license to be included in distributions. In truth, this is probably neither necessary nor practical to satisfy the need for notices. To best effectuate the purposes of open source, licensees need to know:

- What components are open source
- Whether components are modified or unmodified
- Where source code can be obtained
- What license governs use

As a consequence, many developers take a practical approach to complying with notice requirements. They use a spectrum of strategies, usually recognizing that none of them will meet the requirements of all the licenses. In general, companies deeply dislike having to include notices in print product manuals. These manuals are not only expensive to produce but hard to maintain. Companies also believe, not without reason, that most users do not want their product manuals cluttered with dozens of pages of legal notices. Another approach is simply to list the copyright notices but not include all the text of the licenses. Some companies eschew all paper notices and instead elect to point their customers to a publicly available web page that can be easily and frequently updated as the open source components change. However, some companies dislike doing this because it puts information about their product components on public display. In these cases, companies may put the notices on pages that can be accessed only with valid customer registration codes. All of this, of course, applies just to binary distribution. The easiest way to comply with notice requirements in source code distributions is simply to avoid changing the notices that are already there.

CHAPTER 7

Patents and Open Source

I ssues regarding patents and open source fall into two categories: infringement and portfolio management. But before that analysis, it is important to understand the politics of patents in the open source world.

PATENT DEBATE*

There is an enormous amount of discussion on the question of whether software patents are desirable from a policy perspective. The open source community is strongly set against the existence of software patents. For instance, the introduction to the GNU General Public License (GPL) contains a statement that "any free program is threatened constantly by software patents"[1] and the Free Software Foundation (FSF), recently in connection with the Public Patent Foundation (PUBPAT),[2] sponsors both political activities to discourage patent protection of software and projects to "bust" (via prior art) existing patents. Whether open source software is particularly vulnerable to litigation based on patent infringement is an open question upon which open source lawyers are divided.

To understand the contours of the debate, it is necessary to understand some of the basic principles of patent law. Those who are not familiar with

---

*An earlier version of this section appeared in "The Fuzzy Software Patent Debate Rages On," *Linux Insider,* February 25, 2005.
[1] Preamble to GPL2. www.opensource.org/licenses/gpl-license.php.
[2] www.pubpat.org/About.htm.

intellectual property concepts often find patent law quite counterintuitive. Patent rights are sometimes called *nonenabling rights*. In other words, owning a patent does not secure for the owner the right to engage in any particular activity. A patent is exclusively the right to exclude others from engaging in certain activities. Contrast copyright law, under which an author, simply by virtue of authoring software, will have certain rights to exploit it. This ability to exploit the work arises because, in copyright law, independent authorship is a defense to claim to infringement.[3] In other words, if you write a software program yourself from scratch, you have certain rights to exploit it under copyright law—or, better said, others cannot prevent you from doing so by making copyright infringement claims. If you apply for and receive a patent, you do not have the right to do anything except stop others from practicing the inventions you have claimed.

In contrast, independent invention is not a defense to patent infringement. The holder of a patent can exclude others from practicing the inventions claimed in the patent, even if those others have separately come up with the same invention without access to the patent. This occurs in part because the existence of a patent acts as constructive notice to the world that the owner of the patent claims that invention for its own use. In fact, the word "patent" comes from this aspect: The invention is laid open in a patent manner. However, from a practical perspective, the expense and difficulty of searching patents makes that constructive notice somewhat of a fiction. The problem is exacerbated by the risks attendant to searching, which include exposing the searcher to knowledge of patents that might result in a finding of willful infringement, and the related exposure for treble damages.

Therefore, the holder of a patent may rightfully claim that another person who has authored software without awareness of the patent and without copying any other person's code could infringe the patent. This is the basis of the argument that software is threatened constantly by software patents. Persons who write software on their own, without having engaged in any act that would usually be perceived as improper—such as copying other persons' code—can be liable for patent infringement.

---

[3]The same is true with respect to trade secret law. Thus copyright and trade secret are both sometimes called *enabling rights*.

However, it is both tempting and misleading to make this argument in a vacuum. Patents are expensive to get and even more expensive to enforce. Whether there is enough incentive, in the real world, for patent holders to bring patent infringement litigation against purveyors of software—and open source software in particular—is a different question. Most companies that seek patents do so primarily for defensive reasons. A so-called defensive patent portfolio allows a company to have a legitimate basis for counterclaim if a competitor sues that company for patent infringement. Therefore, many patents go largely unenforced, and their value depends heavily on the decision of their owner not to enforce them. Many observers liken this to the "mutually assured disaster" scenarios of the cold war. Refraining from use of the weapon is as powerful as using it. It is the threat, and not the enforcement, that matters.

To underscore the logistics of patent infringement suits, consider these facts. It costs $10,000 to $20,000 to draft and file the average patent in the United States.[4] Any significant objections by the patent office that must be addressed prior to issuance may cost even more. Prosecution in foreign countries requires additional costs and fees. Patents are jurisdictional in nature, and unlike copyrights, they are not enforceable in any jurisdiction other than the one in which they are issued.[5]

Patent litigation is far more expensive than prosecution. The minimum cost to bring a patent infringement lawsuit is approximately $1 million, and rising. The price tag of $1 million generally includes prosecution of the lawsuit through the summary judgment stage.[6] Patent litigation is one of the more high-value, high-risk areas of legal practice. (In the legal trade, it is sometimes called the sport of kings.) Consider, for instance, that

---

[4]This includes filing fees, but more significantly, fees to engage a patent agent or lawyer to draft and prosecute the patent.

[5]Roughly the same application can be filed in multiple countries due to treaties such as PCT; however, multicountry prosecution is costly and requires separate filing actions subject to separate local filing rules.

[6]Included is the so-called Markman hearing, named after *Markman v. Westview Instruments, Inc.* 116 S.Ct. 1384 (1996) in which the Supreme Court held that the interpretation of patent claims was an issue of law for a trial judge rather than a jury. This means the pace and expense of patent litigation is front-loaded in the litigation process.

certain investment funds focus on patent litigation; this fact means that such litigation has a risk-and-reward profile similar to the creation of venture-backed businesses.[7]

Patent infringement lawsuits tend to be brought overwhelmingly in the United States, because the United States is not only an enormous market for goods, but also it supports high patent infringement damage awards, including treble damages for willful infringement.[8] Patent litigation exists worldwide, of course, but the rest of the world is pretty much a drop in the patent litigation bucket compared to the United States.

Patent infringement suits are brought, basically, by one of two kinds of plaintiff patent holders. The first kind of patent holder is a company that has prosecuted a patent that covers its own products or planned products. Keep in mind that having a patent does not allow the company clearance to sell its products because patents are nonenabling rights. Companies that seek patents on products they sell tend to do so largely for defensive purposes. In other words, they are preparing to be sued for patent infringement by their competitors and are making a strategic calculation that a patent that covers their own products may potentially cover their competitors' products, giving competitors the basis to countersue for infringement of their own patents.

The other type of patent plaintiff is what has recently become known as a troll (a reference to fairy-tale characters who hide under bridges and demand fees for crossing). A troll company does not engage in the sale of products, but uses patents primarily for offense rather than defense. In other words, the company threatens lawsuits and seeks to sell licenses to the patents to generate revenue. Companies in this position do not value their patents as a defensive measure, because they have no products to protect.[9]

In between these two are companies that use patent licensing as a both a defensive tool and a revenue business model. However, it is generally

---

[7]See, e.g., Altitude Capital Partners, www.altitudecp.com/.
[8]See 35 USC Section 284.
[9]Naturally, some companies are both strategic patent plaintiffs and trolls. They may have patent litigation initiatives and product sales for the same product line, or for different product areas.

understood that licensing as a business model is not of much use unless the licensor is willing to bring a patent infringement lawsuit against the potential licensee. Therefore, companies with significant licensing programs, such as IBM, are situated similarly to trolls in this regard.

Although data are very hard to come by, relatively few patent infringement claims have accused open source software projects. The data are hard to come by because most patent infringement threats, whether related to open source or not, are resolved informally by granting patent licenses before the threat ever reaches the stage of the filing of a formal lawsuit. Keep in mind that the threat is powerful, and once a suit is filed, defendants often defend to the best of their power, to avoid gaining a reputation as an easy target. Prior to the filing of a lawsuit, the dispute is generally considered confidential and not publicly disclosed. Confidentiality is key because the public threat of a lawsuit can hurt a company almost as much as the lawsuit itself. Private companies facing a threatened suit may have difficulty attracting investors or key employees; stock prices of public companies may plummet when a lawsuit is announced.

Companies that use patents primarily as a defensive measure generally have no interest in bringing suits to enforce them. However, companies that maintain patent portfolios as a defensive measure sometimes engage in patent infringement litigation to eliminate competitors. In such cases, an open source project may be vulnerable to such a suit if it is perceived as a competitor to a proprietary product. An example of this might be Linux, which is a competitor to Windows; Apache, which is a competitor to Sun Java System Web Server; and Firefox, which is a competitor to Microsoft Internet Explorer. However, notably, none of these products appears to have been the target of a patent lawsuit at this time. Interestingly, Microsoft Internet Explorer was accused in a troll suit, and Firefox was not.[10]

The reason for this lack of enforcement lies partly in the public relations problems with bringing suits against open source projects. This difficulty was illustrated most famously in the case of *SCO v. IBM,* in which the SCO Group, Inc. gained great notoriety for making perceived threats

---

[10]The suit was brought by EOLAS, which posted a policy offering royalty-free licenses to noncommercial open source projects: www.eolas.com/licensing.html.

against open source.[11] Although this was not a patent case, it predicts the maelstrom that would attend any such significant patent claim. In 2005, the Alexis de Tocqueville Institution released a controversial paper on why companies refrain from pursuing their intellectual property rights against open source projects.[12] However, the controversy was whether such "unchallenged infringement" was a net social loss or gain, not whether it existed. Public relations issues are, of course, of relatively little concern to trolls, who have no product reputations or trademarks to risk.

With this backdrop in mind, here are some arguments against the proposition that open source is particularly vulnerable to patent infringement suits.

- **Early discovery and constructive notice.** Patent holders who are interested in filing patent infringement suits have baseline evidentiary problems with proprietary software: access to source code. Access to the source code is necessary to determine whether a prima facie case for infringement can be pled, because the patent will read on a method whose existence is unlikely to be certain from the mere results of the software. It is possible for a potential plaintiff to acquire a copy of the object code and decompile it, but by doing this the plaintiff risks copyright infringement and contract claims, as most proprietary licenses prohibit reverse engineering or decompilation. Thus, there are technical and legal barriers to determining whether the patentee actually has a claim to file.

    In open source, the reverse is true. The patent holder can determine whether he or she has a claim by looking at the freely available source code. Moreover, plaintiffs who have had the opportunity to

---

[11]In truth, most of the lawsuit had little to do directly with open source as it was primarily of breach-of-contract action against IBM. However, the press presented the case as a challenge to open source, and the open source community rallied to the defense of Linux. At this point, the case is interesting mostly for the spectacle it created rather than the legal issues it either presented or resolved. However, it did focus the software industry on the threat of copyright infringement claims in open source.

[12]Gordon G. Waggett and Kenneth P. Brown, "Intellectual Property—Left?" April 4, 2005, www.adti.net/ip/laches.050405.pdf.

discover the infringement and fail to act on it can see remedies erode. If plaintiffs sit on their rights long enough, they can lose their right to remedies (through a doctrine called *laches*), though this extreme result is uncommon. However, if plaintiffs sit on the rights for a while, they can more easily lose the right to injunctive relief—the principal hammer in a patent suit, given damages in the open source arena may be difficult to gauge. Therefore, open source should make claims arise more quickly. Earlier claims are easier for defendants to deal with. The worst case for a patent defendant is having to pull a product from the shelves due to an injunction granted after the product has saturated the marketplace.

• **Quick reengineering of problems.** For most companies, the worst-case scenario for intellectual property infringement is having to reengineer a product. But when translated to the open source context, reengineering may be easier. As soon as a suit is publicly announced against a popular open source product, many software engineers go to work to engineer around the problem and find prior art. Public institutions such as PUBPAT, the Electronic Frontier Foundation, and the Software Freedom Law Center enlist the help of volunteers and public funds to do this. Of course, reengineering does not allow users of infringing code to avoid damages for infringement in the past, but it does temper the threat of injunctions and avoid infringement after the claim is made. For an example of this type of effort, see Chapter 13 discussing the *Jacobsen (for JMRI.org) v. Katzer* case.

• **Lawyers do not work for free.** Those who fear patents are quick to point out that patent litigation is expensive to defend, but it is also extremely expensive to prosecute. Thus, the trick to being a patent plaintiff is to issue threats rather than file suits and to go after the choke points that will yield the biggest damages: developers and distributors. Going after individuals is expensive. But many of the distributors in the open source space are not good targets for money damages. Many open source projects are not-for-profit or marginally profitable. Large distributors of open source code, such as Novell or Red Hat, would be more profitable targets. But they are also sophisticated about patent defense and therefore the most likely to defend their position with all their resources, not capitulate to demand letters.

- **The pillory.** As the SCO case demonstrates, litigating "against open source" is a scorched-earth strategy. Any company that undertakes it risks excommunication from the software community and a public relations nightmare. As mentioned, this risk does not apply to trolls, only companies with products whose sales can suffer from public relations problems.

- **Nonobviousness.** The success of patent lawsuits is tempered by doctrines of patent law like nonobviousness. A patent can be invalidated—and indeed never should issue—if the teachings of prior art render the claimed invention obvious. All open source code is by definition publicly available for use as prior art. Those who believe open source represents innovative development must also conclude that the more open source code is published, the fewer valid software patents will issue; the effect of the open source releases is to put great quantities of inventions in the public domain. This does not discourage lawsuits, because invalid patents can and do issue. But it makes patent lawsuits less successful. However, part of the problem with this argument is that patent examiners may not have the proper access to open source code to find it in their examination process. Several initiatives have been attempted to provide this kind of nonpatent prior art in a useful and searchable fashion.

In the spirit of full disclosure, I do not believe open source software is particularly vulnerable to patent infringement. (This does not mean it is not vulnerable at all, simply that it is no more vulnerable than proprietary software). I present the opposite view next, which I have prepared based on comments from colleagues who disagree with me. I am certain I will not do that view justice. However, a legitimate objection to my arguments is that they are what are called *should/would arguments*. In other words, I am not arguing about whether software patents are normatively right or wrong, but whether they have a significant practical detrimental effect on open source. Opponents of software patents generally feel that it is wrong to deny the programmers the ability to use code they wrote themselves. However, this is not a book about policy, and I will not go into that question in detail. But to me, the anti-patent argument is seldom properly drawn as an argument against software patents, and so it must apply to patents in general. I, like most lawyers and businesspeople, will probably never be convinced that the entire patent system should be scrapped or that it should be redrawn for a single industry.

- **No champion.** Proprietary products tend to have defensive patent portfolios to back them, but open source projects do not. Because many open source projects are noncommercial, and because the free software community is generally anti–software patent, there is no motivation or funding to seek patent protection relating to open source projects. The entity most likely to be able to file patents on a particular piece of software is the one that actually wrote it.[13] If open source code is written either by hobbyists, by open source businesses that refuse as a matter of principle to seek patent protection, or by corporate engineers donating their time, likely no patent will be filed. Then, if a patentee sues for patent infringement, there is no one entity to respond and defend the product. There have been initiatives to build patent portfolios to defend open source—one is the Open Invention Network[14]—but whether they will be successful remains to be seen—or not, because their success will be measured by a lack of patent lawsuits.

- **Competitive threat.** While trolls may have little motivation to sue open source software projects for patent infringement, proprietary software companies may have more. The main goal of strategic patent plaintiffs is to interfere with the sale of competing products. Proprietary software companies may see competing open source products as significant competitive threat. In a sense, open source products are the worst kind of competitive threat—one that reduces the price of substitute goods to zero. This use of open source is a legitimate and ever more popular business strategy. (See Chapter 11.)

- **Political antipathy.** Some proprietary software vendors—though certainly fewer and fewer as time goes on—are simply opposed to free software for normative reasons, just as free software advocates are opposed to proprietary software. Such companies might use patent

---

[13]However, it is not necessarily the only one. Others could have invented the methods embodied in the software previous to and outside the scope of the project.

[14]www.openinventionnetwork.com/about.php.

infringement suits as a weapon to create "FUD" (fear, uncertainty, and doubt) to discourage adoption of free software. It is true that lawsuits over free software, such as the SCO case, cause free software users to reexamine their choice, if not to actually change it.

PATENT PORTFOLIO MANAGEMENT

Companies that distribute open source software or release code under open source software licenses often are very concerned about the effect on their patent portfolios. Such questions are handled in Chapter 11. However, companies that make no contributions to open source projects but merely redistribute open source software need to understand the effect of this redistribution on patent portfolios. (See Exhibit 7.1.)

Patent license provisions in open source licenses are not terribly different from those in proprietary licenses, so anyone familiar with patent licensing generally will find these provisions familiar territory. However, patent licensing can be daunting for the novice. Patents contain various "claims" that state the scope of the rights claimed by the patent owner. Claims do not describe the invention that forms the basis of the patent per se; that is described in another part of the patent called the *specification*. Here is an example of a patent claim (from the famous LZW compression patent,[15] edited for the sake of brevity):

> Claim 1. In a *data compression and data decompression system*, compression apparatus for compressing a stream of data character signals into a compressed stream of code signals, said compression apparatus comprising (1) storage for storing strings of data character signals, (2) searching said stream of data character signals by comparing said stream to said *stored strings* to determine the longest match, (3) inserting into said storage means an extended string comprising said longest match extended by the next data character signal following said longest match, (4) assigning a code signal corresponding to said stored extended string, and (5) providing the code signal associated with said longest match so as to provide said compressed stream of code signals.

---

[15]U.S. Patent No. 4,558,302 issued December 10, 1985. This is the patent associated with GIF files. This patent was an infamous "submarine." A tongue-in-cheek history called "Sad day. . .GIF patent dead at 20," appears at www.kyz.uklinux.net/giflzw.php.

EXHIBIT 7.1 PATENT TERMS OF OPEN SOURCE LICENSES

License	Licensed Patents (Originator)	Licensed Patents (Contributor)	Patent Grant (Originator)	Patent Grant (Contributor)
Mozilla 1.1	1.10.1. any patent claim(s), now owned or hereafter acquired, in any patent Licensable by grantor 2.1(b) infringed by the making, using or selling of Original Code	1.10.1. any patent claim(s), now owned or hereafter acquired, in any patent Licensable by grantor 2.2(b) infringed by the making, using, or selling of Modifications made by that Contributor either alone and/or in combination with its Contributor Version	2.1(b) to make, have made, use, practice, sell, and offer for sale, and/or otherwise dispose of the Original Code. 2.1(d) no patent license is granted: 1) for code that You delete from the Original Code; 2) separate from the Original Code; or 3) for infringements caused by: i) the modification of the Original Code or ii) the combination of the Original Code with other software or devices.	2.2(b) to make, use, sell, offer for sale, have made, and/or otherwise dispose of: 1) Modifications made by that Contributor; and 2) the combination of Modifications made by that Contributor with its Contributor Version. (d) No patent license is granted: 1) for any code that Contributor has deleted from the Contributor Version; 2) separate from the Contributor Version; 3) for infringements caused by: i) third party modifications of Contributor Version or ii) the combination of Modifications made by that Contributor with other software or other devices; or 4) under Patent Claims infringed by Covered Code in the absence of Modifications made by that Contributor.

(continued)

EXHIBIT 7.1 (CONTINUED)

License	Licensed Patents (Originator)	Licensed Patents (Contributor)	Patent Grant (Originator)	Patent Grant (Contributor)
CDDL	1.11. any patent claim(s), now owned or hereafter acquired, in any patent licensable by grantor. . . . 2.1(b) infringed by the making, using or selling of Original Software	1.11. any patent claim(s), now owned or hereafter acquired, in any patent licensable by grantor. . . . 2.2(b) infringed by the making, using, or selling of Modifications made by that Contributor either alone and/or in combination with its Contributor Version (or portions of such combination)	2.1(b) to make, have made, use, practice, sell, and offer for sale, and/or otherwise dispose of the Original Software. (d) no patent license is granted: (1) for code that You delete from the Original Software, or (2) for infringements caused by: (i) the modification of the Original Software, or (ii) the combination of the Original Software with other software or devices.	2.2(b) to make, use, sell, offer for sale, have made, and/or otherwise dispose of: (1) Modifications made by that Contributor (or portions thereof); and (2) the combination of Modifications made by that Contributor with its Contributor Version (or portions of such combination). (d) no patent license is granted: (1) for any code that Contributor has deleted from the Contributor Version; (2) for infringements caused by: (i) third party modifications of Contributor Version, or (ii) the combination of Modifications made by that Contributor with other software (except as part of the Contributor Version) or other devices; or (3) under Patent Claims infringed by Covered Software in the absence of Modifications made by that Contributor.

CPL	SAME Patent claims licensable by a Contributor which are necessarily infringed by the use or sale of its Contribution alone or when combined with the Program.	2(b) A non-exclusive, worldwide, royalty-free patent license under Licensed Patents to make, use, sell, offer to sell, import and otherwise transfer the Contribution of such Contributor. This patent license shall apply to the combination of the Contribution and the Program if, at the time the Contribution is added by the Contributor, such addition of the Contribution causes such combination to be covered by the Licensed Patents. The patent license shall not apply to any other combinations which include the Contribution.	SAME
Eclipse	SAME Patent claims licensable by a Contributor which are necessarily infringed by the use or sale of its Contribution alone or when combined with the Program.	2(b) A non-exclusive, worldwide, royalty-free patent license to make, use, sell, offer to sell, import and otherwise transfer the Contribution of such Contributor. This patent license shall apply to the combination of the Contribution and the Program if, at the time the Contribution is added by the Contributor, such addition of the Contribution causes such combination to be covered by the Licensed Patents. The patent license shall not apply to any other combinations which include the Contribution.	SAME

(continued)

EXHIBIT 7.1 (CONTINUED)

License	Licensed Patents (Originator)	Licensed Patents (Contributor)	Patent Grant (Originator)	Patent Grant (Contributor)
GPL Version 3	A contributor's "essential patent claims" are all patent claims owned or controlled by the contributor, whether already acquired or hereafter acquired, that would be infringed by some manner, permitted by this License, of making, using, or selling its contributor version, but do not include claims that would be infringed only as a consequence of further modification of the contributor version. For purposes of this definition, "control" includes the right to grant patent sublicenses in a manner consistent with the requirements of this License.	SAME	Each contributor grants you a non-exclusive, worldwide, royalty-free patent license under the contributor's essential patent claims, to make, use, sell, offer for sale, import and otherwise run, modify and propagate the contents of its contributor version.	SAME

Claim 2. The *compression apparatus of claim 1* in which each said *stored string* of data character signals comprises *a prefix string of data character signals and an extension character signal,* wherein said prefix string corresponds to a stored string.

Claim 3. The compression apparatus of claim 2 in which *said compression apparatus comprises a digital computer* responsive to said stream of data character signals and programmed to compress said stream of data character signals into said compressed stream of code signals. [Emphasis added.]

Claims can be independent or dependent. In the example, claim 2 (compression apparatus using a prefix string of data character signals and an extension character signal) depends on claim 1 (data compression and data decompression system), and claim 3 (compression apparatus using a prefix string of data character signals and an extension character signal implemented on a digital computer) depends on claim 2. Therefore, if the device at issue is a data compression and data decompression system as described in claim 1, but it does not use the prefix and extension approach in claim 2, it might infringe claim 1 but not claim 2. If it infringes claim 2 but is not implemented via a computer program, it might not infringe claim 3.

Patent grants in open source licenses are carefully drawn not to extend to downstream modifications. Here is the patent license provision from the Common Development and Distribution License (CDDL) (also edited for brevity):

2.2 Contributor hereby grants You a world-wide, royalty-free, non-exclusive license: . . .

(b) under Patent Claims infringed by the making, using, or selling of Modifications made by that Contributor *either alone and/or in combination with its Contributor Version (or portions of such combination),* to make, use, sell, offer for sale, have made, and/or otherwise dispose of: (1) Modifications made by that Contributor (or portions thereof); and (2) the combination of Modifications made by that Contributor with its Contributor Version (or portions of such combination).

. . .

(d) Notwithstanding Section 2.2(b) above, no patent license is granted: . . . (2) for infringements caused by: (i) third party modifications of

Contributor Version, or (ii) the combination of Modifications made by that Contributor with other software (except as part of the Contributor Version) or other devices. [Emphasis added.]

If the software version to which the contributor contributed infringed one claim of the patent (say, claim 1 but not claim 2), this language does not grant a license under claim 2. Downstream developers may add the prefix and extension functionality of claim 2, but that would constitute an infringement caused by a third-party modification. It is important to understand that the patent license grant in CDDL did not have to be limited in this way; it could have covered all downstream modifications. However, the drafters of open source licenses, in limiting patent licenses in this way, have responded to the concerns of patent-owning companies that want certainty about what patent licenses they have granted. If a downstream modification could invoke additional patents or claims, then the contributor would have no idea which of its patents were being licensed. This theoretical scorched-earth approach has not been adopted by any major license, even GPL version 3 (GPL3).

It is important to understand that open source licensing is a model that grants rights directly from the author to all licensees. The effect on patent portfolios of distribution of open source software is much easier to contemplate if you keep in mind that the distributor is not the licensor under an open source license. Therefore, distributors (at least under the major hereditary licenses) generally are not required to grant any rights when they redistribute. Companies that are redistributing unmodified open source software within products generally will have the choice to redistribute under the exact same terms—in other words, passing the licensing rights directly from the author to the customer—or relicensing on different terms, assuming that the inbound open source license is a permissive license. If the distributor causes the rights to be passed directly from the author to its licensee, then none of the license-granting language in the document will apply to the distributor. Exhibit 7.1 illustrates that none of the major hereditary open source licenses grants patent rights to unmodified programs on behalf of noncontributing distributors.[16]

---

[16]Note that in CPL and Eclipse, "Contributor" includes nonmodifying distributors, but the patent license grant extends only to that Contributor's modifications.

Distributors and users, as opposed to contributors, are generally more concerned about the effect of patent license termination provisions. These provisions affect distributors as well as licensors, because they place restrictions on the actions of licenses. Distributors and even users worry that these licenses will effectively prohibit them from undertaking certain patent enforcement or defense activities, or risk jeopardizing their continuing rights in the software granted under the license. For instance, consider the patent license termination provision of the CDDL:

6. TERMINATION

6.2. If You assert a patent infringement claim (excluding declaratory judgment actions) against Initial Developer or a Contributor (the Initial Developer or Contributor against whom You assert such claim is referred to as Participant) alleging that the Participant Software (meaning the Contributor Version where the Participant is a Contributor or the Original Software where the Participant is the Initial Developer) directly or indirectly infringes any patent, then any and all rights granted directly or indirectly to You by such Participant, the Initial Developer (if the Initial Developer is not the Participant) and all Contributors under Sections 2.1 and/or 2.2 of this License shall, upon 60 days notice from Participant terminate prospectively and automatically at the expiration of such 60 day notice period, unless if within such 60 day period You withdraw Your claim with respect to the Participant Software against such Participant either unilaterally or pursuant to a written agreement with Participant.

Section 2 refers to the patent license provision of the document, and in fact it is not unusual in licensing agreements for a patent license to terminate if the licensee sues the licensor for patent infringement.

The patent termination provision of the Mozilla Public License version 1.1 (MPL1.1) is broader. Some companies consider this provision of concern.

8.2. If You initiate litigation by asserting a patent infringement claim (excluding declaratory judgment actions) against Initial Developer or a Contributor (the Initial Developer or Contributor against whom You file such action is referred to as "Participant") alleging that: . . .

(b) any software, hardware, or device, *other than such Participant's Contributor Version,* directly or indirectly infringes any patent, then any

EXHIBIT 7.2 PATENT TERMINATION PROVISIONS

License	Termination Trigger	Rights Terminated	Comments
Mozilla 1.1	8.2. You initiate a patent litigation infringement claim (excluding declaratory judgment actions) against Participant alleging: (a) Contributor Version infringes any patent or (b) any software, hardware, or device, other than such Participant's Contributor Version, directly or indirectly infringes any patent.	8.2(a) All rights granted by Participant to You under copyright or patent licenses terminate prospectively. 8.2(b) Any rights granted to You by Participant under patent grants are revoked effective retroactively.	Only license with retroactive termination. Broad patent license termination provision terminates all rights if a claim is brought related to the project.
CDDL	6.2. If You assert a patent infringement claim (excluding declaratory judgment actions) against Initial Developer or a Contributor alleging that entity's contributed software directly or indirectly infringes any patent.	6.2 All rights granted to You by all Contributors terminate prospectively.	Broad patent license termination provision terminates all rights, copyright and patent, but only for claims relating to the project.
CPL	7. If Recipient institutes patent litigation against a Contributor with respect to a patent applicable to any software (including a cross-claim or counterclaim in a lawsuit). If Recipient institutes patent litigation against any entity (including a cross-claim or counter-claim in a lawsuit) alleging that the Program itself (excluding combinations of the Program with other software or hardware) infringes such Recipient's patents.	Any patent licenses granted by that Contributor to such Recipient terminate prospectively. Recipient's rights under patent license from any Contributor terminate prospectively.	Patent license termination provision terminates patent rights only.

Eclipse	7. If Recipient institutes patent litigation against any entity (including a cross-claim or counterclaim in a lawsuit) alleging that the Program itself (excluding combinations of the Program with other software or hardware) infringes such Recipient's patent(s).	Such Recipient's patent rights granted under Section 2(b) terminate prospectively.	Same as CPL except narrower patent license termination provision.
Apache 2.0	3. If You institute patent litigation against any entity (including a cross-claim or counterclaim in a lawsuit) alleging that the Work or a Contribution incorporated within the Work constitutes direct or contributory patent infringement.	Any patent licenses granted to You under this License for that Work shall terminate as of the date such litigation is filed.	Patent license termination provision terminates patent rights only.

rights granted to You by such Participant under Sections 2.1(b) and 2.2(b) are revoked effective as of the date You first made, used, sold, distributed, or had made, Modifications made by that Participant. [Emphasis added.]

The aspects of this provision that cause the most concern are termination of the copyright license under section 2.1 and retroactive termination of the patent license.

Exhibit 7.2 lists the patent license termination provisions of the major licenses.

CHAPTER 8

Trademarks and Open Source

TRADEMARK LAW AND OPEN SOURCE LICENSING*

In the open source context, the function of trademarks can be quite complicated. By definition, any open source license allows modification and distribution of software royalty-free.[1] But that does not mean that these activities are allowed under the trademarks applied to the software. Open source licenses primarily grant rights under copyright and, to some degree, patents. They never include trademark licenses.

To understand the interaction of trademarks and open source, you must first understand trademarks in general—an often misunderstood form of intellectual property. Trademark law is very different from copyright and patent law. In fact, some lawyers do not feel trademarks should be called intellectual property at all, although they usually are. First, in the United States, rights in trademarks do not arise from creation, as they do in copyright or trade secret law. Rights in trademarks arise from use in commerce. In the United States, you can apply for a trademark registration much as you can apply for a patent—and to the same governmental entity, the U.S. Patent and Trademark Office. But unlike patents, trademark registrations are only evidence of ownership, not ownership itself.

---

*An earlier version of this chapter appeared in "Mark My Words—Trademarks and Open Source,"*Linuxworld Magazine,* November 13, 2004.
[1]See the open source definition at www.opensource.org/docs/definition.php.

Trademark law is easiest to understand when you start from the premise that trademarks are instruments of consumer protection. Owning a trademark allows the trademark holder to sue for damages for trademark infringement, and in this way trademark is similar to other intellectual property rights. But whether the trademark is infringed depends on the effect on consumers. Trademarks are protectible only to the extent they represent the quality or reputation associated with a product—and this is called *goodwill*. Because consumers rely on the quality control represented by a trademark to make buying decisions, trademark laws are strong and the penalties for violating them can be high. A company that infringes a trademark is not just hurting the owner of the trademark, it is hurting all consumers, everywhere.

As a corollary, if the owner of the trademark does not police the uses of the trademark—and, say, allows it to be used on goods of random quality—then the trademark no longer protects consumers and no longer represents the goodwill associated with the product. Trademark law is, loosely put, a use-it-or-lose-it regime; better said, it is a use-it-correctly-or-lose-it regime. This rule is called *dilution, genericness,* or *blurring*. The trademark owner must exercise quality control over products bearing the trademark, or trademark rights may become generic to the point that such rights are no longer enforceable. The poster child example here is "aspirin"—once a trademark, now a generic designation with no trademark value.

There are two basic kinds of trademark infringement: passing off and reverse passing off. If you write your own accounting program and call it Quick Books, that is "passing off" your goods as those of another. Consumers will think your product was produced by Intuit, and thus be confused. If you take a copy of Quick Books and put it in a new box with your own brand, that is called reverse passing off. You will be confusing consumers because they will think you are the source of the product rather than Intuit. In the first case, you are trading on Intuit's reputation. In the second case, you are trading on the quality of Intuit's product to boost your own reputation.

Therefore, while open source licenses allow anyone to modify software, no trademark owner can allow use of its mark on that software without controlling the nature of the resulting product. In this way, trademark law and open source licensing are fundamentally at odds.

TRADEMARKS IN THE OPEN SOURCE WORLD

Most open source projects recognize this dilemma and try to set guidelines for trademark use, such as the policies for the use of the Red Hat fedora, the GNOME footprint, the Debian swirl, or the Mozilla red lizard.[2] All of them impose some kind of criteria for products bearing the mark. These criteria range from quality, to interoperability, to the amount of open source code the product contains.

The most popular logo in the open source world, of course, is the penguin named "Tux." This trademark has not been managed with systematic trademark use policies. Consequently, the reputation and trademark strength associated with the mark may be weak.[3] The most common representation is the bowling-pin-shape tuxedo-marked cartoon bird designed by Larry Ewing, but even the average computer programmer, much more so than the average consumer, would be hard pressed to say exactly what product it represents. The only condition for use of this logo is acknowledgment of the author of the logo; there are no conditions regarding the product on which it is placed. This type of condition is associated more with copyright than trademark.

There is, of course, a copyright in the appearance of any logo. But a logo that represents neither a source for products nor a level of quality for products is, in the end, not really a trademark. Tux is usually described by the software community as a mascot rather than a trademark, and this probably is a more accurate description.

"Linux," on the other hand, is a trademark registered by Linus Torvalds. The use of the Linux mark is policed by the Linux Mark Institute (www.linuxmark.org). The institute was created after a dispute over ownership of the trademark arose. This dispute arose because the mark was not being policed and was not registered—a state of affairs that allowed others to claim rights in it. Linux has been used more consistently

---

[2]www.redhat.com/about/trademark_guidelines.html, http://mail.gnome.org/ archives/foundation-list/2003-November/msg00098.html, www.debian.org/ logos/, and www.mozilla.org/foundation/licensing.html, respectively.
[3]The use of the penguin has provided fodder for plenty of amusement (see the discussion of the meaning and history of Tux on http://en.wikipedia.org/wiki/Tux).

than the Tux logo. However, some would argue that it too is generic and may not be enforceable.[4]

The open source business community handles the issues of passing off and reverse passing off much as any other industry. Even the Berkeley Software Distribution (BSD) license, the quintessential permissive license, contains an express statement limiting the licensee's right to use trademarks. For instance, the form of BSD license available on the Open Source Initiative web site says:

> Neither the name of the <ORGANIZATION> nor the names of its contributors may be used to endorse or promote products derived from this software without specific prior written permission.

This line might suggest that any organization granting such a license is not concerned about reverse passing off. However, even the BSD license requires the licensee to display appropriate copyright notices, and earlier versions contained the "advertising requirement" that became so unpopular in the open source community.

AT&T UNIX BATTLE

There is a storied history to trademarks and open source, but not many people know it. As described in Chapter 1, at one time AT&T licensed UNIX freely to universities in source code form, and those universities openly shared improvements and adaptations of the code—a practice that became the social template for the free software movement. One of the recipients of UNIX was the University of California at Berkeley, which modified UNIX extensively, most notably developing networking code that made UNIX work with Transmission Control Protocol and Internet

---

[4] Confusion over what constitutes a "Linux" product is evidenced by the strophic explanation of the difference between Linux and GNU/Linux by the Free Software Foundation. The GNU code base includes a set of tools promulgated by the GNU Project. These tools usually are part of a product distribution that contains the Linux kernel. See Wikipedia's definition of "Linux": "Strictly, the name Linux refers only to the Linux kernel, but it is commonly used to describe entire Unix-like operating systems (also known as GNU/Linux) that are based on the Linux kernel and libraries and tools from the GNU project" (http://en.wikipedia.org/wiki/Linux).

Protocol (TCP/IP)-based networking products. When the consent decree was lifted and AT&T stopped licensing the UNIX source code freely, it turned UNIX into a proprietary product and began charging high prices for licenses. Berkeley, responding to popular demand, began distributing its own version of UNIX, called "Networking Release 1," under the BSD license.[5]

A few versions later, Berkeley Software Design, Incorporated (BSDI) was formed to distribute a commercially supported version of the Berkeley UNIX code. That product, unsurprisingly, was known as BSD UNIX. AT&T released its own, closed-source, version of UNIX, called System V. But BSDI was selling its open source product for 90 percent less. So AT&T sued BSDI, making both copyright and trademark claims. The court found that AT&T had lost its copyright interest in the UNIX code used by Berkeley. The case was settled. Essentially, BSDI won. But BSDI promptly agreed to stop using the trademark UNIX.[6]

The moral of this story is that copyrights are fragile, but trademarks are forever. Copyrights can be lost and engineered around.[7] Patents, too, can be engineered around, and half of them are invalidated when their owner tries to enforce them. Patents, and to a lesser extent copyrights, can expire, but trademarks can last forever. Trademarks claims are often so fearsome that a defendant in a trademark infringement suit will give up without a fight. BSDI fought AT&T's copyright claims and won. It gave up the trademark battle voluntarily.

This may be more than just a cautionary tale but rather a peek into the realities behind how intellectual property works for open source

---

[5]To be precise, the facts were more complicated. Berkeley tried to engineer all of AT&T's copyrightable code out of the product. Whether it succeeded is a moot point, given the disposition of the lawsuit described below.

[6]Once again, the facts were debated. Whether BSDI actually used the UNIX trademark in an infringing way was disputed—and mooted by BSDI's agreement to cease using the mark.

[7]Since the events in the case occurred, the law has changed. It is not so easy to lose the rights in a copyright today. AT&T lost its copyright under the pre-1978 rule, under which publication without copyright notice caused a work to fall into the public domain. Today, a positive statement ceding a work to the public domain is necessary to lose a copyright.

in the business world. Companies commercializing open source have a few basic models: services, support, and widget frosting. (For more detail, see Chapter 11.) Those models may or may not be protected by copyright or patent, but any business model is protected by trademark. Companies can, arguably, exercise even more control over their licensees via trademark than they can via copyright.

In fact, the existence of officially sanctioned versions is hugely important in the open source world. Skeptics often ask what keeps open source code from forking infinitely. The open source community relies heavily on consensus: Licensees trust the official releases of open source code because of the reputation of the stewards and the collective will of the community. Some forking has taken place in the open source world, and trademark battles have not ensued. But if two factions want to maintain competing versions of an open source program, battles over who has the right to use the project name to designate its project could be complicated and costly.

The day may come when those who determine the official versions of large open source projects like Linux will control some of the most valuable pieces of intellectual property in the world: the name by which the project is known. While many in the open source world are poised for a patent fight, trademark fights may be far more complicated and destructive. Patents are a threat from outside the open source community. Trademark disputes are a lurking threat from within.

CHAPTER 9

Open Source and Open Standards

Now that open source has become a media buzzword, it has been applied to many things to which it is completely irrelevant. Now we see discussions of "open source" biotechnology, open source religious texts, and even open source yoga. Open source, though, is a paradigm fairly specific to software. Its basis is the idea that people should have access to a human-readable form of information or technology, not just an unreadable form.

What most people mean when they apply the term "open source" to items other than software is instead an open standard or public domain. Much has been written on open standards, and a full discussion of them is beyond the scope of this book. However, the interaction of open source and open standards is significant, so it is important to understand the broad strokes.[1]

Standards formulation is much older than open source and older than software itself. A time-worn example is that of nuts and bolts. At the beginning of the industrial era, every nut and bolt had unique threads. Of course, that meant every nut could be used only with its own bolt.

---

[1]For in-depth information on standards and the implementation of the intellectual property rules of standards bodies, see Jorge L.Contreras (ed.), *Standards Development Patent Policy Manual* (Chicago: American Bar Association Publishing, 2007).

Eventually, industry developed a standardized[2] system of thread manufacture, so nuts and bolts could be interchanged. It is generally accepted that standardization of technology is good. The question is: Whose standard? We have all experienced competing standards, like those underlying VHS and Betamax videotapes or the Macintosh and PC platforms. Lack of standardization makes consumers delay product-buying decisions, which decreases demand, and makes companies delay investments, which decreases economic development.

Standards promote commerce only when there is a critical mass of product manufacturers willing to adhere to the standards. Therefore, it is common for major industry participants (called *promoters*) to cooperate to develop and promote standards. Doing so can be risky for participants, however, because they must exchange confidential information in the course of standard development, and they must expose themselves to the antitrust liability that might result from horizontal agreements in restraint of trade.[3]

An even more difficult problem arises when a standard emerges, but invokes intellectual property rights owned by a party that can prevent or tax others who wish to practice the standard. Standards are almost exclusively protected by patents, so this issue is largely a patent policy issue. What constitutes an "open" standard is both unclear and controversial,[4] but there are essentially three kinds of open standards: nonproprietary, RAND (reasonable and nondiscriminatory), or RAND-z.

A nonproprietary standard is one in which there is no known intellectual property interest to restrict practice of the standard. The qualifier "known" is important because of the nature of patents; it is possible for

---

[2]Though dizzying, as any novice who has been to a hardware store will attest.

[3]The Department of Justice Guidelines generally consider intellectual property licensing to be pro-competitive. Antitrust Guidelines for the Licensing of Intellectual Property, April 6, 1995, Department of Justice, www.usdoj.gov/atr/public/guidelines/0558.htm. However, license arrangements can stray into the prohibited area of horizontal output restraints or price fixing. Recently Rambus, Inc. was subjected to a protracted legal battle over the failure to disclose intellectual property related to a standard in the course of a standards development process. www.ftc.gov/os/adjpro/d9302/060802commissionopinion.pdf.

[4]For a definition formulated by Bruce Perens, see http://perens.com/Open Standards/Definition.html.

patent rights (or incipient rights, in the form of unpublished applications) to exist without the knowledge of the standard's promoters. Many types of intellectual property may subsist in a standard. Patents may cover the standard by describing it in their claims. Copyright may subsist in the specifications for the standards, but this right will not prevent practice of the standard, as copyright would merely prevent the copying of the specifications document that describes the standard. Trade secrets can subsist in the standard but will not exist once the standard is published, as trade secrets do not protect information that has been released for publication. Finally, trademarks can cover a standard via certification marks, such as Underwriters Laboratory Inc. (UL) or Dolby marks. A nonproprietary standard generally means that the parties who have come together to develop the standard have no patents or applications covering the standard or, to the extent they do, have ceded those rights.

A RAND standard is one in which the standards promoters have all agreed to license the claims of their patents and applications that are required to practice the standard (called *necessary claims*) on reasonable and nondiscriminatory terms, to all who wish to practice the standard. Therefore, while such a standard is not available to those who cannot pay the fees, this means no adopter can be excluded from practicing the standard, and there is a level playing field for those who do: All pay the same royalties and agree to roughly the same terms to license the necessary claims. This distinction helps fend off potential antitrust claims that might result from horizontal competitors conspiring to drive certain other competitors out of the market.

The term "RAND-z" is used to describe a standard that is licensed by the promoters on reasonable and nondiscriminatory terms, but is royalty-free. The lack of a requirement to pay royalties obviously makes a standard more inclusive, but that does not mean it is without cost. RAND-z licenses usually contain restrictions such as cross-licensing of patents or promises not to build substitute products that do not adhere to the standard.

Different standards bodies have different policies about what kind of licensing is acceptable and what constitutes an open standard. For instance, the Institute of Electrical and Electronics Engineers requires RAND,[5] the World Wide Web Consortium (W3C) has historically required RAND-z

---

[5]http://standards.ieee.org/faqs/copyrightFAQ.html.

licenses,[6] and the Internet Engineering Task Force requires RAND.[7] Proposed moves by W3C to allowing RAND standards have been controversial. Those in the open source community often point out that the freedom to modify and develop source code is illusory if restrictive patent licenses that are necessary to develop a product will expose the developer to patent infringement liability. Thus they emphasize that open standards are necessary to open source. Also, often it is not possible to collect royalties for open source products, so royalty-bearing patent licenses might effectively prevent open source implementation of standards covered by RAND and not RAND-z. Open source advocates argue, and quite convincingly, that open source is an excellent vehicle for implementation of standards, because it encourages quick adoption by removing restrictions on copying and modification of code implementing the standard.

---

[6]www.w3.org/Consortium/Patent-Policy-20040205/.
[7]ftp://ftp.rfc-editor.org/in-notes/bcp/bcp79.txt.

CHAPTER 10

Developing a Corporate Open Source Policy

A sample open source policy appears in Appendix 10A. This chapter discusses the pros and cons of creating such a policy and outlines some of the major issues it should address.

It is not crystal clear yet whether having a written corporate open source policy is a best practice, although most lawyers today would probably say it is. While policies have certain settled legal effects in other areas of law (e.g., the case of employment policies, which help avoid liability for discrimination and harassment), the effect of policies in the open source arena is untested. Corporate policies generally serve two purposes: to communicate corporate management's decisions about open source to employees and to provide evidence that the corporation is not willfully ignoring legal issues relating to open source code. It is a common suggestion today that the Sarbanes-Oxley Act (SOX), the corporate responsibility laws enacted in response to the financial scandals of the early 2000s, requires a written open source policy. In brief, this is not true. A written policy may be a best practice, but SOX is not the only—or even the principal—reason for this.

SOX requires each public company to have a special audit committee that signs off on all of the financial auditing procedures for the company. However, some companies may want the audit committee to address other procedures as well, to further insulate the company, or its individual officers and directors, from liability. In such a case the audit committee may attend to intellectual property risks such as those arising with respect to open source. SOX also requires the company to provide a mechanism for persons to report breaches of corporate fiduciary responsibility anonymously and without reprisal. This mechanism is sometimes referred to as "whistleblowing." Companies have generally embraced this practice because it is a relatively inexpensive and effective way to limit liability for the company.

Entirely separate from SOX, public companies need to report all material risks in the yearly and quarterly reports they are required to file with the U.S. Securities and Exchange Commission. Because open source, particularly the copyleft requirements of the GNU General Public License (GPL), and patent licensing provisions of most of the hereditary software licenses are now generally perceived to have significant potential impact on the value of a company's intellectual property assets, public companies have gravitated toward disclosing the risks they face in this area.

A written open source policy may give the audit committee some comfort and help convince auditors to sign off on the company's financial condition. But a policy is not mandated by SOX. The benefit of a written policy comes primarily from communication and enforcement of the policy rather than creation of it. Software engineers are notorious in corporate legal departments for ignoring directives to avoid open source; engineers perceive the directives as slowing down development for the sake of legal technicalities. If a written policy helps convince or cause engineers to follow corporate directives on open source, then a written policy is worth writing.

Thus, there are actually two parameters in this equation: whether a policy will be in writing and whether it will be enforced. Although a written policy may be helpful in reducing corporate liability, a written policy that is ignored is probably the worst case, because it is likely to be used as evidence of corporate mismanagement. A written policy, as opposed to an unwritten one, can be useful in large companies with geographically scattered development groups or in companies with siloed development teams. However, almost no company will include anything controversial in such a policy, so difficult questions like the fine points of the border dispute of GPL version 2 (GPL2) are often reduced to a directive to consult with the legal department.

Here are some of the subjects that should be covered by a corporate open source policy.

- **Corporate open source philosophy.** Whether the company is a significant supporter of open source or wishes to avoid use of open source completely, the policy can help communicate the general approach of the company.
- **Black lists, white lists, and gray lists.** Most companies develop lists of licenses that are acceptable or not acceptable or that require review on a case-by-case basis. Because licenses can be hard to identify if they are not clearly titled, this section should explain the differences between permissive and hereditary licenses and how to identify the licenses on the various lists. Distributors will have a different approach to this portion of the policy from users, because companies that include open source in products bear significantly more compliance risk for adherence to copyleft requirements triggered by distribution. (For more explanation, see Chapter 14.)
- **LKM policy (if applicable).** A company doing Linux kernel adjacent development may wish to state categorically that it does not approve binary loadable kernel modules (LKMs) or that it requires legal review on a case-by-case basis. (For more explanation, see Chapter 14.)
- **Notices.** Most open source licenses require copyright notices or acknowledgments to be included with a product. Any distributors of products that include open source code will likely have developed a policy to formulate, maintain, and communicate notices. This portion of the policy will help ensure that the proper information is collected and recorded and that the company takes a consistent approach to notices across product lines. (See Chapter 6.)
- **Patent considerations.** Code distributed under an open source license can affect a company's ability to secure and later enforce patents. Any company that is contributing to open source projects or releasing code under open source licenses usually will require legal review of its patent position prior to the release. In addition, some open source licenses contain patent termination provisions that can affect patent enforcement strategy. Therefore, users as well as distributors must consider how to ensure that the use of open source code is in sync with its patent strategy and policy. (See Chapter 7.)
- **Source code check-in and storage considerations.** Companies expend significant resources keeping track of which open source

code has been used, modified, or included in products, using the Concurrent Versioning System (CVS) and similar tools. This will be a major point in the policy for most distributors. (See Chapter 4 for more discussion on the due diligence process.)

- **Procurement guidelines.** This section discusses interaction among purchasing, legal, and engineering departments. Companies may want to give guidance on whether to choose open source or commercial options for products with dual licensing models. Policies for use of open source development tools may include checks on whether tools use run-time distribution libraries that create compliance concerns. (See Chapter 4 for more discussion on the due diligence process.)

- **Reversioning.** Some companies prohibit contributions to open source projects by their employees; some support and encourage them with sabbaticals, bonuses, or improved employee reviews. (See Chapter 11.)

Open Source Corporate Policy

This appendix is an example of a corporate open source policy. Corporate open source policies vary significantly in substance, complexity, style, and length. If you are developing a policy for your company, you should consult a lawyer experienced in open source issues.

[COMPANY] OPEN SOURCE SOFTWARE POLICY

I. Introduction

The availability of open source software has fundamentally changed the way software is acquired for use and development. Company wishes to provide guidelines and policies to assist its engineers and managers to participate in the open source movement—to allow Company to efficiently develop software and to maximize the benefit to Company's customers—at a minimum of risk to Company.

By definition, open source software is software that, when licensed, is made available in source code format. Open source software is plentiful, and is either free of charge or much less expensive to acquire than commercially available code. Open source software also often can be culled from a variety of sources, which helps Company avoid being locked into the support, maintenance, and development constraints associated with dependence on a single supplier. Perhaps most important, open source software is constantly being tested, debugged, and upgraded by the open source code community—composed, in the main, of the same programmers that Company might otherwise have to pay to perform that work.

Still, the decision to incorporate open source software poses a potentially critical downside: the need under certain open source licenses to make available the source code of proprietary modules that link or interact too closely with open source modules. Company's failure to abide by such licenses can expose Company to sanctions ranging from pressure from the open source development community to lawsuits seeking to require Company to disclose its proprietary source code.

This policy is intended to help Company maximize the benefits of incorporating open source software while still minimizing the risks of doing so.

This policy addresses the best practice to manage these risks:

- Exposure to intellectual property infringement lawsuits
- Public relations problems if Company does not act as a good corporate citizen
- Compliance with "viral" licenses and the effect on Company proprietary code
- Inadvertent patent licenses

II. Open Source Licenses

Open source software licenses range from the permissive ("Here's my code—do what you want with it") to the restrictive ("Dynamically link to this code and divulge your application's entire source code"). In theory, the variety of potential open source software licenses is as unlimited as the number of developers working within the open source software movement, since each developer has the right to condition the use of his or her code as he or she sees fit.

For the most part, though, open source licenses follow one of several common formats, each a vestige or incarnation of a license used or written by one of a handful of open source institutional pioneers. The most common of those formats include, from the most to the least restrictive, the Free Software Foundation's GNU General Public License ("GPL") and GNU Lesser General Public (or Library General Public) License ("LGPL"); the Mozilla Public License; the Perl Artistic License; the Apache Software Foundation's Apache Software License; and the Berkeley Software Distribution License ("BSD"). The following section focuses on the most restrictive of those licenses—the GPL—since it is that license that gives rise to the thorniest practical and legal problems.

One important thing to remember about open source licenses is that they never absolutely require the disclosure of source code. Even the GPL does not require an end user to lay open the source code of software that the end user never redistributes. The obligation to lay open source code is triggered only when software is redistributed. However, redistribution may be defined more broadly than you expect.

A. GPL   The GNU General Public License, or GPL, is the most widely used open source license. The GPL is a "viral" license, meaning that any changes to GPL code must be relicensed under GPL terms. The language of the GPL is very informal. As a result, much legal and software community discussion and analysis about what the GPL means bears little direct relation to that language.

In general, the GPL allows anyone to use, copy, distribute, and modify the "Program," which means the code published under the GPL, and requires redistribution under GPL terms of any "work based on the Program." There is much division in the legal and software community about what constitutes a work based on the Program. The Free Software Foundation, which promulgates this license, has publicly stated that any code linked to GPL code is part of a work based on the Program.

At least in theory, violations of the GPL can be can be met with a variety of sanctions, ranging from the enmity of the open source software community to a termination of the license to a lawsuit seeking that the violator divulge proprietary source code. To avoid those outcomes, Company should never publish software containing modules—or any portion of modules—licensed under the GPL without prior legal review.

B. LGPL   The GNU Library General Public License, or LGPL, is similar to the GPL in many ways. It is "viral" in the sense that it requires relicensing of any modifications under LGPL terms. However, it is less restrictive than the GPL, in that it explicitly permits dynamic linking of proprietary code with code licensed under the LGPL. This explicit permission is subject to a limitation of 10 lines for in-line functions.

C. Mozilla Public License, Common Public License, and Other Viral Licenses   Other "viral" open source licenses are more corporate in style and intent. The Mozilla Public License, and the Common Public

License, for instance, are drafted in a style more typical to intellectual property licenses—having, for instance, explicit patent license grants and express definitions. The licenses are easy to comply with, although they still require redistribution of modifications on their same terms.

D. Other Open Source Licenses   Two additional common source software licenses are the Apache Software License and the BSD license. While differences exist between the two, they resemble each other in that they impose few practical restrictions on Company's redistribution of modules licensed under them. On the whole, the Apache Software License and BSD license require only that applications incorporating modules licensed under them contain appropriate copyright and warranty notices.

III. Protecting Company Intellectual Property in the Open Source Context

For years, smart software publishers have recognized that their ability to survive and prosper depends in large part on their ability to protect those facets of their products that make them unique—and uniquely valuable to customers. With increasing frequency, software companies seek patent protection for novel algorithms. Prior to the filing of the pertinent patent applications, software companies generally do not release such algorithms in source code under any circumstance. Furthermore, software companies universally accompany proprietary code—whether in source or object format—with copyright notices designed to increase the penalties available against those who misappropriate that code.

The incorporation of open source components poses yet an additional challenge to software publishers. Some open source software licenses—in particular the GPL—require that publishers incorporating open source software make available not only the open source modules themselves, but also all proprietary code that links or otherwise interacts too closely with those modules. This requirement is sometimes called the "viral" element of the GPL. Where the interaction between open source code and proprietary code results in the proprietary code having to be released in source format, that code is described as having been "contaminated" by the open source code. In addition, any license that requires all modifications to be released in source code format is described as "viral," because once the code is covered by that license, it must always be covered by that license.

The good news is that with a little planning, organization, and communication, Company can effectively insulate itself against most compliance issues.

A. Open Source Compliance Issues and the Effect on Company Proprietary Code

1. GPL Compliance Issues: The Most Common Kind   The risk of compliance issues is highest among products that incorporate open source modules licensed under the GPL. When using code licensed under the GPL, avoid doing anything that might later result in proprietary code being classified a "work based on the Program":

- Develop a system for identifying and clearly separating components licensed under the GPL from proprietary code.
- Compile or link Linux kernel header files—all of which are licensed under the GPL—with proprietary code only after legal review.
- Release Linux kernel updates made by Company separately from updates of Company proprietary code.
- Never "cut and paste" or otherwise intermingle Company and Linux kernel code.
- If you want to use functionality already contained in the Linux kernel, ask Company managers to consider making the enhancements in kernel source code and then making that source code available to the development community.

If Company is required to provide its modifications in source code format, it is best to cooperate with the community, for two reasons. First, cooperation maximizes the goodwill to Company from use of the open source code. Second, if the modifications are incorporated into a generally accepted source tree, they will be maintained by the community.

When using GPL code, developers should always seek assistance from Company managers and legal staff. It is best to do this early in the development process, since a compliance problem can at a minimum delay the release of a product and in a worst-case scenario require that Company release source code consisting of Company's most valuable intellectual property.

2. LGPL Compliance   The LGPL is less restrictive than the GPL, in that it permits a wider range of interaction between proprietary and open source code without imposing the requirement that the proprietary code be made available in source format. For example, an application may compile and even link Company proprietary code with code licensed under the LGPL without fear of compliance issues. Still, careless handling of LGPL code can pose a risk of compliance issues. To avoid that risk:

- Implement a system for identifying and clearly separating components licensed under the LGPL from proprietary code.
- Avoid cutting and pasting code from modules licensed under the LGPL into Company proprietary modules, and vice versa.
- Restrict the use of in-line functions, according to the LGPL's terms. (The LGPL allows linking of LGPL code to proprietary code, but this does not apply to in-line functions over 10 lines in length.)

3. Mozilla Public License, Common Public License, and Other "Viral" Licenses
Other viral license agreements operate in a manner that is similar to the LGPL. However, different licenses have different requirements for the integration of proprietary and open source code. For instance, the Mozilla Public License allows distribution of proprietary code as long as it is segregated into a separate source file. If you are integrating code under viral agreements, check with Company legal staff to be sure you are complying with the requirements necessary to prevent Company from having to release key proprietary code in source code format.

4. Compliance Issues under Apache and BSD-Type Open Source Licenses   For the most part, using open source components licensed under Apache and BSD-type licenses does not pose a threat to Company's intellectual property. Still, as with open source code taken under other licenses, developers should err on the side of caution by bringing any questions— in particular about the scope of a particular license—to their manager or Company's legal department. Furthermore, in the interest of avoiding a situation in which developers cannot later say which license governs which open source component, developers should separate open source software from proprietary code and should save a copy of the license under which each open source component is taken.

B. Patent Considerations   Company may have an interest in protecting its intellectual property by seeking patent protection. Any code that is released by Company under an open source license of any kind can compromise Company's ability to secure and later enforce any patents covering that code. That is because, when a company licenses software, it can be argued under patent law that the company has granted an implied license to any patents that would otherwise be infringed by the use of that software. The scope of this "implied patent license" is unclear as a matter of law. Therefore, prior to releasing code under an open source license, Company must weigh carefully whether an open source release will compromise its rights in patents or potential patent filings.

C. Avoiding Intellectual Property Infringement Suits   All software is subject to intellectual property infringement lawsuits by third parties, whether that software is distributed under an open source license or not. Some kinds of intellectual property infringement can be avoided more easily than others. For instance, a company's proprietary code can violate the patent rights of another even if that code was written by Company from scratch. This is because patent rights protect inventions, methods, or algorithms, regardless of the lines of code that embody them. Code designed and written in-house by the Company's own programmers is unlikely to infringe another's copyrights or to misappropriate another's trade secrets. Open source projects reopen the door to copyright and trade secret lawsuits, since open source components often have many contributors, most of whose backgrounds are not known.

To minimize the risk of intellectual property infringement lawsuits, Company should receive open source code only from reputable open source projects. Organizations like the Free Software Foundation, GNOME, Mozilla, and Apache keep careful tabs on intellectual property issues—in particular copyright issues—and have defined intellectual property policies. By contrast, ad-hoc projects, or projects not operated by a definitive management group, are more prone to intellectual property infringement problems.

D. Source Code Storage Considerations   Because Company may have an obligation to provide modified open source code to its licensees, it is important to keep track of which open source code has been modified and which has not. To facilitate that process, Company developers should always:

- Clearly separate materials licensed under open source licenses from proprietary code.
- Make sure that updates, modifications, improvements, or enhancements to open source materials are easily identifiable, and separately released.
- Notify developers whenever material licensed under an open source license is in any way modified.

One important note about downloading open source components: Regardless of the source, each time a developer downloads open source code, he or she should print and save the license agreement under which that code is taken. Internet links and license agreements change over time, and open source projects sometimes change their licensing terms without warning. The outcome of a dispute over Company's compliance with the terms of an open source license can hinge on the exact license under which the code was taken. The only way to know what license governs the code is to capture and save the license at the time of download.

E. Making Open Source Community Contributions Under certain circumstances, Company may decide to release proprietary code under an open source license. This may occur either because Company is required to do so due to viral open source licenses or because Company has made an independent decision to make the release. Releasing source code can increase Company's visibility in the open source community and engender cooperative feelings within open source development circles and the marketplace. Prior to deciding what code to release under an open source license, Company will consider:

- Contributions to the open source community are required only when one or more open source components are distributed along with Company's products. Where open source code is never provided to anyone outside Company, the publisher need not make its source code available. However, the definition of what constitutes distribution is very broad, and can include alpha testing, beta testing, and hiring outside consultants to do development.

- Open source contributions should follow an established management approval process that includes, at the least, review by Company's lawyers. Company will consider whether any of its patent rights will be compromised by the release.

Always work with the recognized keepers of an open source tree. Other approaches can cause forking that may undo the public relations benefits that open source contributions can garner for Company. Developers who make key changes to components licensed under the GPL or LGPL should contact the component's copyright holder (usually available from the materials being updated, as well as from the current developers and maintainers of the work) to see whether and how the copyright holder and other interested parties would like to receive the changes.

IV. Open Source Code Procurement and Support

Although a plethora of open source code is freely available on the Internet, Company may choose instead to acquire open source code and support services from commercial open source redistributors. This section discusses the pros and cons of that approach.

A. Procurement Guidelines   Much, if not most, open source software is available on the Internet free of charge, either directly from an open source development tree or from well-known public web troves such as SourceForge or Freshmeat. Nevertheless, a number of commercial redistributors of open source software also provide open source components. Commercial redistributors offer a number of important advantages over other code sources. They include:

- Warranty protection (varying in duration and scope, depending on the supplier)
- Intellectual property indemnification (varying in scope, depending on the supplier)
- Quality assurance
- Availability of updates
- Availability of documentation
- Support services (usually at additional expense)

Of course, procuring open source code from commercial redistributors also has its disadvantages. One is that commercial redistributors do not offer the variety of components (in terms of versions and features) available on the Internet. Another is cost. Commercial redistributors charge for their code and other services. In fact, Company's fees to a commercial redistributor may be comparable to Company's fees to vendors of proprietary products. The bulk of savings derived from using open source components may come later, as the total cost of ownership (including support, maintenance, compatibility, and security costs) of open source comes into play.

B. Dual Licensing   Many open source developers, suppliers, and projects offer multiple licensing terms. Multiple licensing ranges from those who provide a choice between open source and commercial licenses (such as MySQL and SleepyCat), to open source projects that provide the opportunity to take code under multiple open source licenses (such as Mozilla, which offers its code under the GPL, LGPL, or Mozilla Public License). When you investigate procurement sources, be sure to advise your legal team of the licensing options available, and make the procurement decisions based on both cost savings and intellectual property protection.

C. Acquiring Support Services   As with open source code, there generally are two sources for open source software support: commercial redistributors of open source products, such as MontaVista, IBM, Red Hat, and Novell, and the numerous online resources of the open source software community, such as mailing lists and newsgroups. These sources offer continuous support from the same developers that maintain and, in many cases, wrote the open source components.

D. Open Source Development Tools   A growing number of companies make tools—compilers, linkers, debuggers, and other performance aids—designed to assist open source software publishers. When choosing an open source development tool, Company will keep in mind these points:

- Consider purchasing open source tools from a corporate supplier rather than simply pulling them off the Internet. Suppliers like Red Hat and MontaVista may supply these tools under commercial terms.

- If the decision has been made to download open source tools from an open source tree, consider using only known Internet distributors with good reputations, such as Red Hat, Mandrake, and SuSe.
- Open source development tools that are themselves distributed under open source licenses can be used in the development of Company proprietary code without that code becoming contaminated. However, this does not apply to run-time libraries or sample source code that is actually incorporated into Company products. For example, a C compiler itself will not contaminate Company code, but standard C libraries might. Because it may be impossible to use one without the other, compilers and other development tools should be considered with care. Tools for testing and debugging, which do not usually incorporate code into a product, may not present the same concerns.

V. Considerations in Marketing Open Source Products

Marketing open source products is, in some measure, different from marketing other software. Most customers do not have a need or desire to know what a software product contains, so long as that product works. Others, though, are biased toward applications based on specific platforms. When marketing products containing open source components:

- Most open source licenses require a copyright notice to be placed on boxes, headers, or documentation for products that incorporate open source code. Company prefers to provide this information in a manner that will be easy to maintain and centralized. Contact Company's legal department if you have questions about when and where you must place notices.
- If the open source code has a logo, brand, or trademark that will appear to Company's customer, and if you have made any change to the code, contact the legal department. An open source developer may have trademark guidelines or qualifications that licensees must comply with. If Company's developers have modified the open source code, Company may no longer have the right to use the open source developer's trademarks.

- Do not remove the trademarks or logos from any unmodified open source code.
- Do not remove copyright or other proprietary notices from header files of any open source code.
- Many open source licenses require that Company make available modifications to the open source code that are included in Company products. Before releasing a product, Company should know which of its source code it plans to disclose and should decide on the easiest, most efficient way to distribute that source code.

CHAPTER 11

Open Source Code Releases

Most companies, and the lawyers and businesspeople who work with them, first become involved in open source involuntarily by having to ensure compliance with inbound open source licenses. Some companies, however, take the additional step of releasing their own code under open source licenses. This step is more deliberate, and is undertaken for many reasons.

The most straightforward case is a company that wishes to make a limited open source code release but not to build a business around it. This option is sometimes attractive for companies trying to revive or leverage commoditized products. For instance, if a software product has become outdated, unprofitable because of competition, or simply no longer commercially viable, a company may elect to release it under an open source license. The goals in doing this are to create goodwill in the open source community, encourage adoption of standards that the company uses, increase the market for complementary products, or disrupt the market for competing products.

Companies considering such an initiative face questions like these:

- What goals will be served by making the release?
- How will the release serve the company's profitability?
- What license should be used?
- What is the effect on the company's patent portfolio?
- What is the effect on the company's trademarks?
- How will company resources be devoted to the project, and how will employees have incentives to contribute?

- Should a new entity be created to administer the project?
- How much control of the project should be transferred to the community?

CHOOSING A LICENSE

The first three questions must be taken together. Although companies often find the choice of a license daunting, the right choice flows naturally once the company's objectives are clear. Exhibit 11.1 outlines some of the most common choices and the licenses used to effectuate them.

The more permissive the license, the more likely the software will be used. The more restrictive the license, the more the company's competitors will be discouraged from exploiting the software commercially. For example, if a company wishes to maximize adoption of a standard, it may choose to release the software embodying the standard under a permissive license like BSD (Berkeley Software Distribution) or Apache, perhaps coupled with an initiative to promote the functionality of the software as a standard using a certification trademark or a patent pool. However, licenses like these allow code adopters to place them in proprietary products, which create the potential for forking and the creation of competing standards. If, in contrast, a company wishes to control the market for plug-ins and add-ons to the software, it might release the code under GNU General Public License (GPL) because this would require its competitors to release under GPL.[1] Some companies, in contrast, are uncomfortable with the drafting of GPL, and for that reason choose a more customarily drafted license such as the Mozilla Public License (MPL), Common Public License (CPL), or Common Development and Distribution License (CDDL). Each of these licenses will have a slightly different effect on the position of competitors.[2]

The business objectives of the release will largely dictate the right license to use. The first step is to identify the most likely class of adopters and how they will want to use the software. Here are some examples.

---

[1]For a discussion of why this is so, see Chapter 14.
[2]See the discussion of patent licenses and patent license termination provisions in Chapter 7.

EXHIBIT 11.1 **LICENSE CHOICE FOR CODE RELEASES**

Licensing Option	Examples	Revenue Model	Competitive Position	Other Business and Intellectual Property Issues
GPL	Red Hat	• Support and services • Hardware sales • Standalone companion products possible	• Maximum restraint of use of code in proprietary competing products, due to "taint" issues • Minimum time negotiating outbound licenses	• Maximum public relations boost in open source community • Patent enforcement issues due to implicit patent grant • Trademark control issues
LGPL	JBOSS	• Support and services • Hardware sales • Dynamically linked companion products	• Allows competitors to develop adjacent, proprietary modules • "Developer-friendly" model	• Compromise public relations position, but still excellent public relations • Patent enforcement issues due to implicit patent grant • Trademark control issues
Other Hereditary Software Licenses	Sun Solaris (CDDL)	• Support and services • Hardware sales • Unintegrated companion products	• Allows competitors to develop adjacent, proprietary modules • Provides more comfort to patent holder developers than LGPL	• Compromise public relations position • Patent enforcement issues, but more certain than implicit grants • "Corporate-friendly" licensing model • Trademark control issues
Permissive Licenses	Lucas OpenEXR (BSD-like)	• Support and services • Hardware sales	• No restraint on competitors • Loss leader • Standards promulgation	• Patent enforcement issues • Trademark control issues • Competitive advantage is control of project

- **Goal: Interoperability.** A videoconferencing services company seeks to create a market for its services. Accessing the services requires the user to download certain client software that configures the user's computer to connect with the service. In this case, the client software is not the company's main product. The company would prefer to maximize the number of persons with the client software on their computers, to drive sales of its videoconferencing services. It is unimportant to the company whether the client software is in a proprietary product. The choice here is a permissive license.

- **Goal: Standard adoption.** A company creating computer graphics seeks to promote its graphics format. It has developed a set of encoders and decoders for the format. This case is similar to the interoperability goal, but the company may be concerned that the ability to modify the code will result in nonstandard implementations. If this is not a meaningful risk—which will generally require that the company has established the standard within the marketplace prior to the code release—then an open source release will encourage quick adoption. If the company wants to control modification to the standard, it may need to pick a different kind of license (such as a freeware license limiting the modifications to those that preserve the standard), or it can control the standard through limited RAND (reasonable and nondiscriminatory) and RAND-z (royalty-free RAND) patent cross-licensing or certification trademarks. (See Chapter 9.)

- **Goal: Sell commercial licenses.** A company has developed a document server application to store, index, and manipulate data files. To interface with other applications, the company has developed a set of library routines. Releasing this code under GPL will mean that competitors will be able to use the code only if they are willing to license their server code under GPL. The company, however, need not do this, because as owner of the code, it will not be subject to the requirements of GPL. Part of the company's goal is to benefit from improvements made by users who take the code under GPL. Note that releasing such code under a license such as Lesser General Public License (LGPL) or CDDL would be fatal to the business goal, because it would allow competitors to use the code with their proprietary server applications. If the company releases the code under GPL but sets up a parallel commercial licensing track to sell licenses of the library to systems integrators and other developers, this scenario is the quintessential model for dual licensing. (See the section on dual licensing later in this chapter.)

- **Goals: Upsell new products and undermine competitors.** The company has a product that is mature and is becoming commoditized. However, the company has developed value-add products that are selling well and are more profitable. The company can release its mature product under an open source license, effectively driving the price to zero and therefore undermining sales of competing products. The company then focuses on selling other products that are compatible. If the company's main goal is to disrupt competitors, a restrictive license like GPL may work best. However, a corporate-style hereditary license like CDDL or even a permissive license will drive down prices, and if the product is commoditized, access to the code will not give competitors any meaningful leverage.

EFFECT ON PATENT PORTFOLIO

Prior to releasing any code under an open source license, the licensor should understand the effect on its patent portfolio. This effect will depend on the license under which the code is released. Such an understanding is particularly important for companies releasing mature products on which patent protection is likely to have been sought at some point in the past. Companies that have made the decision to open source a product may have also decided that patents related to the product are no longer very valuable. However, they may want to reserve the ability to enforce the patent portfolio against competitors who violate the open source license or try to fork any standard being promoted. In addition, some companies effectuating code releases will have patents that apply both to the product being open sourced and others as well.

Companies that want to conserve any significant patent rights should seriously consider releasing code under a license with an express patent grant, such as Apache 2.0 (for the permissive option) or CDDL (for the hereditary option). Doing so will control the scope of the patent grants in terms of how far downstream the grants reach and how broad a scope of downstream modifications will be covered. For instance, a company that releases an open source engine for a text-filtering application may keep in reserve certain add-ons and plug-ins (such as hooks into proprietary programs like Internet Explorer or Outlook) to sell as proprietary products. If the company's patents cover the add-on, it may be concerned that licensees making similar additions under the open source license will enjoy immunity from patent suits, even though the plug-in was not licensed to those licensees.

Companies without patents at risk may find it more strategic to choose a license with no explicit patent provisions, assuming that the scope of the implied license is broader than that of an explicit license. This assumption may or may not be true; competitors with patent portfolios to protect may pause before using code offered under such a license, because they are unsure about the scope of the patent license they would be required to grant.

EFFECT ON TRADEMARKS

Any company launching a business initiative needs to consider branding. Open source business initiatives are no different in this respect, but the trademark policies covering open source products can be trickier than those for proprietary software. The problem is that trademark law and open source are fundamental opposites. (See Chapter 8.) A company can decide to grant the right to modify its software to the community at large, but it must decide how far to let those modifications stray from the official release before the product's branding has to be changed. Different open source companies and projects approach this issue differently. Some allow limited use of the mark associated with the product; some allow none. A savvy open source release requires serious thought about trademark policy and active policing of the policy to avoid compromising of a company's trademark rights.

Releasing an open source product can have a complicating effect on trademark rights. While open source licenses are not trademark licenses, and many explicitly disclaim any grant of license, the name of the open source project to be released will inevitably be difficult to control.

Companies that manage open source products generally have some difficultly policing their trademarks. First, most open source licensees do not understand that the ability of licensees to change the software freely does not mean that the software can be attributed to the licensor. For instance, if a company releases a product called OpenFoobar under the GPL, it has only granted licensees right in the software code and not any right to use the term "OpenFoobar" to designate the software. However, they will inevitably do so, even using it to designate their own versions. If the company allows them to do so, it risks losing any trademark rights in OpenFoobar.

Second, the free software community has a very negative view of heavy-handed trademark enforcement. The reason for both these problems is that most engineers hold normative notions more consistent with academic plagiarism rules than the rules of trademark law. Therefore, they believe that attribution is the right thing to do and that preventing them from attributing the product to the original licensor is actually wrong. Companies should be careful, in the course of trademark enforcement, not to kill the very community they hope to create around their product. The average trademark cease and desist letter sent to an unsuspecting developer or user group will backfire.

A sample trademark policy form appears in Appendix 11A. However, these documents vary enormously depending on context. Companies developing trademark policies for open source releases should consider questions such as:

- How much modification can occur before licensees must remove the company's trademarks?
- If licensees modify the code, will the company request any kind of attribution (such as "powered by" attribution)? Note that some companies address this either in the open source license itself, such as the "Exhibit B" (see Appendix A) license pioneered by SugarCRM, or in separate developer program agreements.
- Will the company allow anyone, such as distributors, user groups, or developers, to register domain names that include the company mark? If so, who will own the domain name?
- Will the company operate a certification program to allow the mark to be used for modified products?

These are business questions that are often addressed as business initiatives, such as developer programs or officially sanctioned user groups.

As a practical matter, companies that make open source or dual-licensed code releases often remove their logos and trademarks from the public source tree. While these companies may make binaries available for download with the logos intact, removing the logos from the source tree may prevent inadvertent misuse of the trademark by licensees.

Open Source Business Models

The concerns of a company mounting an open source code release are magnified when the company actually intends to rest its entire business model on the open source code release.[3]

The most straightforward open source business model sometimes is referred to as a "pure" open source business model. In such a model, the revenue for the business is not generated via licensing fees; the core product of the business is open source software. The best-known example is Red Hat, Inc., a purveyor of enterprise Linux systems. In models like this, revenue comes from ancillary sources, such as customization services and maintenance and support. The value added by the business is access to the latest builds of the software, maintenance and support, customization, and quality assurance—all essentially service revenue.

Much has been written about the flavors of open source business models, but of course these flavors are constantly developing, because the very idea of making money with open source is relatively new. Here are some examples of open source business models:

- **Support and services.** The company makes revenues from supporting and customizing open source products. Example: Red Hat.
- **Loss leadering.** The company gives away an open source version of the product and sells a different version with additional functionality, such as features to deploy it on enterprise servers. Examples: Many dual-license businesses, the original Netscape model.
- **Widget frosting.** The company sells hardware products that use open source software. Examples: Digium (which sells telephony hardware

---

[3]There is much written on the Web about open source business models. However, it is difficult to attribute what is written to a clear original source. See, e.g., Frank Hecker, "Setting Up Shop: The Business of Open Source Software," at http://hecker.org/writings/setting-up-shop.

that works in conjunction with Asterisk PBX software), Silicon Graphics (which sells file server hardware with Samba SMB/CIFS software).

- **Service provider.** The company gives away an open source product, usually client software, and sells online services or drives traffic to an ad-supported service. Example: Boingo (which sells Wi-Fi Internet access).

- **Picks and shovels.** The company sells educational products or development tools that assist open source developers. Examples: O'Reilly Media (which sells books and educational materials) and SourceForge, Inc. (which operates a web site that hosts thousands of open source projects), or newspapers, magazines, or web sites devoted to open source topics. Also lawyers.

It is worth noting that none of these is a particularly new business strategy. Mostly they can be summed up by loss leadering, sometimes referred to as selling razor blades (a term coined by, perhaps apocryphally, Gillette). The important thing is that the company has a plan to reap revenue, and it does not rest on licensing revenue.

Dual Licensing

In a dual-licensing business model, a company that markets a commercial software product gives its licensees the choice of two licensing options: open source and proprietary.[4] The customer can choose to license the software under the terms of an open source license, such as the GPL. Alternatively, the customer can choose a proprietary license with more conventional licensing terms that limit its ability to relicense the product or restrict it to object code sublicenses only. (See Exhibit 11.2.)

The theory behind the dual-licensing model is that it helps both the open source community and the commercial software licensee. The open availability of source code allows the software to be improved by those who wish to contribute changes. The proceeds from commercial licensing

---

[4]An earlier version of this section appeared in "Dual-Licensing Open Source Models," *Linuxworld,* April 2005.

EXHIBIT 11.2 DUAL LICENSING CHOICES

Model	Examples	Revenue Model	Competitive Position	Other Business and Intellectual Property Issues
"Pure" dual licensing—same product, different licenses	• MySQL • Sleepycat	• Licensing revenue • Support and customization	• Dual licensing path usually involves GPL or free software licenses • Reduces negotiation resources re: escrows, assignment, revenue recognition (try before you buy)	• Contribution agreements can be a challenge • Trademark control issues
"Value-add" dual licensing—different product, different licenses	• Active Endpoints	• Licensing revenue • Support and customization	• Dual licensing path usually involves GPL or free software licenses • Reduces negotiation resources re: escrows, assignment, revenue recognition (try before you buy) • Most popular dual licensing model for new ventures	• Contribution agreements can be a challenge • Trademark control issues

help fund additional development and help establish the product as a commercial standard.

Several companies have broken ground by launching dual-licensing models. The best known is MySQL AB, which offers an open source database. MySQL has two license options: a commercial license and a modified GPL license, which allows the licensee to distribute mySQL code under GPL side by side with other open source licenses and a proprietary license. The two licensing models cover identical products.

Active Endpoints, Inc., uses a different strategy, having launched a separate open source product that complements its commercial products. The open source ActiveBPEL engine is a run-time environment for executing processes based on the WSBPEL specification (WSBPEL refers to Web Services Business Process Execution Language.). The ActiveBPEL engine is also the core of Active Endpoints' ActiveBPEL Enterprise Server family of products. Active Endpoints licenses the ActiveBPEL engine under the GPL and its ActiveBPEL Enterprise products on commercial licensing terms.

This is an example of a value-added dual model, where certain core technology is available under an open source license and additional functionality is available under proprietary terms. One common use of this model is to provide a core set of functions under open source and provide the tools or integration that enables its use in enterprise network systems under proprietary terms. From a business perspective, this means the enterprises that have more resources will choose to take a license to the product on commercial terms, but individuals or hobbyists have access to the software free of charge.

Another well-known dual-license company is Sleepycat Software, Inc., recently acquired by Oracle Corporation. Sleepycat sells an embedded database product called Berkeley DB. This product was originally licensed under a permissive license, but then released under the dual-license model in 1997.[5] The Sleepycat license is a strong hereditary license. Its commercial license is a fairly customary commercial distribution one.

Many open source projects offer licenses under multiple open source options, such as the Mozilla Foundation, which uses a trilicense model

---

[5]For an interesting discussion of several dual-licensing companies, see http://opensource.mit.edu/papers/valimaki.pdf.

including the Mozilla Public License (MPL), GPL, and LGPL. This multiple licensing model is not a business strategy so much as an effort to address licensing compatibility problems (see Chapter 4).

Companies contemplating a dual-licensing model sometimes expend great effort choosing a license to use. However, dual licensing does not work well with permissive licenses. Dual-licensing models tend to use the onerous nature of the copyleft restrictions to drive licensees toward the commercial model. Therefore, the most common licenses used for this purpose are GPL, GPL + FLOSS exception, and occasionally the so-called Exhibit B licenses—variants of MPL with trademark requirements.

"UR-LICENSOR" AND OPEN SOURCE DECISION MODELS

Some in the open source community mistakenly believe that it is a violation of GPL for a company to release its code simultaneously under GPL and other licenses. This misunderstanding arises from the nonreciprocal nature of the obligations under GPL.[6] Only the licensee is bound by the copyleft obligations of GPL. The licensor is not bound by these obligations, unless the licensor is also a licensee (or has taken part of its code from another licensor under GPL). This distinction is critical; it is only the ultimate licensor—the initial developer of the code—who can make the decision to "fork" the licensing terms for the code that the licensor wrote.

CONTRIBUTION AGREEMENTS

The premise of dual licensing is that the community can contribute to the product's code base to build better code.[7] Assuming a company has the right—by virtue of having written its code—to give its licensees a choice of open source or commercial terms, it must decide how to manage contributions from the open source community. There are two ways to go about it: by requiring contributors to assign all rights to their contributions

---

[6]It is for this reason that I disfavor calling hereditary licenses "reciprocal"—it may add to this confusion.

[7]An earlier version of this section appeared in "Legal Issues: The Contribution Conundrum,"*Enterprise Open Source Journal* (July 2006).

to the company or by requiring the contributors to grant a license to the company that is broad enough to allow redistribution on both commercial and noncommercial terms. There is also a third option, which is to use no agreement at all; although this approach has some support in the open source community, most lawyers do not recommend it.

Views in the open source community are mixed but mostly come out in favor of contributor agreements. In 2004, in the wake of the *SCO v. IBM* case, Linus Torvalds publicly supported improvements in the house-keeping measures for the Linux kernel, acknowledging that keeping a project's intellectual property house in order was the most important challenge to adoption of open source and that professional due diligence procedures would help dispel copyright infringement fears for open source adopters. The Free Software Foundation generally requires that all rights to contributions be assigned to it.[8] Apache uses a contribution agreement that is generally regarded as a standard in the industry; and some open source projects like Sleepycat do not accept contributions from people outside the corporation that runs the project.[9]

Simply stated, a contribution agreement is an agreement by which a contributor to an open source project grants sufficient rights for the parties operating the project to release the contribution as part of the project. These agreements are usually quite straightforward. When stripped of their bells and whistles, they consist of a broad license grant or an assignment of rights. Assignments, rather than licenses, also generally grant back to the assignor a broad right to use the code.

Contribution agreements come with a handful of variations:

- Limitations of the actions of the project (such as keeping the source code open)
- Grant back to the contributor
- Representations and warranties (such as a warranty that the contributor wrote the code or is not employed by a company that will claim rights in it)

---

[8]www.gnu.org/licenses/why-assign.html.

[9]Interview with Sleepycat president and chief executive officer Michael Olson, October 29, 2001, winterspeak.com, www.winterspeak.com/2001_10_01_archive.html.

- Assistance with enforcement against those violating the rights in the code
- Corporate versus individual agreements (corporations often are asked to grant more patent rights or make more representations about the noninfringing nature of the code)
- Extending grant to all projects run by the company (if the company is running multiple projects)

The typical arguments against use of contribution agreements include:

- **Contribution agreements make you give up your rights in the code.** This is true only of assignments of rights rather than licenses, and then it is true only of those that do not license any rights back to the assignor; currently no such contribution agreements are in use with any major project. Only a few projects (most notably the GNU Project) require assignments from their contributors, and largely to preserve standing to enforce the copyright in the entire open source work. Most contribution agreements are simply broad nonexclusive licenses.
- **Misuse of code.** Contribution agreements allow the project to "go proprietary." It is true that some contribution agreements allow the project to use contributions in commercial software. In this sense, though, such an agreement is essentially equivalent to a permissive license such as BSD and MIT. Some contribution agreements have restrictions on outbound licensing that require that the project license the contribution to others only under an approved open source license.
- **Contribution agreements are not necessary because of implied licenses.** This argument goes like this: The contributor provides the contribution to a project covered by GPL; therefore, obviously the project can license the contribution under GPL, because that clearly was the intention of the contributor, from the objective circumstances of the contribution. Unfortunately, implied intellectual property licensing is a murky area of law. Projects find it difficult to state what implied or oral licenses govern the use of copyrightable works. In any case, implied licenses generally are revocable at will, which means that the project cannot rely on the license. Moreover, implied licenses may or may not allow the project to use a subsequent

revision of its own license agreement. Open source projects also legitimately change their license terms (other than revisions of the same license) from time to time—usually from one open source license to another. If they have accepted contributions under an implied license theory, they cannot change their license terms unless they get the permission of every contributor. Backtracking to get permission may be feasible when there is a small group of known contributors with good, current relations with the project. But if contributors are numerous, unavailable, or even hostile, it will be impossible.

- **If most projects use contribution agreements, this will lead to the conclusion that those projects that do not use them cannot rely on implied licenses.** Courts imply licenses based on the facts of the particular case rather than the practices of an industry at large.

- **Contribution agreements do nothing to address the greatest threats to open source: software patents.** That statement is true, but the argument is specious. The purpose of contribution agreements is not to clear patent infringement. However, contribution agreements (such as the Apache agreement) can be used to clear the patent claims of the contributors.

- **Contribution agreements are unfair because they pave the way for projects to sue contributors.** This is an argument not against contribution agreements but against overdrafted ones. A contribution agreement, like any agreement, should be drafted based on context. Contributors who provide code for free should not have to sign up to the same terms as those who license code for money. It is reasonable to ask a contributor to warrant that the contribution is his or her own original work, and that the contributor's employer does not lay claim to it. This is the minimal level of comfort for a project to manage the rights to its code. But it is less reasonable to make contributors sign up to long and onerous warranties and indemnities or ongoing obligations, such as support and updates. I know of no case of a project ever suing a contributor over a contribution agreement. Suits have been threatened, however, by contributors who contributed under the implied license theory and later fell out with the projects.

This last point underscores the importance of contribution agreements as form as well as substance. Written agreements regarding inbound intellectual property rights are considered a baseline for professional due diligence. It has taken many years for corporate developers to accept the risks attendant with the open source development model and the idea that open source is not simply a collection of infringing bits of code, whose broken provenance will compromise their organizations. Even if a contributor were never to argue with a project about an implied license, many licensees might refuse to use open source code if the project does not engage in a baseline of diligence on its contributions.

REISSUING CODE

A licensor that chooses to release code under one open source license may later choose another license, with the caveat that licenses granted under the prior license do not evaporate. Thus, if a project releases code under LGPL, and later decides to release it under GPL, not only can the licensees who took the code under LGPL continue to use it under those terms, but those licensees can also pass the code on under those terms. So, if a licensor makes a decision to reissue the code under another license, it does not make much sense to move from a less restrictive license (here, LGPL) to a more restrictive license (GPL). The licensees who took the code under LGPL will always be able to avoid the restrictions of GPL. However, it may make sense to reissue code under a more restrictive license in conjunction with a major revision, because the newly revised or added code in the revision will be subject to the more restrictive terms. Naturally, this problem does not occur when moving from a more restrictive license (such as GPL) to a less restrictive one (such as BSD). When that occurs, a rational licensee would take the code only under the less restrictive license.

For this reason, if a licensor is unsure which license to use in a code release, the licensor usually will choose to start with a more restrictive license, with the option of moving to a less restrictive one if circumstances so dictate.

CORPORATE ORGANIZATION

Companies pursuing a dual-licensing strategy should consider the lesson—learned too dearly and too late by many startups—that distinct businesses are better separated into different operating entities. While many in the business community have embraced open source as a development method or a business model, some still consider it a substantial negative. A startup may find that a potential acquiror or investor dislikes the idea of buying or investing in open source assets or, at least, does not place substantial value on those assets. A company may therefore find it useful to segregate its open source business into a separate entity. Doing this on the eve of an acquisition can be difficult—and at a minimum will make the deal more expensive, more complex, and slower to finalize. The longer a business operates, the more complex it is to segregate multiple business lines into distinct entities. Assets such as copyrights, trade secrets, trademark rights, and goodwill can be difficult to separate once they are mingled.

Creating dual entities to handle a dual-licensing model may also help compartmentalize liability—this is always the result of creating multiple corporations. But creating the entity is not a silver bullet; it is necessary actually to operate the entities separately to preserve this advantage.

Some companies designate the entity handling the open source channel as a not-for-profit entity. Many open source projects operate through public benefit corporations (classified under 501(c)(3) of the Internal Revenue Code). However, before expending resources on establishing such a corporation, it is important to consult a tax attorney experienced in this area to understand whether the benefit is worth the expense. Not-for-profit entities are obligated to operate for the benefit of the public at large, and an entity created only to run a corporate open source project may not qualify. Transfer payments between for-profit and not-for-profit entities can cause tax problems and compromise a not-for-profit status. This status has other more important benefits: It encourages donations and grants and garners goodwill with the community. However, it requires significant corporate formalities, usually including an independent board of directors. Tax advantages alone may be more easily addressed by a limited liability company (LLC) with a pass-through tax structure or other means.

$11A$

Open Source Trademark Policy

This Form Is an Example of a Policy for a Dual-licensed Open Source Product. Foobar Trademark Policy

The trademark FOOBAR signals quality, dependability, and robustness in the world of memory leakage control. Foobar, Inc. ("Foobar") is proud of its reputation for excellent software products, and wishes to maintain that reputation for the benefit of Foobar and its open source community. This trademark policy (the "Policy") describes the ways in which the trademarks, service marks, and logos of Foobar relating to the Foobar memory leakage product ("Trademarks") may or may not be used. If you use any of the Trademarks, you must abide by this Policy. We encourage communication to prevent misunderstanding. If you have any questions or comments, please contact as described at the end of this Policy.

Foobar's trademark policy attempts to balance two competing interests: Foobar's need to ensure that its trademarks remain reliable indicators of quality, and Foobar's desire to permit community members to contribute to the development and success of the Foobar software. Striking a proper balance can be difficult, and we hope this Policy will help us to do that.

Underlying Foobar's trademark policy is the general law of trademarks. Trademarks exist to help consumers identify the source or origin of products. When a company makes a good product or a bad one, consumers begin to associate those qualities with the name and trademarks of that company. The reputation of a company can be a key factor in a consumer deciding to use one product or another. Allowing others to place a company's trademarks on other people's products can affect this reputation. Trademark law exists, at least in part, to help consumers avoid being confused about the source and quality of the goods they are using.

As a baseline, any use of the Trademarks should not be confusing or misleading. Beyond that, this Policy describes uses of the Trademarks that are allowed and not allowed. When we refer to "Trademarks," we refer not only to the logo of Foobar but the name Foobar as well.

Trademarks and the GPL

As you know, certain noncommercial versions of the Foobar software are distributed under the GPL. Please keep in mind that the GPL does not grant any trademark rights. Although you may distribute and modify certain software under the GPL, you may use our Trademarks in connection with those modifications and distributions only as described in this Policy.

Modified Software and Unmodified Software

Genuine Foobar software, which is sourced by Foobar and thus properly bears the Trademarks, is the software in the exact binary form that it is distributed by Foobar, without modification of any kind. Once any change has been made to the software, even if that change may be permissible under the GPL, the software should no longer bear the Trademarks. The public has a right to know when it is receiving a genuine Foobar product that is quality assured by Foobar.

Uses that Are Not Approved by This Policy. The following uses are not allowed. If you feel you need to use the Trademarks as described below, and have a legitimate reason to do so, please contact us. Some such uses may be acceptable under a written license agreement negotiated between you and Foobar. However, Foobar will decide this at its discretion on a case-by-case basis.

- **Certain web uses.** You must not use any Trademark in a web page title, titletag, metatag, or other manner with the intent or the likely effect of influencing search engine rankings or results listings.

- **Combination marks.** You must not use any Trademark in a manner that creates a "combined mark," or use that integrates other wording with the Trademark in a way that the public may think of the use as a new mark (e.g., SuperFoobar, or Foobar Lite, or Foobar by Goober).
- **Company names.** You must not use any Trademarks as part of your company name, trademark, or logo.
- **Domain names.** If you want to include all or part of a Foobar Trademark in a domain name, you must first receive written permission from Foobar. This includes uses for user groups, developer groups, or international groups. We approve many such uses, but we need to do this on a case-by-case basis.
- **Misuse.** You must not use the Trademarks in a manner that is unethical, offensive, disparaging, defamatory, illegal, or in bad taste.

Uses Permitted under This Policy

The following uses of the Trademarks are permitted, but in all cases you must use the Trademark only as otherwise required by this Trademark Policy. Also, if you use the Trademarks in violation of this Trademark Policy in any way, Foobar may revoke your right to use the Trademarks, even as allowed under this Trademark Policy.

Developers and Affiliates

Foobar has created special logos for use by its business affiliates, such as developers or value-added resellers. For more information on our affiliate programs, please see [URL]. These logos may be used only by parties who have entered into our affiliate program agreement. In addition, you may wish to engage Foobar to certify your product as compatible with the Foobar software. For certified products, Foobar has created a special certification logo. For more information on our certification programs, please see [URL].

Unaltered Binaries. You may distribute binaries downloaded from the Foobar web site to anyone, without receiving any further permission from Foobar. However, you must not remove or change any part of the official binary, including Foobar trademarks. On your web site or in other materials, you may truthfully state that the software you are providing is an unmodified version of a Foobar application. If you choose to provide visitors to your web site the opportunity to download Foobar binaries, you must do so by means of a link to our download site, to help ensure faster, more reliable downloads.

If you choose to distribute Foobar binaries yourself, you must make available only the latest released version.

Modified Versions.   Foobar's source code repository does not contain any digital version of Foobar's logos. You may not use the Trademarks with any modified program (including a modified configuration or build) that you create using this source code, and you may not use the Trademarks in any way to designate a modified version, except that you may truthfully state that the software you are providing contains portions that are derived from the Foobar software, and then only by using the Trademarks in their word form. You may not use any Foobar logo on any modified version. If you want to build an unmodified version, you should instead use our binary distribution only.

Extensions and Plug-ins.   If you want to distribute extensions or plug-ins, you may not use the Trademarks to refer either to the extensions or plug-ins, or to a product that consists of unmodified Foobar software built or installed together with your extensions or plug-ins. You should use the Trademarks only to refer to unmodified versions of the Foobar software alone. If you are in doubt about how to do this, you should consider contacting us or joining our developer program.

Linking

Foobar invites you to link to Foobar's web site, for the purpose of allowing your visitors to download the Foobar software by using this hyperlink: [Insert "Get Foobar" button]

Services Related to Foobar Software

If you offer services related to Foobar software, you may use Foobar's Trademarks in word form to describe and advertise your services, so long as you do not suggest that you are the origin of the Foobar software. For example, your web site might say "Customization services for the Foobar utility available here." It must not say "Foobar services sold here," or "custom Foobar software available here."

Proper trademark use. If you use the Trademarks as described in this policy, here is how they should be used.

- **Proper form.** Foobar's Trademarks should be used in their exact form, neither abbreviated nor combined with any other word or words. Do not vary the spelling, add hyphens, make one word into two, or use a possessive or plural form of the Trademarks. Do not abbreviate a Trademark to create an acronym. When using a logo, you must never modify the design, add or delete any words, or change any colors or proportions. The logo may be scaled proportionally. The logo may in its entirety be displayed in black on white background or using the exact colors used by Foobar.

- **Use of word mark.** We encourage you to use the word form of the Trademark (as opposed to the logo), because using the word form is easier to do without violating this Policy. You may use the word form of the Trademarks either in all capitals (FOOBAR) or by capitalizing only the first letter (Foobar). No other capitalization should be used. Use of the word form of the trademark should be in the same font and style as the surrounding text.

- **Trademarks are adjectives.** Always use the Trademarks as adjectives, and not as a verb or noun or in the possessive or plural forms. Examples of proper use: Foobar Software, Foobar Software application. Examples of improper use: Custom Foobar I Foobar-ed my system.

- **Accompanying symbol.** The first or most prominent mention of a Foobar Trademark should be accompanied by a symbol indicating whether the mark is a registered trademark ("®") or an unregistered trademark ("™"). Please see our Trademarks below for the correct symbol to use.

- **Attribution.** The fact that the Trademarks are owned by Foobar should be stated (e.g., "[FOOBAR] is a trademark of Foobar, Inc.") in a footnote or similar place, in a reasonably legible positionand size.

- **Separation.** The Foobar logos must be used as standalone icons, without any other third-party logos and/or trademarks combined or associated with them. A margin of at least the size of [describe letter or graphical feature of the logo] in the logo should be left empty around the logo in the background color of the displayed logo.

Trademarks.   [Display the Trademarks here.]

Possible Infringements.   Please help us by reporting any possible infringement of any Trademark by contacting us at the e-mail address below. [Insert e-mail address.]

POLICY UPDATES

Foobar reserves the right to modify this Policy at any time. You should review this Policy from time to time so that you will be aware of any updates. Any updates will apply as soon as they are posted on this page.

QUESTIONS

Foobar has tried to make this Policy as comprehensive and understandable as possible. If you are considering a use of a Trademark that is not covered by the policy, and you are unsure whether that use would run afoul of this Policy, please feel free to contact us. Also, we welcome your suggestions as to how to make this Policy better and more workable for our community. We like hearing from you!

PART TWO

Understanding Risks

Two major risks arise from open source: infringement risk and compliance risk. Infringement risk is the risk that infringing code has entered the open source code base due to the collaborative development model. In other words, this risk arises from the open source development model. Compliance risk is the risk that the licensee is not complying with the open source licenses that apply to the code. In other words, this risk arises from the open source licensing model. Infringement risk is addressed via due diligence, which is discussed in detail in Chapter 4. This part focuses primarily on compliance risk. Over the years, the focus of risk management for open source has shifted from infringement to compliance risk analysis.

CHAPTER 12

Technical Background: Operating System Kernels, User Space, and Elements of Programming

A computer functions by executing extremely simple instructions—but executing so many instructions so quickly that its actions seem complex. It can do this because computer programming allows programmers to use theoretical "layers" of functionality, which are sometimes called *levels of abstraction*. These layers are fundamentally arbitrary, but they must be used by everyone if programs are to be reusable from computer to computer. In the lowest level of abstraction, which is generally called the *operating system,* the computer executes the basic functions for the machine's processor to interface with the physical devices attached to the machine. In higher levels of abstraction, programmers can write a simple line of script (such as Hypertext Markup Language or HTML) that directs the computer to perform extremely complex tasks, because each line of code represents many low-level instructions. When analyzing certain open source issues, most significantly the border dispute of GNU General Public License version 2 (GPL2) in the area of Linux kernel development, it is essential to understand how this works.

Exhibit 12.1 shows a very abstract depiction of how a Linux kernel powers a computer. In the exhibit, the code in user space talks to the code in operating system space via system calls. System calls are the interface

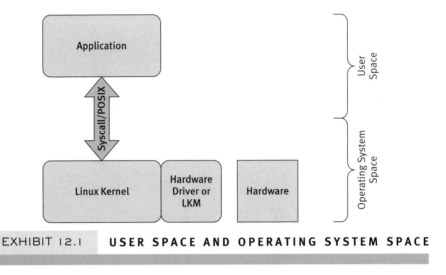

EXHIBIT 12.1   USER SPACE AND OPERATING SYSTEM SPACE

between the lowest level of abstraction—the operating system—and high levels, such as applications. The SYSCALL library is a description of the entry points into the Linux kernel. If you are building a Linux kernel, you actually use a library of files called the SYSCALL library. More than 200 function calls are available in the latest version of SYSCALL. They include functions that perform tasks related to file systems, virtual memory, and control of application programs. They also set the compatibility standard for Linux. In other words, if you write a program that uses SYSCALL, you have written a program that works with Linux.

Because of its UNIX heritage, SYSCALL is compatible with a standard called *POSIX* (Portable Operating System Interface[1]), which is a UNIX-to-UNIX interoperability standard maintained by the Portable Application Standards Committee of the Institute of Electrical and Electronics Engineers (IEEE). POSIX is now evolving into the Single UNIX Specification, which is being hammered out by a cross-industry cooperation including IEEE, the Austin Group, and The Open Group, with heavy participation from the software industry. About 80 percent of SYSCALL functions are identical to corresponding functions in POSIX.

---

[1]The *X* is an artifact of the UNIX naming convention that all "flavors" of UNIX end in *X*.

What Is the Difference Between an Application and an Operating System?

All computer programs written in a language such as Java or C, no matter whether they are part of the most fundamental operating system, or essential operating system tools, or high-level applications, operate in essentially the same way. They consist of procedures that talk to each other through defined interfaces.

The way in which functions must be invoked is sometimes called an applications program interface (API). An API is a specification that tells you how to use certain software code. Remember the explanation of the black box in Chapter 1? The API describes how to use the box. It dictates how a function is called and what data flow to and from it.

All well-written code is written in modules, more or less. For lawyers, it is difficult to understand how one program (called a *kernel*) and another program (a *library*) and yet other (an *application*) can be viewed so differently when assessing copyright questions. After all, each is a literary work in the form of a computer program that operates by passing information to other functions, and each is treated identically under copyright law. The software community views these types of programs quite distinctly, because programmers are more focused on practicality, whereas lawyers are focused on the application of an abstract law to the facts. To a lawyer, analyzing an operating system kernel versus an application under copyright law is a distinction without a difference. It is like distinguishing among a letter agreement, a memorandum of understanding, and an agreement. They look different, but they are all contracts.

Applications are the easiest kind of code for nonprogrammers to understand, because they are visible to users. An application could be a spreadsheet, or a word processor, or an Internet browser. In a Windows interface, you can see an application on your desktop. It has an icon. You tell it to run by selecting it from the program menu or clicking on it.

But there are lots of programs that run when you do not manually direct them to. If you load a music compact disc (CD) into your computer, a media player may run automatically to play your CD. That, too, is an application. But it appears to be an automatic part of Windows. What makes it an application, exactly? Programmers make these determinations by determining the "permissions" that a program has. These permissions dictate availability of computer memory and function to the program.

Suppose you are browsing the Internet and typing a URL into the input window. Would you like that line you are typing to be able to overwrite the operating system and change the default settings of your disk drive? Probably not. You want what you are asking the computer to do to be limited to those things it ought to be doing. Anything else is a recipe for disaster. So, in a sense, we define an application not by what it is, but by what it is not.

What Is an Operating System Kernel?

A kernel is the core of an operating system, providing the basic functionality that allows software applications to interact with the hardware they are running on: It controls hardware, manages files, and allocates the machine's memory and resources to the programs it runs.

More specifically, a kernel is:

> operating system software that . . . has access to the hardware's privileged registers. . . . The kernel is not a separate process running on the system. It is the guts of the operating system, which controls the scheduling of processes to achieve multitasking and provides a set of routines, constantly in memory, to which every user-space process has access.[2]

A kernel controls all programs running on the computer. It is the only program on a computer that is always running. Other programs, such as applications and loadable modules, can run at the same time, and it is the kernel's job to keep them all from interfering with each other.

An operating system sets aside certain portions of the computer's memory for operating system tasks, such as running programs and accessing disk files. For instance, the space in memory that contains the operating system must be reserved for the operating system alone. If not, an application could use that memory and cause the system to forget what it was doing, and crash.[3] You may recall that operating systems like UNIX and Linux are written in C, which is a very powerful language that allows

---

[2]Moshe Barr, *Linux Internals* (New York: McGraw-Hill, 2000), xiii.
[3]It is not as if this never happens. It is just not supposed to happen.

programmers to manipulate memory by direct address. For instance, it is easy (ask any beginning C programmer with a wild look in her eyes) to write a C program that instructs the computer to overwrite important memory. A C program can actually tell the computer to "go to memory address 10,000 and write a 1 there" without having any idea what it is overwriting. But a good operating system will not let an application program do that. Thus, applications are limited to using certain memory. The memory used by applications often has less priority or speed of access than that used by lower-level programs like operating systems and device drivers. Computers are designed this way because you want your operating system to control your applications, not vice versa.

What Is an Application?

These conventions tell us what applications are. Applications in user space cannot address portions of the computer's memory that are declared off limits by the operating system. In addition, applications can only call the functions available to user space. Thus, a program in user space can make the kernel perform its functions only through the 200 or so functions in SYSCALL. In contrast, a program in kernel space can make about 10,000 direct function calls to the kernel without going through SYSCALL. Think of this like a key in a hotel. Some people have access to any room. Some have access to low-security areas. Applications are like programs with low-level security clearance.

Just to be clear, an application in "user space" could occupy the same bits in memory as a kernel program, at different times. It is not the physical location of the memory that matters. It is the permission of the program to access whatever memory is set aside at that moment for user space and to access functions available to user space.

To understand Linux, you must also understand that making an operating system kernel usable requires various utilities and related software, such as compiler tools and shell tools. These utilities, among other things, provide the "shell" that allows the user to communicate with the operating system and installers that contain the boot and shutdown scripts. Utilities for Linux were developed by the GNU Project. The combination of the Linux kernel and these tools is known as a *Linux distribution*. The Free Software Foundation owns the GNU tools. Linux and the GNU tools are inseparable.

For instance, compiling Linux with anything but the GNU C compiler (GCC) probably will not work.[4]

DYNAMIC AND STATIC LINKING, AND INLINE CODE

It is possible to write a program by writing one huge source code file with a long list of instructions that execute in sequence. But this is not how it is done. Most programs are written using modular sets of instructions that can be reused many times within the program. These pieces are called *functions*, and they perform the same task many times when called from somewhere in the program. For example, you may want to have a user input a date into a program. But the date will not be useful unless it is a valid date, so it is useful to write a function that rejects invalid entries (such as 4/31/99). All distributions of programming languages, thus, include some form of a "date verify" function. In fact, low-level[5] languages like C do almost everything using functions. Some extremely basic tasks are built into the language: addition, subtraction, multiplication, and division, for example. But even the most basic tasks of accepting input from a keyboard or reading from a disk file are implemented as functions. Why? Because the procedure for accepting a keystroke from a keyboard might vary from computer to computer. If the acceptance of the keystroke is implemented as a function, the program does not need to be rewritten for different computers; only the basic functions must be adapted.

When a program uses a function, it passes data to the function, and the function returns different data, the result of the function's operation. Functions save time and space because the same function code can be recycled many times when a program runs. But they also "hide" certain details about the computer's operation from the programmer. When a program is well designed, it is modular. So, for instance, if the date functions need to

---

[4]Barr, *Linux Internals,* 19.

[5]This means the language operates closer to the hardware and can manipulate hardware more directly. C is a low-level language: fast but sometimes cumbersome to write. HTML is a high-level language: powerful but too slow to perform critical computer functions.

be changed (e.g., to account for whether there is a leap year in A.D. 3000), they can be changed, recompiled, and no other code needs to be changed. Moreover, a different programmer can work on a date verification routine and a date entry routine. As long as the input and output data are standardized, they need not know each other or work together.

Languages like C allow programmers great flexibility in determining how a product will be implemented using their various functions. When a program gets distributed to end users, it is usually not one single file. It includes many code files. How those files talk to each other—through functions—is a crucial part of program design. A well-designed program operates quickly and within the memory space allowed. Programmers use concepts called *dynamic* and *static linking* to achieve optimal program design. The process of implementing various source files and functions in a software product is called *creating a build*.

Exhibit 12.2 illustrates three ways to build the same application, which uses a library routine to verify a date that has been input by a user.

If the function is dynamically linked, it can be read into and deleted from memory as needed. This means programmers can write programs that run in smaller memory space. The dynamic linking implementation in

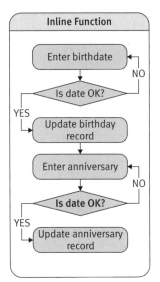
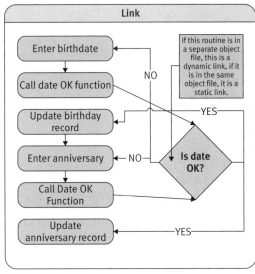

EXHIBIT 12.2   **METHODS OF LINKING**

Exhibit 12.2 results in the smallest program. It allows the shaded library routine (which verifies date input) to be loaded into memory as it is needed. The inline implementation results in the largest program: one object file that includes two copies of the library routine. The static linking implementation results in a smaller program than the inline implementation, because the library routine has been included only once. When the library routine is in memory, the dynamic and static linking implementations are similar. But when the library routine is not in memory, the dynamic linking implementation is smaller.[6]

Programming is always a trade-off between speed and size. Every time a program uses a function, it must look for the function, find it, pass data to it, and get data from it. All this takes processor time. The alternative is to put small, frequently accessed functions into the main program without linking them. Doing so enables the code to be referenced more quickly.[7] But it also makes the program bigger and thus uses up memory space. In C, this alternative can be accomplished by using "inline" functions. By designating a function as inline, the programmer tells the compiler actually to copy the function code into the place where the function is referenced. If a function is small, this will save time without much expense in size. If it is not, it will result in "code bloat," and the program will become too big. Also, when inline functions are used, every change to the function requires recompilation of all the code, not just the function code.

Programmers can choose, with almost complete discretion, what kind of build to use. Programmers use linking, both static and dynamic, and inline functions to maximize performance and ease of maintenance, but these methods are readily interchangeable. And they can be changed with very small changes—or no changes—in the source code being linked.

---

[6]Naturally this is a gross oversimplification. In the simple procedure presented, the library routine would always be in memory. But it still is possible to save space. If multiple processes referenced the same library date routine and if the library routine was properly segregated into a designated code library, the code could be shared by multiple processes.

[7]Nothing is ever this easy! Sometimes inline functions make code faster, sometimes they do not. There is plenty of discussion on the Web about efficiency concerns in building software.

More important, these methods of interface are sometimes substituted without human intervention. Some compilers or linkers will ignore the programmer's directives on how to link functions. When an inline function would be more efficient, the compiler might implement the function that way regardless of the programmer's instructions; and when a link would be more efficient, the compiler might ignore the directive to use an inline function. As compilers become more sophisticated, the method of building software becomes more transparent to programmers. Computer compilers and linkers today will generally "optimize" the build of a program by choosing the method of interface based on efficiency or other technical parameters.

HEADER FILES

As we know, a well-written function is like a black box: data go in, data are processed, and data come out, but to use the function, it is not necessary to know how it works. All that matters is that it works correctly. This is sometimes referred to as *transparency*.

Header files are the means by which code in one source file talks to code in another file. For instance, in our date verify routine, the input data might be a date in the form 00/00/0000, and the output data might be a single bit (0 for OK, 1 for not-OK). The header file for our date routine, therefore, might look like this:

```
extern int dateOK(int mm, int dd, int yyyy);
```

This header information tells the calling program what information the date verification routine needs and what it will return. Here, the keyword "extern" indicates that this function may be used by code in another source file. The variables mm, dd, and yyyy are the input variables, and they are called arguments to the function—in this case three integer numbers (represented by the data type "int"). The "return type" of the function is also an integer—yes or no (which will be represented by 0 or 1). This information is all the calling program needs to know about this routine to use it. The "guts" of the date verification—the way it verifies dates—is transparent to the calling program. Thus, if you wanted to substitute another date system (such as year, day, dynasty), you need rewrite the date verify routine only, not the calling program. Conversely, if you want to rewrite the way the date verification routine is used in the calling program (get a hire date instead of a birthdate), there is no need to rewrite the date routine. The header files set the standards for using library routines: what goes in and what goes out.

A header file contains relatively simple information: the name of the function, the number, type and order of arguments, and the return type. It is not quite software code; it is more like software design: a set of parameters for using software code. It is not possible to interface with a library function without using a corresponding header file.

However, it is important to understand that most headers are more complicated than the one just given. For one thing, there are other kinds of routines than functions, which are the simplest kind. Object-oriented languages like C++ use "objects" that can contain complex interfaces consisting of multiple functions, routines, and data structures.

MONOLITHS AND LOADABLE KERNEL MODULES

Operating systems such as UNIX are said to have a "monolithic architecture," in which all device drivers are part of one big kernel.[8] In Linux, however, device drivers—the software that runs peripheral devices—can also be loaded and unloaded from memory through dynamic links and even through user commands. Such a structure sometimes is called a micro-kernel architecture.[9] Thus, it is not strictly correct to say that an operating system kernel is always running. At least, not all of it is always running.

When a Linux system boots, the kernel must create and populate all the tables needed for its normal functioning. Almost all of these tables are statically allocated and initiated when the program is compiled.[10] However, as mentioned, Linux is not an entirely monolithic architecture. So, certain modules can be directed to load after the initial kernel executable. This aspect of Linux design is important in the analysis of the meaning of GPL2, discussed in Chapter 14.

---

[8] Barr, *Linux Internals,* xiii.
[9] Ibid., 220.
[10] Ibid., 68.

CHAPTER **13**

Enforcement of Open Source Licenses

PAST ENFORCEMENT

Compared to proprietary software licensing, open source licensing has seen relatively little formal enforcement activity.[1] Open source license enforcement is a moving target, of course, so cataloging all enforcement efforts in a book is not feasible.[2]

The Free Software Foundation (FSF) is in some ways the de facto enforcer of the GNU General Public License (GPL)— whether the license covers the FSF's own software or not—and to date, the FSF has only once fileda lawsuit to enforce the conditions of the license.[3] Because open source

---

[1]In writing this section, I relied on materials prepared by Hank Jones and Jason Haislmaier, who were kind enough to share presentations they gave on the subject.

[2]The best general source for up-to-date information is probably www.groklaw.net, but it is source information rather than summary.

[3]Shortly before this manuscript went to press (September 2007), the Software Freedom Law Center filed suit in the United States District Court for the Southern District of New York against Monsoon Multimedia on behalf of the developers of BusyBox, Erik Andersen and Rob Landley. BusyBox is a lightweight set of UNIX utilities used in embedded systems. Monsoon develops digital video products, including a Slingbox-like device that enables remote TV viewing. www.infoworld.com/article/07/09/20/Lawsuit-charges-open-source-license-violation_1.html? APPLICATIONS.

licenses flow directly from the author/owner to the licensee, the only party in a legal position to enforce the GPL is the author or owner of the copyright. Intermediate distributors do not have the power to enforce except with respect to any contribution they may make.[4] The FSF's enforcement activities for non-FSF code take place due to the FSF's position in the free software community and its resources for enforcement rather than to its legal right to bring enforcement actions. For the past few years, informal enforcement activities have been run through the Software Freedom Law Center (SFLC), a not-for-profit organization that assists the FSF in certain legal matters.[5]

While the FSF and SFLC have not filed lawsuits to enforce the GPL, the FSF filed an amicus brief in the *Nusphere* case (described later). (An *amicus curae* brief is one in which a nonlitigant seeks to sway the court's opinion, and such briefs often are filed by public interest law advocates.) Open source lawyers generally anticipate that the FSF or SFLC will seek to file amicus briefs in any meaningful suit involving the GPL where those organizations are not parties. The FSF conducts a compliance laboratory that investigates violations and is available for hire to assist companies to comply.[6]

The most widely publicized enforcement action of the FSF involved Cisco, Linksys, and Broadcom.[7] Facts regarding this action are challenging to verify but have been described publicly to some extent.[8] Linksys, a WiFi router company, was acquired by Cisco Systems in March 2003. After the acquisition, complaints appeared on Web discussion boards claiming Linksys was violating the GPL by not providing source code. The Linksys product included both the Linux kernel and other GPL code. The FSF undertook and coordinated enforcement.

Cisco was unaware of the problem when it bought Linksys. Linksys was probably unaware of the problem as well; the chipsets containing the

---

[4]Under United States law, only copyright owners or exclusive licensees have standing to bring a suit for copyright infringement.

[5]www.softwarefreedom.org/services/.

[6]www.fsf.org/licensing/compliance.html.

[7]An earlier version of this section appeared in "Open Source and the Legend of Linksys," *Linux Insider,* June 28, 2005.

[8]See, e.g., Dan Lyons, "Linux Hit Men," *Forbes,* October 14, 2003.

GPL code had been purchased from Broadcom. Broadcom was also probably unaware, because it outsourced the development of the firmware for the chipsets to an overseas developer. A negotiation of several months ensued, and Linksys eventually released the source code at issue. Open source advocates are quick to point out that doing so ultimately increased sales of the Linksys product. But this is just one story with mostly non-public details and no formal lawsuit. The only conclusion to draw from it is that open source is potentially risky—but anyone who is reading this book presumably already knew that. Actions by FSF and SFLC remain almost entirely confidential and sub rosa.

The main active formal enforcer of GPL is Harald Welte in Germany and the other volunteers organized around www.gpl-violations.org. Some, but not all, of the cases brought by this organization relate to Welte's own software.[9] The German system of jurisprudence allows actions that may not be as easy to bring in the United States. For instance, German courts allow ex-parte actions for injunction—a suit for an injunction brought by the plaintiff where the defendant does not participate, and the plaintiff pursues the injunction directly with a court.[10] This difference may explain why the enforcement strategy of FSF and Welte is different. The Legal FAQ on www.gpl-violations.org states:

> From a [German] legal point of view, damages are a totally different issue from the "cease-and-desist" issue. So in all cases that went to court so far, we've only enforced the latter.

The most widely publicized enforcement action by this group was against Fortinet UK. A Munich district court granted a preliminary injunction against Fortinet prohibiting distribution of the company's products absent compliance with the GPL. Welte also claimed that Fortinet was obfuscating the existence of GPL code in its product, a fact that Fortinet disputed.[11] Fortinet eventually agreed to make certain source code in its products available under GPL.

---

[9]A list of successful enforcement actions appears at http://gpl-violations.org/news .html. These include both lawsuits and informal enforcement.

[10]Germany is a jurisdiction particularly friendly to the granting of intellectual property injunctions. www.managingip.com/?Page=17&ISS=21425&SID=614860.

[11]http://gpl-violations.org/news/20050414-fortinet-injunction.html.

A few other lawsuits have involved the GPL, although none has specifically addressed the key issues of enforceability or the "boundary dispute" (discussed in Chapter 14). Some rightly observe that the results in some of the cases to be discussed imply that the GPL is enforceable, but that is not the same as a court stating that it is enforceable. Our system of law in the United States is called a *common law* system. When judges make decisions in such a system, they rely on case law—which means the written opinions on matters of law that were published previously by courts. For the most part, courts inquire into only those issues that litigants raise. If this were not so, the legal system would be even more clogged than it is. If you bring a suit to enforce the GPL, and the defendant does not deny that the GPL is enforceable, the issue is not litigated, nor is it decided by the court. In a common law system, the hard questions often do not get answered, because the enunciation of legal principles is driven by the controversy of the case, not by what legal scholars want to know. So far, in GPL enforcement, no case has enunciated the central legal issues in open source law, such as whether linking code creates a derivative work, or whether the GPL is a contract.[12]

Some of the more notable cases involving open source (not necessarily GPL) follow.

- *SCO Group, Inc (SCO). v. IBM, Novell, Red Hat, AutoZone & Daimler-Benz.* While this set of related cases was by far the most publicized in the open source world, the SCO cases were primarily breach of contract cases and did not seek to enforce any open source license. In fact, IBM raised SCO's breach of the GPL as a counterclaim, but the issue has not yet been settled.[13]
- *MontaVista Software v. Lineo.* MontaVista sued its competitor, Lineo, claiming Lineo was distributing software written by MontaVista

---

[12]Shortly before this book went to press (September 2007), an order was handed down in the *Jacobsen v. Katzer* case speaking to this issue. See below.

[13]The brief is available on Groklaw at www.groklaw.net/pdf/IBM-826.pdf. A Memorandum Decision and Order in the related *Novell* case (*SCO Group, Inc. v. Novell, Inc.* (Utah Dist. Ct.2004)(Civil No.2:04CV139DAK)), dated August 10, 2007 holding that Novell, and not SCO, owns the rights to UNIXWare probably means the *SCO v. IBM* case is effectively over.

with the copyright notices removed.[14] The case was settled. The issue in this case—the stripping of notice—was not specific to open source.

- **Progress Software and NuSphere v. MySQL.** NuSphere and MySQL had a business relationship in which NuSphere marketed several products that included both MySQL software and other proprietary software. Proprietary code (called Gemini) was statically linked to MySQL code in the NuSphere MySQL Advantage product. Although MySQL alleged a breach of its GPL license, the case was decided on trademark grounds, with the court sidestepping the GPL issues.[15]

- **Monotype v. Red Hat.** Monotype sued Red Hat claiming copyright and trademark infringements. The suit was settled and, in December 2003, the parties entered into a license agreement that provided Red Hat the right to distribute certain Monotype commercial fonts over a five-year period. The license cost Red Hat $500,000. This was not a suit to enforce any open source license; it was an infringement suit regarding proprietary software.[16]

- **Jacobsen (for JMRI.org) v. Katzer.** This case involved a developer who created toy train control software called Java Model Railroad Interface. Jacobsen received a demand for $203,000 for allegedly infringing a patent. Jacobsen filed an action for declaratory relief asking the court to rule that the patent was invalid. In an article on the web site Groklaw.net, there is a general call for community assistance to help find prior art to support invalidation of the patent. This case is still pending.[17]

---

[14]Steven Shankland, "Linux Companies Settle Copyright Suit," C/Net News.com, October 13, 2003 http://news.com.com/2100-7344_3-5090704.html.
[15]For the court's order, see http://pacer.mad.uscourts.gov/dc/opinions/saris/pdf/progress%20software.pdf.
[16]See Red Hat's 10-K dated 2/29/04, www.secinfo.com/d14D5a.12Mg6.htm.
[17]www.groklaw.net/articlebasic.php?story=20060514233436196. On August 17, 2007, an order was issued in the Northern District of California granting in part and denying in part defendants' motion to dismiss. The order was notable in stating that the plaintiffs' claims for violation of an open source license sounded in contract rather than copyright (page 9). However, this ruling is unlikely to be the last word on the subject.

- *Drew Technologies Inc. v. Society of Auto Engineers (SAE).* This case was filed in November 2003 and settled in early 2005. Drew Tech released a program under GPL, which was posted by an employee of Drew Tech on a message board run by SAE. Drew Tech sued to compel the removal of the posting, and the case was settled and the posting removed. No reported opinion resulted, but the result suggested the GPL was enforceable.[18]

ENFORCEMENT OBSTACLES

Many have commented that there may be limits to the enforceability of GPL under law.[19] However, many of these comments have been specious and are not treated at any length there. For instance, in its lawsuit against IBM, SCO pled that the GPL violated the U.S. Constitution[20]—an argument so poorly reasoned that most legal commentators did not expend much effort to refute it. Recently a lawsuit was brought claiming that the GPL violated antitrust law. The court ruled, not surprisingly, that it did not.[21] Here are some of the more interesting enforceability arguments and a brief discussion of their merits.

Lack of Track Record: GPL Has Never Been Tested in Court

This "oft-repeated mantra"[22] of open source detractors has lost some of its trenchancy given the recent actions of gpl-violations.org, but it still continues to be heard. Such an argument is quite misguided. Contracts need not have been previously tested in court (i.e., adjudged enforceable) to be valid; indeed, most contracts are written ad hoc and could not

---

[18]The Groklaw posting about the case is at www.groklaw.net/articlebasic. php?story=20050225223848129.
[19]For an excellent article on the topic, see Jason Wacha, "Taking the Case: Is the GPL Enforceable?" reprinted at www.open-bar.org/docs/GPL-enforceability.pdf.
[20]Open Letter on Copyrights from Daryl McBride, President and CEO, The SCO Group, Inc., December 4, 2003, www.sco.com/copyright.
[21]Order dismissing *Wallace v. Free Software Foundation, Inc.* (S. Dist. Ind., October 28, 2005).
[22]See note 19, 469.

feasibly be tested in advance. Such a requirement would put the courts in a position of telling people what they could agree to by contract—which would be a significant limitation of freedom of contract and therefore a limitation on political freedom.

Waiver/Estoppel: Occasional and Selective Enforcement of GPL Means It Is Unenforceable

Suits to enforce GPL are thought to be copyright claims rather than contract claims. (See the discussion in Chapter 15.) Copyrights are very hard to lose through estoppel—harder than trademarks (which must be policed to be enforceable),[23] patents (whose enforcement will result in lower damages if not enforced),[24] and trade secrets (which evaporate if the owner does not use reasonable efforts to maintain their secrecy).[25] In addition, any waiver or estoppel will be particular to the copyright at issue and not the license that covers it. A contract claim can be waived through estoppel as well, but this is also a difficult argument to win and fact-specific.

Formation: GPL Is Not Validly Accepted by Licensees

The FSF actually takes the position that the GPL is not a contract. However, assuming it is a contract, this argument takes the additional step that therefore the GPL's terms are unenforceable. For a contract to be enforceable, it must have three elements: offer, acceptance, and consideration. Clearly the GPL contains an offer by the licensor, because the licensor has made the code available under the license. Consideration (or quid pro quo) is not in much doubt either, given that the licensor is granting a license (i.e., forgoing a suit for copyright infringement) and the licensee must agree to many conditions, including copyleft conditions. The problem is acceptance. The law on this topic lies in case law and statute—the latter mainly for states that have adopted the Uniform Computer Information Transactions Act

---

[23]*McCarthy on Trademarks,* Section 18:42 (2004).
[24]35 USC Sections 286, 287.
[25]Uniform Trade Secrets Act, Section 1(4).

(UCITA).[26] Under the *ProCD* line of cases (discussed in Chapter 15), online terms are enforceable if the user has sufficient notice of the existence of the licensing terms prior to purchase. Acceptance could be effectuated in any manner reasonable under the circumstances—which is the formulation of the Uniform Commercial Code in Section 2-106(a)(1). The license terms in *ProCD* were inside the box, and the court ruled the agreement enforceable even though there was no opportunity to view them prior to purchase. In the post-*ProCD* world, it is fairly clear that click-to-accept agreements are enforceable if presented as a condition to software download or otherwise correctly within the transaction process. The problem with translating this rule to an open source context is that no transaction actually takes place, no money is paid, and there is almost never a click-to-accept implementation. In this way, GPL acceptance is more akin to the classic "shrink-wrap" agreement where breaking the seal constituted acceptance. The question of contract formation is fact-specific and will depend on whether the licensee knew or should reasonably have known about the terms. In today's world, it strains belief to think that a licensee of a major open source project such as Linux or GNU could be unaware that GPL terms applied to the code.

GPL Constitutes Copyright Misuse

Copyright misuse is an equitable doctrine that will prevent a licensor from getting relief for copyright infringement in violation of a license if the licensor has acted improperly. The misuse doctrine is fairly well developed under patent law,[27] and less so under copyright law. Misuse usually arises when the licensor places obligations or conditions in the license that are unlawful (such as anticompetitive obligations that violate antitrust law) or that attempt to "disrupt a copyright's goal to increase the store of creative expression for the public good."[28] The true extent of this doctrine is unclear. Although courts have held that clauses attempting to control ideas rather than expression may constitute copyright misuse,[29]

---

[26]For a general discussion of online assent rules, see Ian Ballon, *E-Commerce and Internet Law* (Glasser Legalworks, 2003), chapter 26.

[27]The seminal case is *Morton Salt Co. v. G.S. Suppiger,* 314 U.S. 488 (1942).

[28]*Video Pipeline, Inc. v. Buena Vista Home Entertainment,* 342 F.3d 191 (3d Cir. 2003).

[29]*Lasercomb America Inc. v. Reynolds,* 911 F.2d 970 (4th Cir. 1990).

the boundaries of this doctrine are extremely unclear. A defendant may argue that the scope of the GPL goes beyond the control of the works to which the licensor owns the copyright. Presumably the position of the FSF that the boundary of a work based on the program is coterminous with the extent of a derivative work of the program is, in part, an attempt to avoid application of this doctrine. A potential litigant making this argument probably would point to the phrase in paragraph 2 of the GPL stating that the license is intended to cover "collective works"—a category that the copyright owner does not have the right to prohibit.

Joint Work Arguments

Joint work arguments turn on whether an open source project is a work of joint authorship or the combination of many works of authorship. Under U.S. law, joint copyright owners each have the right to freely license their rights in the whole work.[30] Therefore, if one author sues for copyright infringement, courts often require all authors to be parties to the suit—to address the problem that any one of those parties could have granted a license that would be a defense to infringement. Joint authors need not be conjoined in time or geography.[31] The copyright law states that a joint work arises when both authors intended, at the time the work was created, "that their contributions be merged into inseparable or interdependent parts of a unitary whole." The Second Circuit has stated that

> [p]arts of a unitary whole are "inseparable" when they have little or no independent meaning standing alone. . . . By contrast, parts of a unitary whole are "interdependent" when they have some meaning standing alone but achieve their primary significance because of their combined effect.[32]

Whether a work is a joint work may turn on the intent of the authors. Nimmer observes:

> The distinction lies in the intent of each contributing author at the time his contribution is written. If his work is written "with the intention

---

[30]*Oddo v. Ries,* 743 F.2d 630 (9th Cir.1984).

[31]See, e.g., *Edward B. Marks Music Corp. v. Jerry Vogel Music Co.,* 140 F.2d 267 (2d Cir. 1944).

[32]*Childress v. Taylor,* 945 F.2d 500, 505 (2nd Cir. 1991).

that [his] contribution . . . be merged into inseparable or interdependent parts of a unitary whole," then the merger of his contribution with that of others creates a joint work. If such intention occurs only after the work has been written, then the merger results in a derivative or collective work.[33]

There is a split of opinion on whether the individual authors need contribute copyrightable expression, or whether contribution of ideas alone will suffice.[34] Contributors to an open source project may find it difficult to argue that the work is not a joint work. Rhetoric abounds about open source being a collaborative development model, where the intent is to create a single, cohesive work regardless of the number, geography, or timing of contributions. It seems unlikely that a court would conclude that each author has the ability to license all the code on terms of his or her choice; it is more likely to find that the authors jointly intended to limit licensing of the whole work to the open source license. However, if an open source project is found to be a joint work, courts may require all or many of the authors to be joined to the suit, as described in the next section. Such arguments will be fact-specific and will be more significant for projects with a large number of significant contributors, particularly if the project does not use contribution agreements that might clarify enforcement rights.

Standing and Joinder Arguments

Standing and joinder arguments are potentially significant limitations for open source projects with many contributors. Under U.S. law, only the author or copyright owner has standing to bring a lawsuit for infringement. The converse is also true, to a point: All authors must join a suit for copyright infringement. Under 17 United States Code Section 501(b), a court "may require the joinder, and shall permit the intervention, of any person having or claiming an interest in the copyright." Although theoretically any author may sue for infringement of his or her own portion of the project, a court may require that a critical mass of owners

---

[33]*Nimmer on Copyright* Section 6.05 (2005).
[34]*Ashton-Tate Corp. v. Ross,* 916 F.2d 516 (9th Cir. 1990).

of the infringed material be joined to the case. This requirement is to a large degree up to the court, which will decide whether it is equitable to allow separate suits.[35]

Most companies that are assessing the likelihood of enforcement are less concerned about the enforceability of the GPL than with its interpretation. However, enforcement cases to date have not addressed any of the difficult enforcement issues. One FSF spokesman has said, "In nearly every enforcement case I have worked on in my career, that fact that infringement had occurred was never in dispute."[36] The lesson to be learned is that fine questions of interpretation may not receive court attention for some time yet—at least not at the behest of the FSF, which appears to have its hands full enforcing clear violations of the license.

---

[35]*Edward B. Marks Music Corp. v. Jerry Vogel Music Co.*, 140 F.2d 268 (2d Cir. 1944) held that co-owners were not indispensable parties; for the opposite view see *Key West Hand Fabrics v. Serbin, Inc.*, 244 F. Supp. 287 (S.D.Fla. 1965). Case law on the subject is scant.

[36]Brad Kuhn, former director of the Software Freedom Law center. www.soft warefreedom.org/technology/blog/2007/may/08/infringement-1. See also Jason Haislmaier, "Open Source License Enforcement Actions: What You Can Expect When There Is a Knock on Your Door," PowerPoint presentation given at Open Source Business Conference, May 23, 2007, available at www.hro.com/resources/custom/publications/HRO%20Publications/opensourceppt.pdf.

CHAPTER 14

The Border Dispute of GPL2

DEFINING THE BORDER DISPUTE

There is one central, crucial question of GNU General Public License version 2 (GPL2) compliance whose importance to commercial developers eclipses all others, the question that I refer to as the *border dispute*. The "border" at issue is that between a "work based on the Program" and everything else.

As we know, the GPL is a hereditary license whose copyleft provisions apply to the original work (the "Program") and works "based on the Program." However, what constitutes a work based on the Program, and is thus covered by GPL, versus a new work can be very difficult to determine.

Resolving this border dispute is crucial to developers of proprietary technology products. Before I explain why this is so, it is worth observing who is not concerned. Mere users of GPL materials are not concerned about this issue. The boundary dispute matters only when you are concerned about the obligation to lay open source code in distributions. The reason is because the copyleft obligations of the GPL attach only to code that is distributed,[1] not to code that is merely used.

On the other end of the spectrum, companies using a pure open source business model are not concerned either, because the hereditary nature of the GPL does not compromise their goals. They release all code in open source format because they want to, not because they must. But this is a

---

[1]See Chapter 16 for a discussion of distribution issues relating to GPL2.

relatively small constituency. Of all the companies today using free software in their products, only a small subset employ a true open source business model.

In contrast, a great many other companies use open source software in their products but are not open source companies. For instance, some companies build products that consist of standard Linux systems with specialized application software, such as security devices (physical or virtual), communications products, or office-in-a-box. For these companies, open source assets are a component of their products, but the companies have not made a decision to use open source as a business model. These companies comply with hereditary open source requirements to the extent they must, not because they choose to.

It is these developers to whom the border dispute is of such critical importance. These developers want to know whether the code they develop on their own, using company resources, will need to be laid open under the GPL. If it must, investors will perceive the code as having a lower commercial value, and competitors will have access to it. Companies with proprietary business models that are making design decisions related to the GPL want to know whether they will be required to lay open source code before they engage in developments with high nonrecurring costs. If the source code must be laid open, they will be less inclined to engage in expensive development. But these companies often are very confused about where the border truly lies. Their confusion arises because of the blurred line of demarcation between works based on the Program and independent, separate, or nonderivative works—in other words, the border dispute.

What the GPL Says

In the text of the GPL, the border between code that is covered by the GPL and code that is not turns on what composes a "work based on the Program." The "Program" means the code received under the GPL. A "work based on the Program" must be relicensed under the GPL's terms.

Paragraph 0 of the GPL says (emphasis below added):

> This License applies to any program or other work which contains a notice placed by the copyright holder saying it may be distributed under

the terms of this General Public License. The "Program," below, refers to any such program or work, and *a "work based on the Program" means either the Program or any derivative work under copyright law: that is to say, a work containing the Program or a portion of it, either verbatim or with modifications and/or translated into another language.*

According to Paragraph 2:

You may modify your copy or copies of, thus forming a work based on the Program.

Paragraph 2(b), the copyleft provision of the GPL, says:

You must cause any work that you distribute or publish, that *in whole or in part contains or is derived from the Program or any part thereof,* to be licensed as a whole at no charge to all third parties under the terms of this License.

Also in Paragraph 2:

These requirements apply to the modified work as a whole. If identifiable sections of that work are *not derived from the Program, and can be reasonably considered independent and separate works in themselves,* then this License, and its terms, do not apply to those sections when you distribute them as separate works. But when you distribute the same sections as part of a whole which is a work based on the Program, the distribution of the whole must be on the terms of this License, whose permissions for other licensees extend to *the entire whole, and thus to each and every part* regardless of who wrote it.

Thus, it is not the intent of this section to claim rights or contest your rights to *work written entirely by you;* rather, the intent is to exercise the right to control the distribution of *derivative or collective works based on the Program.* In addition, *mere aggregation* of another work not based on the Program with the Program (or with a work based on the Program) on a volume of a storage or distribution medium does not bring the other work under the scope of this License.

Paragraph 5 states:

You are not required to accept this License, since you have not signed it. However, nothing else grants you permission to modify or distribute the Program *or its derivative works.*

RULES OF CONTRACT CONSTRUCTION

To understand the difficulty in interpreting the overlapping language of the GPL, it is first necessary to understand the rules by which contracts are interpreted. Although some claim that the GPL is a license and not a contract, the rules of interpretation for most legal documents, such as contracts and statutes, are quite similar.[2] The rules to be discussed are taken from the Restatement (Second) of Contracts, which is a scholarly statement of the general rules of contract law,[3] and the Uniform Commercial Code (UCC), which has been adopted in all states of the United States and Article 2 of which applies to contracts involving the sale of goods. Licenses of software are generally considered to be covered by the UCC Article 2.[4]

The first of these rules of contract interpretation sometimes is called the four corners rule. According to this rule, the meaning of the language of a contract is the intent of the contracting parties, as objectively determined from the contract language, on its face. The second rule is the "parol evidence rule," which states that if a written document exists, prior or contemporaneous oral agreements are not considered competent evidence of interpretation. The third rule is that, where possible, a document is interpreted as a whole, giving effect to all parts of the document. It is therefore not an option simply to ignore part of the document and use other parts. The interpretation must give meaning to all the parts.

Thus, interpretation focuses on the exact words of the document, and not what others say about them. Remember that the meaning is that of

---

[2]Lawrence Rosen posits that the rules for interpreting bare licenses may not be similar to those used for contracts; see www.rosenlaw.com/Rosen_Ch04.pdf.

[3]Contract law in the United States is state law, so there are potentially 50 different sets of rules. The UCC applies only to the sale of goods, so the laws regarding contracts generally are broader than this. We turn to the Restatement rather than state law because the GPL does not have a governing law selection. Assuming the analysis is taking place under U.S. law, the Restatement is the closest thing to a general statement of law that exists. In any case, these principles are not controversial, and most lawyers learn them as axioms of contract law.

[4]A seminal case was *Step-Saver Data Sys., Inc. v. Wyse Tech.,* 939 F.2d 91 (3d Cir. 1991).

the contracting parties, not others. Interpretation is accomplished in levels of precedence. First, the words in the document are assigned their ordinary, plain meaning. Courts interpreting documents look to dictionaries and similar references for what constitutes ordinary meaning. If a court determines that the terms are unambiguous (susceptible of only one reasonable meaning), then the court may presume that the parties intended what they stated and enforce the contract as written. However, if a court determines that the terms are ambiguous (susceptible of more than one reasonable meaning), then the court must use established rules of contract construction to resolve the ambiguity.[5]

Once a court determines that a term is ambiguous, other evidence, including evidence of the way in which the parties to the contract interpret the language, can be used to determine its meaning. Also, the meaning given to a word by a trade or profession will supersede the ordinary or popular sense of words, where such usage would more nearly approximate the understanding of the parties. In the case of GPL interpretation, technical meanings are obviously very important.

These rules of law use two types of evidence that are often confused. One is "course of performance," which the Restatement describes as "repeated occasions for performance by either party with knowledge of the nature of the performance."[6] The other is "usage of trade," which is defined in the UCC as "any practice . . . having such regularity of observance in a place, vocation, or trade as to justify an expectation that it will be observed with respect to the transaction in question."[7] In other words, course of performance describes how the exact parties to the agreement perform the agreement. Usage of trade describes how the industry generally does so.

Finally, if the rules of contract construction fail to resolve the ambiguity, then, under the rule of *contra proferentem,* any ambiguity must be construed against the drafter of the contract.[8]

---

[5]See Restatement (Second) Contracts Section 202 (1981).
[6]Ibid.
[7]UCC Article 2, Section 1-303. The UCC and the Restatement are almost identical on this topic.
[8]Restatement (Second) Contracts Section 206 (1981).

APPLYING THE FOUR CORNERS RULE TO GPL2

To determine the true meaning of a "work based on the Program" under law, you must apply the rules of contract construction to the many "definitions" of that phrase in the text of the GPL. If the GPL were drafted in a more traditional fashion, the term "Work Based on the Program" would be capitalized whenever used and defined once, and only once, at the beginning of the agreement.[9] But it is not.

To resolve this ambiguity, we need to assess the boundary or overlap between, on one hand, "works written entirely by" the licensee, works combined by "mere aggregation" on the same storage volume or medium, and works that "can be reasonably considered independent and separate works in themselves"; and, on the other hand, a work "that in whole or in part contains or is derived from the Program or any part thereof." Keep in mind that we do not have the option of discarding any of these phrases. Every term of the document must have meaning.

This is why attorneys who read the GPL quickly come to the conclusion that this phrase—upon which entire companies and development projects depend—is irretrievably vague. To illustrate this point, Exhibit 14.1 is a Venn diagram of the various definitional phrases of the language of GPL2.

This diagram represents a hypothetical software product for a commercial technology company, which would contain:

- Code received under the GPL (the Program)
- Modifications to the Program written by the licensee
- New code (which forms part of a derivative work composed by the Program plus the new code)

---

[9]See, for instance, the handling of "Covered Code" in the Mozilla Public License, which was drafted in a more corporate style, and the program boundary is more clearly set: Any code segregated into a distinct source code file is outside the program boundary. Thus, even though this licenses is hereditary, it does not trouble developers or lawyers much. It is easy to avoid laying open source code simply by segregating closed-source code in a separate file—a design decision that will likely have little effect on technical efficacy because of the flexibility of modern linkers and compilers.

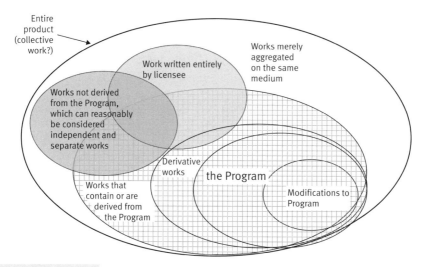

Entire product (collective work?)

Work written entirely by licensee

Works merely aggregated on the same medium

Works not derived from the Program, which can reasonably be considered independent and separate works

Derivative works

the Program

Works that contain or are derived from the Program

Modifications to Program

EXHIBIT 14.1   DEFINITIONAL PHRASES OF THE LANGUAGE OF GPL2

- Code written by the licensee that is not part of the work based on the Program
- Code written by others but included on the same distribution medium

In a properly drafted license,[10] the cross-hatched portions on the exhibit, which represent code covered by the GPL, would not overlap with the shaded portions, which represent code that escapes coverage. The overlap

---

[10]To provide context for nonlawyer readers, drafting unique (in the document) and unambiguous definitions is considered a baseline lawyering skill in transactional practice. Doing otherwise is generally a sign that the drafter is not a lawyer or, more precisely, does not have baseline drafting skills. If this seems harsh, consider that many programming languages require one, and only one, definition of a user-defined variable. (Some languages allow multiple definitions, or "overloading," but using this feature requires intimate knowledge of the rules used by the compiler or interpreter to resolve them.) Failing to understand these rules properly creates bugs. So, in a sense, multiple or conflicting definitions in a legal document, without express rules to resolve them, is a "bug" in drafting.

occurs because, taking the various definitional phrases of GPL2 at face value, a work can contain the Program but include code not derived from it (see the overlap of the largest cross-hatched circle and the lower shaded circle). Also, work that is written entirely by the licensee can be part of a derived work or not (see the relation between the largest cross-hatched circle and the upper shaded circle).

This pastiche of meaning was certainly not the intention of the stewards of the GPL. However, the fact that the meaning is so difficult to parse is underscored by the extensive frequently asked questions (FAQ) on the topic published by the Free Software Foundation (FSF). Some have likened the GPL to a holy text, and the FAQ to the dogma of the faithful. The simile is not without its merits.

APPLYING THE RULES OF CONTRACT CONSTRUCTION TO GPL2

For reasons just outlined, the four-corners legal analysis of the literal meaning of a "work based on the Program" in the GPL is of less practical use in making design decisions than a commercial developer might hope. So, when corporate lawyers try to interpret the GPL, they tend to assume, instead, that the interpretation of the various phrases in the GPL that would define "work based on the Program" is irretrievably ambiguous. If that is the case, then there are several alternatives. These include:

- Relying on trade usage evidence
- Engaging in a derivative works analysis (discussed later)
- Using a "legal realism" approach by laying aside an actual interpretation and focusing on the risk of enforcement

"Legal realism" is, of course, very attractive to most companies making real-life risk decisions. They select open source code to avoid expense, so they are highly unlikely to be willing to undertake the expense necessary to resolve the ambiguity through the legal process: filing an action for declaratory relief that would likely become the most controversial and celebrated software licensing case of the nascent century.

Trade Usage and Other Extrinsic Evidence

When plain meaning and the four corners of the document do not suffice, contract law allows for alternative evidence of meaning.[11] It may be a prerequisite that parties be aware of the trade usage for it to be relevant to interpretation.[12] Therefore, to the extent a court follows interpretations of community leaders such as the FSF, it will do so only to the extent that those interpretations are widely accepted and known within the industry. However, it would be misguided to rely on the assumption that courts are likely to accept trade usage evidence when interpreting "derivative works." A derivative work is clearly a creature of copyright law; even the FSF admits that the meaning of "derivative work" is coterminous with its meaning under relevant copyright law. If this is the case, the FSF's positions on the meaning of "derivative work" are unlikely to be treated as competent evidence. Trade usage is used in interpreting private contracts (and licenses) because the object of interpreting contracts is to determine the intent of the parties. Trade usage is evidence of what the parties believed at the time they entered into the contract. Interpreting statutory language, in contrast, is an attempt to determine the intent of the legislative body that passed it. Trade usage is therefore not relevant.

In the context of contract interpretation, the GPL is an unusual phenomenon. Although many standard contracts have been developed for various industries (particularly insurance and health care), GPL is arguably the most widely used standard contract[13] in the world, in the sense that many parties use it to cover many unrelated transactions.

Consider that the GPL is probably more like a statute than a contract: a single document that is applied to many situations and many persons. It is possible, therefore, that the traditional approach to contract law may

---

[11]In exact fact, neither the UCC nor the Restatement (Second) of Contracts strictly requires a showing of ambiguity before trade usage is introduced. Restatement (Second) Contracts Section 220 comment d.

[12]UCC Article 2, Section 1-303(d).

[13]Assuming it is a contract. See Chapter 15.

not be the best way to interpret the document. If contract interpretation is not appropriate to apply to GPL, though, what is? If FSF is viewed as a quasi-legislative body, what it says about the contract may be paramount. But the problem is that the FSF is not bounded by the same rules as a legislative body, whose statutory enactments have the power to affect many people's lives. It is, after all, simply a not-for-profit corporation, which ultimately does not answer to an electorate.[14] Therefore, it may be best from a policy perspective to reexamine the way such a document is interpreted and consider whether different rules should apply, as a general case. But that is theory, and as interesting as it may be, our job is to turn to the nuts and bolts of the legal analysis.

DERIVATIVE WORKS QUESTION

Perhaps, at least in part, in tacit recognition of the ambiguous language defining a "work based on the Program" in the GPL, the FSF has publicly declared that it considers the definition of "work based on the Program" identical to that of a "derivative work" under copyright law.[15] This is consistent with the FSF's position that the GPL, as a conditional license only, can control only what is controlled by background copyright law.

Derivative works are more complicated to assess in the context of computer programs than in the context of other copyrightable works. Indeed, some have suggested that, like the language of the GPL, the extent of copyright coverage of software and its derivative works is irretrievably vague.[16] Much computer source code text is dictated by function;

---

[14]www.fsf.org/about.

[15]In writing this section, I have relied heavily on the excellent materials written by Thomas Graves for the University of Washington Shidler Center conference on open source in March 2006, www.law.washington.edu/lct/Events/FOSS.

[16]Greg Aharonian's position is that software source code is outside the scope of copyrightable subject matter and that the application of copyright law to software is unconstitutionally vague. Personally I find his analysis rather persuasive, but the court did not. See the order dismissing his case at www.iplaw-quality.com/lawsuit/i-lose.pdf.

for instance, there is only one way to write a loop[17] in many languages, and the expression of a loop thus cannot be copyrightable.[18] Copyright, however, does not protect functional elements, only expression. This principle is sometimes called the idea/expression dichotomy or the merger doctrine.

To understand the analysis of derivative works, you must first understand copyright's application to software generally. Courts assume that software code is a literary work. Although the statutory basis for this assumption is murky, most courts rely on the legislative history to conclude that computer programs are literary works, a category that is the subject matter of copyright law.[19] However, courts also recognize that not all portions of software code can be protected, because much of software is dictated either by efficiency or by the constraints of the language in which it is written.

The analysis that follows is written in roughly the form it would be presented in a legal brief. For those readers who are not lawyers, do not lose heart. Legal argument is not that difficult to follow. It is mostly reasoning by analogy—something that any good engineer or businessperson does every day. Do not be discouraged by the case names and the citations. These names (*Plaintiff v. Defendant*) and numbers (982 F.2d 693) simply tell lawyers where to find the written opinions being relied on. In legal writing, it is fundamental to include them; citing written authority for statements in the argument is a baseline requirement.

Legal argument is, however, written in a formulaic way. It has a particular structure: issue, rule, argument, conclusion (called IRAC by law students learning its practice). This structured argument is preceded by a

---

[17]A loop is a section of code that executes repeatedly, usually until a particular condition occurs.

[18]There are a few ways to do it in C++ or Java, for instance, and which one a programmer selects is a matter of style. That selection is an example of a copyrightable element: If three kinds of loops will work just as well as each other, the selection is creative. If, however, there is only one type that will do, the selection is not a copyrightable element. The latter case is an example of the merger doctrine: Because there is only one way to express this idea, the idea and the expression merge into an unprotectable element.

[19]Pub. L. 96-517, 94 Stat. 3015, 3028 (1980).

statement of facts.[20] The "rules" in legal argument are statutes and written judicial opinions, or case law. Copyright law in the United States is federal law only; there is no longer any state law of copyright.[21] Therefore, the principal statutory authority in this argument is Title 17 of the United States Code, which is the statutory expression of the Copyright Act.

For nonlawyers, the idea of controlling case law might be new. Because the United States is a common law country, while statutes certainly apply, if a court of sufficient authority issues an opinion interpreting a statute in a certain way, then that opinion is law for the jurisdiction of the court.[22] Courts also can rely on the opinions of other noncontrolling courts or legal commentators. This is called "persuasive authority," and the court can follow or disregard it as it chooses.[23] Finally, most legal arguments also focus on policy considerations: What is the right result for society? There is no authority for policy arguments, per se, and a court can make the decision it likes. But in our justice system, courts are obligated to follow controlling legal authority and cannot wholesale substitute policy concerns for grounding their decisions in legal rules.

It may be obvious to lawyers, but it is worth pointing out for the sake of others, that commentary on the meaning of the GPL by private parties such as the FSF or Linus Torvalds, persuasive as it may be, can be

---

[20]The facts are stated prior to a legal argument because issues of pure law usually are decided by courts of appeal. Courts of appeal are not fact finders; facts are determined by juries (or, in cases of trial to the court, by the trial court). Courts of appeal take the facts found by the lower court as given and in most cases are not allowed to determine them.

[21]See 17 USC Section 301.

[22]In the text that follows, you will see references to the "Ninth Circuit" and the like. The U.S. Supreme Court is the court of ultimate jurisdiction in the United States, and its opinions apply to all of the United States. The court of appeal below the Supreme Court is divided into 11 circuits. The opinions of those circuit courts apply only in their circuits. The Ninth Circuit is the western states including California, and the Second Circuit is the Northeast including New York. These two circuits often act as thought leaders for the other circuits, even though their opinions are not controlling in other circuits.

[23]In the text that follows, you will see references to the book *Nimmer on Copyright*. This is considered one of the most authoritative treatises on copyright law.

disregarded by courts at their discretion. Such commentary is not controlling authority, and while it may be evidence of trade usage, that analysis depends on facts.

THE FACTS

Although this fact pattern is hypothetical, it is the paradigmatic border dispute case that concerns most developers. An author ("GPL Developer") releases a program ("GPL Utility") under GPL version 2. A corporate developer ("Plug-in Developer") writes, from scratch, a plug-in for GPL Utility that is integrated with GPL Utility via dynamic linking. Plug-in Developer distributes the GPL Utility in source code form under GPL and the plug-in ("Proprietary Plug-in") in binary form under a typical end user license agreement. The recipient of the combined product ("Licensee") has the option of including Proprietary Plug-in in the product build to create an integrated program consisting of GPL Utility and Proprietary Plug-in ("Integrated Product"). GPL Developer sues Plug-in Developer, claiming Plug-in Developer has violated the GPL, and insists that Plug-in Developer either license the Proprietary Plug-in under GPL or cease distributing the GPL Utility.

This is the quintessential case, because it is the "work-around" that corporate developers have posited will comply with GPL. Yet the Free Software Foundation expressly states this is a violation of GPL. From the frequently asked questions (FAQs):

> Q: You have a GPL'ed program that I'd like to link with my code to build a proprietary program. Does the fact that I link with your program mean I have to GPL my program?
>
> A: Yes.[24]

But the FSF has this to say about the scenario above:

> Q: If a program released under the GPL uses plug-ins, what are the requirements for the licenses of a plug-in?
>
> A: It depends on how the program invokes its plug-ins. If the program uses fork and exec to invoke plug-ins, then the plug-ins are separate

---

[24]www.fsf.org/licensing/licenses/gpl-faq.html#LinkingWithGPL.

programs, so the license for the main program makes no requirements for them.

If the program dynamically links plug-ins, and they make function calls to each other and share data structures, we believe they form a single program, which must be treated as an extension of both the main program and the plug-ins. This means the plug-ins must be released under the GPL or a GPL-compatible free software license, and that the terms of the GPL must be followed when those plug-ins are distributed.

If the program dynamically links plug-ins, but the communication between them is limited to invoking the "main" function of the plug-in with some options and waiting for it to return, that is a borderline case.[25]

Note that the FSF does not distinguish between the case where the GPL Utility and the Proprietary Plug-in are distributed together, in one product build, or separately. While technically this may make some difference as to whether the Plug-in Developer is infringing the rights in the GPL Utility, ultimately it will not make a great difference, because if the Plug-in Developer is causing the Licensee to infringe, the Plug-in Developer may be liable for indirect infringement anyway. In any case, the FSF has made it clear that requiring the Licensee actually to make the product build does not make a difference, because regardless, the Proprietary Plug-in is still a derivative work of the GPL Utility.

LEGAL RULES

Copyright in the United States is a list of rights set forth in Title 17. Copyright allows the owner of a copyright in a work of authorship the right to exclude others from copying, distributing, preparing derivative works, publicly performing, and publicly displaying the work. The Copyright Act grants the owner of a copyright the exclusive right "to prepare derivative works based upon the copyrighted work."[26] The Copyright Act says:

A "derivative work" is a work based upon one or more preexisting works, such as a translation, musical arrangement, dramatization, fictionalization, motion picture version, sound recording, art reproduction,

---

[25]www.fsf.org/licensing/licenses/gpl-faq.html#TOCGPLAndPlugins.
[26]17 USC Section 106(2).

abridgment, condensation, or any other form in which a work may be recast, transformed, or adapted. A work consisting of editorial revisions, annotations, elaborations, or other modifications which, as a whole, represent an original work of authorship, is a "derivative work."[27]

The act also defines a category of work called a *collective work*, which is "a work . . . in which a number of contributions, constituting separate and independent works in themselves, are assembled into a collective whole."[28] However, the law does not allow the owner of a work the right to exclude others from creating collective works.[29]

Much of the case law on what constitutes a derivative work or a collective work has to do with whether there is a separate copyright interest in the derivative or collective work, and not whether the derivative or collective work infringes the copyright interest in the original work. Therefore, relying on this case law to determine the latter question can be treacherous. For instance, the primary case law on the nature of a derivative work says that a derivative work or collective work must satisfy the requirements of originality to qualify as a derivative work.[30] But when asking whether the Proprietary Plug-in is a derivative work of the GPL Utility, we are actually asking whether it infringes the rights in the GPL Utility.

To prove copyright infringement, the plaintiff must show that the work has been copied. Because there often is no direct evidence of this, a plaintiff can provide this with two elements: access and substantial similarity. The access prong of the copyright infringement test is generally trivial in the free software context. Free software is by definition freely available, and thus it may be that any defendant has constructive access to it. Moreover, it probably would be impossible for the Plug-in Developer to have developed the Proprietary Plug-in without access to the GPL Utility, to determine its correct interface. Thus, the entire question turns on substantial similarity.

---

[27]Ibid.

[28]Ibid.

[29]Lothar Determann, "Dangerous Liaisons," 21 *Berkeley Technology Law Review* (2006), at 1435.

[30]*Nimmer on Copyright* Section 3.03 (2004).

The case law on what constitutes an infringing work under copyright law mostly does not concern computer software; instead it focuses on traditional copyrightable works, such as music, film, and books. Such cases can be extrapolated to apply to software, but this is a dicey process. Software is a fundamentally different kind of work, and copyright is difficult to apply to it—particularly questions of substantial similarity. As the Supreme Court has observed, "[T]here are, and can be, few, if any, things which, in an abstract sense, are strictly new and original throughout. Every book in literature, science and art, borrows and must necessarily borrow, and use much which was well known and used before."[31] In the case of software, this is true in spades.

To address this complication, some courts have adopted the "abstraction, filtration, and comparison" (AFC) test to determine whether one computer program is a derivative of another. This test involves three steps:

1. Abstract all expressive elements of the programs from their ideas.
2. Filter out all unprotectable elements.
3. Compare all remaining elements of creative expression to determine substantial similarity.[32]

Abstracted elements could include the main purpose of the program, system architecture, custom data types, algorithms, or data structures. Filtration eliminates elements that are unprotectable due to the merger doctrine or due to the lack of protection for ideas rather than expression, due to being in the public domain, or *scenes a faire*.[33] When all the unprotectable elements are filtered out, the original work and the new work are compared. If they are substantially similar, the new work is a derivative work of the original.[34]

---

[31]*Emerson v. Davies*, 8 F. Cas. 615 (1845).

[32]See, e.g., *Computer Associates Intl. Inc. v. Altai, Inc.*, 982 F.2d 693 (2d Cir. 1992). This is only an example; the test has different formulations in different circuits.

[33]*Scenes a faire* means "scenes to be made" and refers to stock or trite elements, particularly in genre works. In the software context, it may include elements dictated by operating system requirements, hardware standards, or compatibility standards for other programs.

[34]Daniel Ravicher notes the circuits that have adopted this test in his paper, "Software Derivative Work: A Jurisdiction Dependent Determination," Linux.com, November 13, 2002, http://community.linux.com/article.pl?sid=02/11/13/117247.

The Ninth Circuit uses an alternative test called the *analytical dissection test*.[35] This test mostly turns the AFC test front to back. The test has an "intrinsic" and an "extrinsic" component. Extrinsic elements or ideas are assessed using objective evidence. Intrinsic elements or expression are assessed "from the standpoint of the ordinary reasonable observer, with no expert assistance." The four steps are:

1. Identify the source of the alleged similarity between the works (similar to comparison step of AFC).
2. Using analytical dissection and, if necessary, expert testimony, determine whether any of the allegedly similar features are protected by copyright (similar to the filtration step in the AFC test).
3. Decide whether similar and protectable elements enjoy broad or thin protection.
   - Fact and ideas get thin protection only by virtue of the manner of their use.
   - Expression itself gets broad protection.
4. Decide whether the works are substantially similar as a whole.

A possible problem with applying the analytical dissection test to the border dispute is that the seminal cases on this test do not involve computer software code and thus focus on ideas and general impressions. The test was first enunciated in *Sid & Marty Krofft Television Productions, Inc. v. McDonald's Corp*[36] and reiterated in *Apple Computer, Inc. v. Microsoft Corp.* The *Apple* case concerned infringement by the Microsoft Windows GUI of the Apple Macintosh desktop GUI. *Sid & Marty Krofft* involved the infringement by McDonald's Hamburgler character of the characters in *H.R. Pufnstuf*. A test of substantial similarity from the view of the "ordinary reasonable observer, with no expert assistance" is undoubtedly more useful for puppets and graphical user interfaces (GUIs) than for operating system kernels, because the nut of the question is the visual nature of the infringed work. At the operating system level, that does not work.

But in a sense the split in the circuits is of peripheral importance, because the AFC and analytical dissection tests are both very difficult to

---

[35]*Apple Computer, Inc. v. Microsoft Corp.*, 35 F.3d 1435 (9th Cir. 1994). The First Circuit (which promulgated the *Lotus* case, described later) rejected the AFC test. Other circuits have not yet adopted a test.

[36]562 F.2d 1157, 1164 (9th Cir. 1977).

apply, and it is unclear that the application of one or the other will produce a different result.

It is crucial here to determine which work is at issue: Is it the linked
program as a whole, or only its components? Assuming for the moment
that we are assessing these two issues separately, the question is whether
the portions of a GPL program that must be reused in linked code for the
sake of interoperation are protectable under copyright. The portion of a
program that must be duplicated in linked code is the header file.[37]

What should be clear at this point is that whether code is dynamically
or statically linked is of relatively little importance to this analysis. No
programmer would be surprised to hear this; methods of linking do not
create any meaningful differences in the exact expression of the code, and
the difference between types of linking probably has nothing to do with the
analysis of copyright infringement.[38]

ANALYZING THE CASE OF TWO WORKS

To drill down on this analysis, we need to recognize that there are potentially two cases here: the case of one work or two. We start with the
assumption that the GPL Utility and the Proprietary Plug-in are two
separate copyrightable works. Therefore, the question is whether the Proprietary Plug-in infringes the rights in the GPL Utility (i.e., whether it is
substantially similar, in whole or in part). Few reported cases at a meaningful level of authority treat in depth the question of what is an infringing
work of software.

In the *Worlds of Wonder*[39] cases, plaintiff was the holder of a copyright
in a toy, namely a talking, dancing bear named "Teddy Ruxpin" whose
programming was contained on cassette tapes. The Ninth Circuit held

---

[37]Header files are explained in Chapter 12.

[38]See, e.g., Lawrence Rosen, *Open Source Licensing* (Prentice Hall, Upper Saddle
River, NJ, 2005). "Nothing in the law of copyright suggests that linking between
programs is a determinative factor in derivative work analyses by courts—except
perhaps as evidence of one of the abstract, non-literal, copyrightable aspects of
the software" (p. 287).

[39]*Worlds of Wonder, Inc. v. Veritel Learning Systems, Inc.*, 658 F. Supp. 351 (N.D. Tex.
1986) and *Worlds of Wonder, Inc. v. Vector Intercontinental, Inc.*, 653 F. Supp. 135
(N.D. Ohio 1986).

that third-party tapes that changed the programming of the bear were infringing derivative works despite the fact that the third-party tapes did not contain any part of the recordings from the original. *Micro Star v. Formgen*[40] involved the creation of alternate levels to the video game *Duke Nukem 3D*, a three-dimensional, first-person-shooter computer game in which the end user controls a character who explores and fights other characters at numerous levels. The game came with a build editor that allowed users to create their own levels. Micro Star downloaded 300 user-created levels and distributed them on CD-ROM. Micro Star did not incorporate any code or artwork from the game but used MAP files created by the build editor to invoke art libraries used in the game. The court found the levels to be infringing, saying:

> A copyright owner holds the right to create sequels . . . and the stories told in the N/I MAP files are surely sequels, telling new (though somewhat repetitive) tales of Duke's fabulous adventures. A book about Duke Nukem would infringe for the same reason, even if it contained no pictures.

In *Lewis Galoob Toys, Inc. v. Nintendo of Am., Inc.,*[41] Galoob manufactured the Game Genie, an after-market device that allowed the user to alter play in video games for Nintendo's NES game platform. The court found the Game Genie did not create a derivative work, because

> [t]he altered displays do not incorporate a portion of a copyrighted work in some form. . . . [T]he Game Genie cannot produce an audio-visual display; the underlying display must be produced by a Nintendo Entertainment System and game cartridge. The Game Genie's display has no form.

However, the court reached this result based on the premise that the Game Genie produced no fixed work of authorship. Presumably, if this case is to be read consistently with those discussed earlier, it was the existence of the tape or the CD-ROM that made the difference. The court also distinguished *Midway Mfg. Co. v. Artic Int'l, Inc.,*[42] which involved a chip that could be inserted in the video game itself to speed up play: "Artic's chip

---

[40]*Micro Star v. Formgen, Inc.,* 154 F.3d 1107 (9th Cir. 1998).

[41]780 F. Supp. 1283, 1289 (N.D. Cal. 1991).

[42]704 F.2d 1009 (7th Cir. 1983).

substantially copied and replaced the chip that was originally distributed by Midway." Ultimately *Galoob,* therefore, is not relevant to the question at hand. Its result turned on the fact that no fixed work was employed.

These cases are notable because they hold that a work can be infringing even if it contains no part of the original—despite clearly enunciated rules that an infringing work "must substantially incorporate protected material from the preexisting work."[43] Unfortunately, though, these cases may not be very instructive. The copyright held by Worlds of Wonder was in the bear as an audiovisual work. An audiovisual work is typically a movie or television show. Software code, however, is a literary work. The test for similarity for audiovisual works was to compare the "total concept" of the allegedly infringing work against the original, and ask whether an average lay observer would conclude they were substantially similar. Moreover, the court in the *Worlds of Wonder* case pointed out that it assessed this threshold based on the children who were the primary audience for the work, who would have difficulty discerning subtle differences. The court in the *Duke Nukem* case also based its analysis on the audiovisual displays of the game rather than the code in it. This shows the tendency of courts to analyze computer software in the same manner it has used for films and novels—based on the experience of the viewer or reader. Applying the Worlds of Wonder logic to the GPL analysis would be like comparing the GUIs of the programs to see if they used the same logic flow. Operating system code, for instance, has no direct user interface. If a court is presented with the question of whether a loadable kernel module (LKM) creates a derivative work, the analysis in these cases may easily break down. It is easy to see why a court can come to the conclusion that a new work that contains no part of the original infringes an audiovisual work, because the core issue is the perception of the work, not the expression of the software code itself.

On the other side of the equation is the First Circuit. In *Lotus v. Borland,* 49 F.3d 807 (1995), the First Circuit considered whether a computer menu command hierarchy could be an infringing copyrightable work:

> When faced with nonliteral-copying cases, courts must determine whether similarities are due merely to the fact that the two works share

---

[43]*Micro Star v. Formgen, Inc.,* 154 F.3d 1107, 1110 (9th Cir. 1998), citing *Litchfield v. Spielberg,* 736 F.2d 1352, 1357 (9th Cir. 1984).

the same underlying idea or whether they instead indicated that the second author copied the first author's expression.[44]

While the *Altai* test may provide a useful framework for assessing the alleged nonliteral copying of computer code, we find it to be of little help in assessing whether the literal copying of a menu command hierarchy constitutes copyright infringement. In fact, we think that the *Altai* test in this context may actually be misleading because, in instructing courts to abstract the various levels, it seems to encourage them to find a base level that includes copyrightable subject matter that, if literally copied, would make the copier liable for copyright infringement.

In *Lotus,* the court considered whether the command hierarchy was not copyrightable because it was a "system, method of operation, process, or procedure foreclosed from copyright protection by 17 U.S.C. § 102(b)." The court found the command menu hierarchy to be an uncopyrightable "method."

The Lotus menu command hierarchy . . . serves as the method by which the program is operated and controlled. . . . The Lotus menu command hierarchy is also different from the Lotus screen displays, for users need not "use" any expressive aspects of the screen displays in order to operate Lotus 1-2-3; because the way the screens look has little bearing on how users control the program, the screen displays are not part of Lotus 1-2-3's "method of operation." The Lotus menu command hierarchy is also different from the underlying computer code, because while code is necessary for the program to work, its precise formulation is not. In other words, to offer the same capabilities as Lotus 1-2-3, Borland did not have to copy Lotus's underlying code (and indeed it did not); to allow users to operate its programs in substantially the same way, however, Borland had to copy the Lotus menu command hierarchy.[45]

This case is crucial because it bears directly on whether headers are copyrightable. If we assume that a command hierarchy is not a protectable work of authorship, it is a small step to include that a header is not copyrightable—or at least a header that is relatively simple and acts merely as a method for invoking and running code.

---

[44]*Lotus,* quoting *Computer Assoc. Int'l, Inc. v. Altai, Inc.,* 982 F.2d 693 (2d Cir. 1992).

[45]Ibid.

Further instruction can be found in the *LEXIS/Westlaw* cases.[46] Both companies publish reference books containing the published opinions of law courts. The text of the opinions is not protected by copyright because works produced by the U.S. government are in the public domain. When Westlaw sued Mead (which operated LEXIS) for copying its material, it based the claim on the pagination of the cases in the books. There was no question that the Westlaw books contained copyrightable material; Westlaw produces summaries of key legal points and commentary that are textual works of authorship. Mead ran an online service offering access to the opinions. Mead introduced a feature allowing a user to skip to a particular page in the opinion as it appeared in the West Reporter.[47] In an initial decision in 1986, the Eighth Circuit found the use to be infringing. The court's decision turned on the fact that allowing a competing service access to Westlaw's pagination would undermine the market for West's reporters, and that West had expended substantial effort in making its compilation of cases and explanatory material. However, in light of the 1990 Supreme Court case *Feist Publications, Inc. v. Rural Telephone Service Co.*,[48] which rejected the "sweat of the brow" doctrine in assessing copyright infringement, the same issue was later otherwise decided by the Second Circuit.[49] As a consequence, use of West's paging is probably not considered infringement.[50]

When reduced to its most basic level, a header file is similar to a paging system in that it provides pointers to memory locations assigned

---

[46]*West Publishing Company v. Mead Data Central, Inc.*, 799 F.2d 1219 (8th Cir. 1986).

[47]This was useful because of the system of case citation used by lawyers. You will note that some of these footnotes contain "pin cites" that indicate the particular page of the opinion on which the referenced text is found. Without being able to locate these, a reader would have to either access the West Reporter or read the entire case.

[48]499 U.S. 340 (1990).

[49]*Matthew Bender & Co., Inc. v. West Publishing Co.*, 158 F. 3d 674 (2nd Cir. 1998) and *Matthew Bender & Co. Inc. v. West Publishing Co.*, 158 F. 3d 693 (2nd Cir. 1998).

[50]Because of the different outcomes of the two circuits, the authority is not perfectly settled. This is known as a circuit split. However, the Supreme Court declined to hear an appeal from the Second Circuit, which may imply it would rule similarly.

to variables in dynamically or statically linked routines. However, headers are obviously more complex than mere page numbers and therefore more likely to contain material protectable under copyright. Whether they do, in actuality, is an unanswered question.

The facts in *Secure Serv. Tech., Inc. v. Time & Space Processing, Inc.,*[51] may also bear on this question. In that case the court found that there was no copyright protection for a securing faxing handshake protocol that dictated the "content . . . length . . . and order" of signals. This information is not unlike that provided by software headers, although here it was provided via communications protocols rather than links. The court here held that neither the base protocol used with the fax machine nor the variation of it was a copyrightable work, citing the exclusion of methods of operation under 17 USC Section 102(b).

Finally, even if the copying would otherwise be infringement, reuse of small amounts of code to achieve interoperability may not be infringing because it is fair use. For instance, in *Sega v. Accolade,* the court held that the decompilation and copying of an initialization code in software for Sega Genesis game cartridges was fair use.[52] Similarly, in *Vault Corp. v. Quaid Software, Ltd.,* the court held that copying and decompilation of a software program key and fingerprint was fair use.[53] As one commentator has observed:

> [A]s a general matter, copyright owners cannot rely on the protections that copyright law affords where they deploy copyrighted works in a software context for the sole purpose of forcing others to infringe (by copying or adapting copyrighted code) in order to establish interoperability.[54]

IS THE RESULT ONE OR TWO WORKS?

It is easy to imagine that a different result would be obtained if the GPL Utility and the Proprietary Plug-in are viewed as one work of authorship instead of two. If they are a single work, the combination of the two can

---

[51]722 F.Supp. 1354 (E.D. Va. 1989).
[52]*Sega v. Accolade,* 977 F.2d 1510 (9th Cir 1992).
[53]*Vault Corp. v. Quaid Software, Ltd.,* 847 F.2d 255, 267–68 (5th Cir. 1988).
[54]Determann, "Dangerous Liaisons," at fn 90.

be one of two things: a derivative work or a joint work.[55] If the two together form a joint work, then the result would be unexpected, as either party may have rights to license the whole on terms of its choice. This result seems highly unlikely, if only because one portion of the work was written before the other.[56] If they form a derivative work, then GPL Developer wins.

The Copyright Act does not contain much guidance on what constitutes a single work. However, the law of statutory damages addresses this issue and is well developed. An author may elect statutory damages for "all infringements involved in the action, with respect to any one work."[57] It applies an economic viability test:

> [W]here separate copyrights have no separate economic value, whatever their artistic value, they must be considered part of [a]. . .work for purposes of the copyright statute.[58]

In the case at hand, it is clear that the GPL Utility has value apart from the Proprietary Plug-in. Thus it is possible that the answer to this question would turn on whether the Proprietary Plug-in can be used in any other situation. A Proprietary Plug-in that works with products other than the GPL Utility (presumably with minor modifications necessary to render it interoperable with those products) might be far more likely to stand on its own and be analyzed as a separate work.

POLICY ARGUMENTS

The quintessential policy goal of copyright is to promote creativity and progress. The provision of the U.S. Constitution that enables the copyright law says:

---

[55]They can also be a collective work, but the exploitation of individual portions of a collective work is not controlled by the author of any other portion, in which case the question is resolved clearly in favor of Plug-In Developer.

[56]Nimmer discusses the effect of time sequence on the existence of a joint work. *Nimmer on Copyright,* Section 6.05 (2005).

[57]17 USC Section 504(c)(1).

[58]*Walt Disney Co. v. Powell,* 897 F.2d 565, 569 (2d Cir. 1990).

The Congress shall have the Power. . .to Promote the Progress of Science and useful Arts, by securing for limited Times to Authors and Inventors the exclusive Right to their respective Writings and Discoveries.[59]

The courts characterize copyright policy as a balance between protection of the rights of authors and the availability of material for use by others without infringement.[60]

The question of which result—a broad interpretation of GPL or a narrow one—would best promote the production of copyrightable works remains an open one. It is part of the larger debate between the proponents of proprietary software, who claim that authors must be rewarded to create incentives to write software, and proponents of free software, who claim that programmers are motivated by other factors and will produce the most (and best) software if all software is under a free software paradigm like GPL. It is likely that courts will focus on this policy question when rendering an opinion on this topic, but it is unclear which camp will be the most persuasive.

Non-U.S. Law Interpretations

The preceding derivative works analysis presumes the application of U.S. law. However, because the GPL has no choice of law provision and relies for its power on background copyright law, the scope of derivative works can be different in different jurisdictions. Unfortunately for the sake of clarity, other nations have widely varying notions of derivative works. For instance, European Union (EU) law does not have a notion of derivative works per se, but may have an even broader definition of modifications controllable under copyright.[61]A thorough analysis of this question is beyond the scope of this book, and might in any case be unique in every country. As hard as GPL interpretation might be in the United States, it is even harder to interpret as a general case—for instance, by a company releasing an international product.

---

[59]U.S. Constitution Article I, Section 8.
[60]*Sony Corp. of America v. Universal City Studios, Inc.,* 464 U.S. 417 (1984).
[61]See, e.g., Mikko Välimäki, "GNU General Public License and the Distribution of Derivative Works," September 4, 2003, www.soberit.hut.fi/~msvalima/gpl_derivative.pdf.

APPROACH OF LEGAL REALISM

The last choice is to leave behind legal analysis entirely and take a legal realism approach. Eric Raymond expressed this idea elegantly, in a discussion thread regarding Linus Torvalds' views on whether LKMs are derivative works of the kernel under the GPL. A previous thread had opined "Linus's opinion on this is irrelevant," and Raymond responded:

> [I]n fact, I agree with his assessment. The key question is whether the particular kind of linking involved with loading binary modules propagates derivative-work status under copyright law. This is a legal question a court may rule on someday. Until one does, anyone who relies on such linking is taking a legal risk . . . [but it] is not quite right that Linus's opinion is irrelevant. It is irrelevant to the underlying legal question, but not to the associated business risk.[62]

This is the nexus of the issue. Statements by Linus Torvalds, the FSF, and others may or may not be evidence of trade usage that is relevant to the legal truth, but evidence of the likelihood of enforcement is clearly relevant to the assessment of business risk. Corporate developers care a great deal about the latter; business risk is exactly what they want to assess. Thus, they want to know: If we distribute an additional module that we wrote, which works with GPL code, and we do not lay open our source code to that additional module, what will happen to us? And most of them would not give a nickel to know the true meaning of "derivative works" under the law.

It is not possible to answer the question of what will happen without mentioning the remedies for breach of the GPL. Clients want to know: (1) Will I have to lay open my source code? and (2) Will I have to pay damages? So ultimately, for most companies, GPL compliance is more of a remedies question than an interpretive one. That in turn necessitates a discussion of the enforceability of the GPL, which is touched on in Chapter 13. I assume for purposes of this discussion that the GPL is an enforceable obligation.[63]

---

[62]http://old.lwn.net/2001/0628/a/esr-modules.php3.

[63]This is two assumptions: first that it is a contract and second that it is enforceable. The FSF claims the GPL is not a contract, which is an interesting but odd theoretical position, and which I believe fails because the FSF cannot avoid a claim by a licensee that it is a contract. See Chapter 16.

OUTSIDE THE FOUR CORNERS

Thanks in part to the World Wide Web, where opinions[64] abound, we have a fair amount of evidence about the likely enforcement of the boundary dispute. There are two main factions here: Linus Torvalds and the FSF. Understanding from the preceding analysis that these opinions are more useful for risk analysis than the abstract legal questions of the meaning of "work based on the Program" or derivative work, here are the main positions.

- **FSF: The boundary is identical to what composes a derivative work under copyright law.** This position is based on the theory that the GPL can control only what is controllable under copyright law and also on some of the phrases in GPL2 used to define the scope of a work based on the Program.
- **FSF: Any linking (dynamic or static) to GPL code is a derivative work within the boundary.** This position is based on the FSF FAQ on GPL2 and FSF comments on the GNU Lesser General Public License (LGPL). The LGPL explicitly allows linking to LGPL code, in which case linked code is outside the boundary. LGPL must be different from GPL or there would not be two different licenses. Thus, linking brings code within the GPL boundary. In truth, the FSF position is not quite this clear-cut. However, many in the industry use this rule because it represents a safe position: If you assume

---

[64]Even legal opinions abound. The Web teems with discussion of legal principles by nonlawyers—so much so that a common way to start such an opinion is "IANAL, but . . ." (I am not a lawyer, but . . .). Reading such discussion, particularly on this topic, is both interesting and useful, but frustrating for lawyers seeking a definitive answer on the subject. For instance, the commentary by leading open source figures like Linus Torvalds is tantalizing, but any lawyer will observe that verifying the identity of the posters would be awkward, many sources are quoted inaccurately or with no sources cited, and legal concepts such as derivative works are frequently undefined or misdefined. My comments here are not intended to cast aspersions on these postings, many of which are quite informative and perceptive, but to warn lawyers to watch their step. When a posted conclusion is not based on correct legal rules, the legal conclusion itself is not reliable. But these postings are very useful for the facts and principles of programming they discuss and for evidence of the industry's behavior in light of its perception of the border dispute.

that all linked code creates a derivative work, you will likely not run afoul of the FSF position.

- **FSF: User space is outside the boundary of the kernel.** The FSF recognizes an exception for interaction between user space and kernel space.[65] This "special exception"[66] is expressly allowed in Section 3 of GPL2, which implies that the FSF considers this to create a derivative work but has allowed an exception for it.

- **Linus Torvalds: User space is outside the boundary of the kernel.** Torvalds and the FSF are aligned on this: Each recognizes that interaction between user space and kernel space does not create a derivative work.

The "user program" exception is not an exception at all, for example, it's just a more clearly stated limitation on the "derived work" issue. If you use standard UNIX system calls (with accepted Linux extensions), your program obviously doesn't "derive" from the kernel itself.

Whenever you link into the kernel, either directly or through a module, the case is just a lot more muddy. But as stated, by default it's obviously derived—the very fact that you need to do something as fundamental as linking against the kernel very much argues that your module is not a stand-alone thing, regardless of where the module source code itself has come from.[67]

- **FSF: Linking to standard language routines does not create a derivative work.** The FSF recognizes an exception for interaction with standard system libraries such as Java standard classes.[68] However, if this is so, it is unclear why the standard C libraries (glibc) are licensed under LGPL.

---

[65] www.fsf.org/licensing/licenses/gpl-faq.html.

[66] "However, as a special exception, the source code distributed need not include anything that is normally distributed (in either source or binary form) with the major components (compiler, kernel, and so on) of the operating system on which the executable runs, unless that component itself accompanies the executable."

[67] http://linuxmafia.com/faq/Kernel/proprietary-kernel-modules.html.

[68] This exception is laid out with greater specificity in GPL3.

- **FSF: Software that interacts via communications protocols such as pipes and sockets is not a derivative work.**

  The FAQ on the GPL2 (version 2) says:

  What constitutes combining two parts into one program? This is a legal question, which ultimately judges will decide. We believe that a proper criterion depends both on the mechanism of communication (exec, pipes, rpc, function calls within a shared address space, etc.) and the semantics of the communication (what kinds of information are interchanged).

  If the modules are included in the same executable file, they are definitely combined in one program. If modules are designed to run linked together in a shared address space, that almost surely means combining them into one program.

  By contrast, pipes, sockets and command-line arguments are communication mechanisms normally used between two separate programs. So when they are used for communication, the modules normally are separate programs. But if the semantics of the communication are intimate enough, exchanging complex internal data structures, that too could be a basis to consider the two parts as combined into a larger program.[69]

- **FSF: Software that interacts via an exec statement is not a derivative work.** See FAQ quoted earlier.
- **FSF: Clean integration (e.g., data sharing).** The FSF's overall position on linked code has more to do with the "intimacy" of integration between modules than their method of integration: dynamic link, static link, or otherwise. One useful approach is to focus on the spirit of GPL rather than its letter, or the exact words of any extrinsic commentary. The spirit of the GPL is to allow licensees to freely use and modify code. The whole question of the border dispute arises because segregating code into linked files is a way to hide functionality in proprietary modules. Any programmer worth his or her salt can move any key functionality into a separate file and obfuscate it in binary form. This violates the spirit of the GPL. Therefore, a company considering distributing a proprietary module should always ask, "How does this affect my licensees?" If the existence of the

---

[69]www.fsf.org/licensing/licenses/gpl-faq.html.

proprietary module means the licensee cannot effectively modify the GPL code, then the spirit of the license has not been served. However, if the interface between the proprietary module and GPL code is simple, clearly described, and creates a true "black box," then the spirit has been served. (A black box means that the programmer modifying the GPL code does not need access to the proprietary code. In other words, the programmer does not need to see the workings of the proprietary module, so it functions as a black box; the interface is all that matters.) This approach is attractive both because it bears directly on risk assessment (by irritating the least number of licensees who want to modify the GPL code) and because it is based on sound engineering principles. Black boxes are good design. Every engineer understands that, without a complex explanation of circuit splits and copyright law. When assessing these issues, here are some questions you may ask:

- Must the proprietary module load at the same time as the GPL module?
- How complex and large are the data structures shared by the modules?
- Does the proprietary module also interact with other software in the same way?
- Is the interface between the modules a standard, published interface?

Naturally, this list of questions is not exhaustive. But it should give an idea of the process for making this assessment.

- **Anything with a GPL header must be covered by GPL.** This statement is heard often, but what it means is not always clear. In a sense it is a truism, because the header is often the file that indicates license terms. However, more often it means that any module linked to GPL code must be under GPL, because a link requires a header to connect the two linked files. Because this line of demarcation seems more an industry adage than a reasoned opinion, I leave it aside in favor of the more detailed cases discussed earlier.

LOADABLE KERNEL MODULES

Because Linux is not a completely monolithic operating system, it is possible to write drivers and other modules for Linux that link dynamically with the kernel. Whether those LKMs must be covered by GPL has been hotly debated for years. Torvalds' position on linked modules like LKMs is not easy to glean with certainty from his postings on the topic—postings that may or may not have been intended to endure the scrutiny they have been given on this question by the industry.

- **Linus Torvalds: Code written prior to Linux is not a derivative work of Linux.**[70] Much emphasis has been placed on the next quotation, which was posted by Torvalds on the Web.

There are (mainly historical) examples of UNIX device drivers and some UNIX filesystems that were pre-existing pieces of work, and which had fairly well-defined and clear interfaces and that I personally could not really consider any kind of "derived work" at all, and that were thus acceptable. The clearest example of this is probably the AFS (the Andrew Filesystem), but there have been various device drivers ported from SCO too.

- **Linus Torvalds: Device drivers that work with Linux and other systems (including UNIX) are not derivative works of Linux.**[71]

Well, there really is no exception. However, copyright law obviously hinges on the definition of "derived work," and as such anything can always be argued on that point. I personally consider anything a "derived work" that needs special hooks in the kernel to function with Linux (i.e., it is not acceptable to make a small piece of GPL-code as a hook for the larger piece), as that obviously implies that the bigger module needs "help" from the main kernel. Similarly, I consider anything that has intimate knowledge about kernel internals to be a derived work.

What is left in the gray area tends to be clearly separate modules: code that had a life outside Linux from the beginning, and that do something self-contained that doesn't really have any impact on the rest of the kernel. A device driver that was originally written for something else, and that doesn't need any but the standard UNIX read/write kind of interfaces, for example.

---

[70]The quotations here are reproduced at http://linuxmafia.com/faq/Kernel/proprietary-kernel-modules.html.

[71]http://linuxmafia.com/faq/Kernel/proprietary-kernel-modules.html.

- **Linus Torvalds: A new module with no overlapping code to the kernel may not be a derivative work.**

Well, see above about the lack of exception, and about the fundamental gray area in any copyright issue. The "derived work" issue is obviously a gray area, and I know lawyers don't like them. Crazy people (even judges) have, as we know, claimed that even obvious spoofs of a work that contain nothing of the original work itself, can be ruled to be "derived."

I do not hold views that extreme, but at the same time I do consider a module written for Linux and using kernel infrastructures to get its work done, even if not actually copying any existing Linux code, to be a derived work by default. You would have to have a strong case to not consider your code a derived work.

- **Linus Torvalds: The more complex Linux gets, the less likely an LKM can be considered a separate work.**

The Linux kernel modules had (a long time ago), a more limited interface, and not very many functions were actually exported. So five or six years ago, we could believably claim that "if you only use these N interfaces that are exported from the standard kernel, you've kind of implicitly proven that you do not need the kernel infrastructure."

That was never really documented either (more of a guideline for me and others when we looked at the "derived work" issue), and as modules were more-and-more used not for external stuff, but just for dynamic loading of standard linux modules that were distributed as part of the kernel anyway, the "limited interfaces" argument is no longer a very good guideline for "derived work."

So these days, we export many internal interfaces, not because we don't think that they would "taint" the linker, but simply because it's useful to do dynamic run-time loading of modules even with standard kernel modules that are supposed to know a lot about kernel internals, and are obviously "derived works."

- **Linus Torvalds: Plug-ins may be derivative works, but a published interface supports the existence of a separate work.**

It's an issue of what a "plug-in" is—is it a way for the program to internally load more modules as it needs them, or is it meant to be a public, published interface?

For example, the "system call" interface could be considered a "plug-in interface," and running a user mode program under Linux could easily be construed as running a "plug-in" for the Linux kernel. No?

And there, I obviously absolutely agree with you 100%: the interface is published, and it's meant for external and independent users. It's an interface that we go to great lengths to preserve as well as we can, and it's an interface that is designed to be independent of kernel versions.

But maybe somebody wrote his program with the intention to dynamically load "actors" as they were needed, as a way to maintain a good modularity, and to try to keep the problem spaces well-defined. In that case, the "plug-in" may technically follow all the same rules as the system call interface, even though the author doesn't intend it that way.

So I think it's to a large degree a matter of intent, but it could arguably also be considered a matter of stability and documentation (i.e., "require recompilation of the plug-in between version changes" would tend to imply that it's an internal interface, while "documented binary compatibility across many releases" implies a more stable external interface, and less of a derived work).

- **MODULE_LICENSE Macros.** Later versions of the Linux kernel support a macro called "MODULE_LICENSE." The code of a module can set the value to be returned by this macro, such as by using the statement "MODULE_LICENSE("GPL")," often as the last statement in the module. (If the module is not under GPL, it might say, for instance, MODULE_LICENSE("Proprietary"). Of course, the setting of a programmatic flag is only an indication of the license covering the module; it is the licensing text itself that designates the license covering the code. GPLONLY flags are a developer's way of warning future developers about possible licensing issues.[72] For developers trying to determine the intentions of kernel module

---

[72]For a technical explanation, see http://linuxdevices.com/articles/AT5041108431 .html, which states that in Linux kernel version 2.5.38, there are 4 symbols (out of 437) so designated. For the explanation of how programmers use flags to designate their views on proprietary modules, see www.tux.org/lkml/#s1-19. For information on what settings designate free modules, see http://lxr.linux.no/ source/include/linux/module.h#L126.

contributors, flags may provide information, however brief, about the contributor's sensitivity to adjacent proprietary development.

THE HARDEST CASES

It is difficult enough to assess the boundary dispute for loadable kernel modules, about which much has been written.[73] It is another task to assess the boundary dispute for similar yet different cases, about which virtually nothing has been written. In such cases the risk assessment is almost as unclear as the legal truth.

For instance, everyone seems to agree that the fact that the Linux kernel is covered by GPL does not affect applications residing in user space that run on top of the operating system and interact with it via standard system calls. However, what about the converse? Can a GPL application run on top of a proprietary operating system like Windows? In fact, in the eyes of the community, this does seem to be clearly acceptable.[74]

Note that all of the preceding discussion of the border dispute takes place within the context of linking and executables. However, some programming takes place at a level below this, either underneath the operating system or in a context in which concepts like linking and executables have less concrete meaning. For instance, a hypervisor is a code layer that allows multiple operating systems to be run on a single hardware platform. With a hypervisor, the standard stack that includes operating system space and user space can have an additional layer. Where a hypervisor is used, the figure depicting user space changes to Exhibit 14.2. Hypervisor interfaces are similar to direct hardware interfaces.

One example of a hypervisor is Xen, a project of the University of Cambridge.[75] The FAQ on its site says: "Operating systems or other applications written to use Xen's hypercall interface are not derived works of Xen, hence may be licensed differently."[76] Xen is licensed under the GPL, so without such a statement it might be unclear whether Xen could interoperate with proprietary operating systems. However, without direction

---

[73]Thanks to Constantine Sapuntzakis for his help on this section.

[74]This result is suggested here: www.gnu.org/licenses/gpl-faq.html#TOCGPL IncompatibleLibs.

[75]www.cl.cam.ac.uk/research/srg/netos/xen/.

[76]http://wiki.xensource.com/xenwiki/XenFaq.

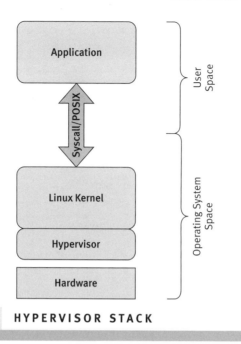

EXHIBIT 14.2   **HYPERVISOR STACK**

from the particular licensor, GPL2 interpretation questions remain vague for hypervisors—including the use of GPL hypervisors with proprietary operating systems and the use of proprietary hypervisors with free software operating systems like Linux.

The existence of these cases arises because the software stack becomes more and more complex as time goes on. As demonstrated by the language of GPL version 3, the general position of the FSF seems to be that horizontal layers in the stack are insulated and vertical divisions are not. Thus, Linux does not require language processors such as Java to be GPL, and Java does not require applications to be GPL, and so forth. This situation allows the developer to draw the boundary between horizontal layers with established and public interfaces. But horizontal combinations like LKMs and linked libraries are not allowed.

LGPL COMPLIANCE

LGPL compliance, while much less difficult than GPL compliance, has its challenges as well. Two provisions of the LGPL are particularly difficult for licensees to sort out. The first centers on the 10-line limit on source code macros. The LGPL generally allows the code covered by GPL to be used as a dynamically linked library and linked to code covered by other licenses, including a proprietary license. The problem is that, while it may be straightforward in most instances to control whether code is dynamically or statically linked, modern compilers are designed to optimize software builds by automatically choosing dynamic or static links, or even inline functions, to maximize the efficiency of code. Thus, build instructions that direct the compiler to create a dynamic link may instead result in the creation of an inline function or static link. Therefore, licensees of LGPL code, even with the best intentions, may violate the literal terms of the license. There seems to have been little or no enforcement of such situations.

This problem is exacerbated by the 10-line macro limits. The LGPL specifically states:

> If such an object file uses only numerical parameters, data structure lay-
> outs and accessors, and small macros and small inline functions (ten lines
> or less in length), then the use of the object file is unrestricted, regard-
> less of whether it is legally a derivative work.

This limitation may have made much more sense when this license was first written in 1999 than it does today. As memory has become cheaper, programmers have tended to use more inline functions. Programming design decisions are often a trade-off between speed and memory. A program will operate most quickly if its instructions are completely sequential. Exhibits 14.3 and 14.4 illustrate this trade-off in a function to calculate the absolute value of a number.

Exhibit 14.3 shows what an inline function looks like. Note the "#include" statement. A C compiler works in stages, one of which is called a preprocessor. The "#include" statement here instructs the C preprocessor to go get the code in the header files so the main program can talk to them. Here the preprocessor will go get the code for the "my_abs" function and compile it directly into the object code for the program. The "inline" designation tells it to copy the function code directly into the object code for the program. It is like cutting and pasting, but in binary code.

The alternative is to do this as a regular function (non-inline), as shown in Exhibit 14.4.

In Exhibit 14.4, a separate source file is used for the function, to save the program from having to duplicate the code calculating the absolute value. However, executing this code will require the computer to locate the function code, execute the function, and return the value to the main program, which saves memory space at the cost of increased processing time. In Exhibit 14.3, the function code is repeated, which will speed up processing at the expense of increased memory usage.

In real-world programming, a programmer can write the code for the function once but change the way it is used simply by making a minor change in the header file to designate the function as inline. As mentioned, modern compilers may do this automatically, making automated decisions about trade-offs between memory and speed.

Once upon a time, when memory was a scarce resource, programmers were more accustomed to focusing on these trade-offs. Now, as memory has become less expensive to manufacture, there is not so much pressure to save space and more pressure to speed up processing. Inline functions have therefore become more prevalent. Combined with the tendency of

EXHIBIT 14.3   INLINE FUNCTION

File	Code	Comments
Header file:	`my_abs.h:`	Name of the header file for the function
	`static inline int` `    my_abs(int x)`	Defines the arguments of the function
	`{ return (x < 0) ?` `    −x : x; }`	The logic of the function; if x is less than zero, change its sign
Main source file:	`test.c:`	Name of the source code file
	`#include "my_abs.h"` `#include <stdio.h>`	Tell the compiler what to include ("stdio" is necessary in almost every program, to handle input and output)

	`int main(int argc,`
	`char *argv[]){`
	`printf ("%d", my_`
	`abs(−5));`
	`return 0;`
	`}`
		Code for the program (called "main"); calls the function "myabs" and prints the result

EXHIBIT 14.4   **NON-INLINE FUNCTION**

File	Code	Comments
Header file:	`my_abs.h:`	Name of the header file that specifies the function
	`int my_abs(int x);`	Defines the arguments of the function
		The logic of the function is *not* in the header file here (unlike inline function style)

Function source file:	`my_abs.c:`
	`int my_abs(int x) {`
	`  return (x < 0)`
	`? -x : x; }`
		In a separate file now

Main source file (the same as for the inline function):	`test.c:`	Name of the source code file
	`#include "my_abs.h"` `#include <stdio.h>`	Tell the compiler what to include ("stdio" is necessary in almost every program, to handle input and output)

	`int main(int argc,`
	`char *argv[]) {`
	`  printf ("%d", my_`
	`abs(-5)); return 0;`
	`}`
		Code for the program (called "main"); calls the function "myabs" and prints the result

compilers to optimize builds, the 10-line limit may be both archaic and impossible to police.

The other problematic provision of the LGPL is the term restricting prohibition of reverse engineering. Section 6 states:

[Y]ou may also combine or link a "work that uses the Library" with the Library to produce a work containing portions of the Library, and distribute that work under terms of your choice, provided that the terms permit modification of the work for the customer's own use and reverse engineering for debugging such modifications.

The problem here is mostly an administrative one. Companies that incorporate LGPL libraries into their proprietary products tend to do so by modifying the proprietary license for the product so that the entire

EXHIBIT 14.5   OPEN SOURCE "CARVEOUT" FOR
                 PROPRIETARY LICENSE

Sample Provision to Be Inserted in a Proprietary License to Account for Open Source Software Whose Rights Will Be Passed through to the Licensee.

Notwithstanding the foregoing [reference license grant], Licensee acknowledges that certain components of the Software may be covered by so-called "open source" software licenses ("Open Source Components"), which means any software licenses approved as open source licenses by the Open Source Initiative or any substantially similar licenses, including without limitation any license that, as a condition of distribution of the software licensed under such license, requires that the distributor make the software available in source code format. Licensor shall provide a list of Open Source Components for a particular version of the Software upon Licensee's request. To the extent required by the licenses covering Open Source Components, the terms of such licenses will apply in lieu of the terms of this Agreement, and Licensor hereby represents and warrants that the licenses granted to such Open Source Components will be no less broad than the license granted in Section [_____]. To the extent the terms of the licenses applicable to Open Source Components prohibit any of the restrictions in this Agreement with respect to such Open Source Component, such restrictions will not apply to such Open Source Component.

product is covered by a proprietary license, except for LGPL portions. Not only do most proprietary licenses contain a restriction on reverse engineering, that restriction often is one of the most important provisions in the license.[77] Companies that implement product licensing in this manner may find that the reverse engineering provisions in their proprietary licenses actually conflict with LGPL. Therefore, it is extremely important, when licensing in a mixed-rights environment, to place an exception in the proprietary license (such as the carveout in Exhibit 14.5) clarifying that any terms of the proprietary license that would conflict with an open source license covering included code will be governed by the open source license rather than the proprietary license.

---

[77]See Heather Meeker, *A Primer on Intellectual Property Licensing,* 2d ed. (Earthling Press, United States of America, 2004), Chapter 1.

CHAPTER 15

License or Contract?

O ne significant unresolved legal issue in open source licensing is whether licenses like GNU General Public License (GPL) and GNU Lesser General Public License (LGPL) should be characterized as contracts. As a baseline, most licensing agreements are just that: agreements. Documents like the GPL, though, specifically state they are not contracts.

In theory, the GPL and similar documents are licenses granted simultaneously to all who wish to take the code under that license, and their restrictions operate as conditions to the license rather than as contractual obligations. Many people, and particularly lawyers who are accustomed to dealing with software license agreements, find this quite confusing.

CONTRACT FORMATION

Under the law, a contract is a promise or series of promises made by two or more parties. Promises are sometimes called *covenants*, but there is no magic about this; a covenant is merely a somewhat old-fashioned word for a promise. Under law, to have a binding contract—one that will be enforced by the law—there must be an offer, an acceptance, and consideration. Consideration is the giving of something of value, or quid pro quo. The law does not generally inquire into whether the bargain is fair or even,[1] but each

---

[1] In law, consideration is sometimes referred to as a peppercorn—in other words, it does not matter if the thing given is of value, so a peppercorn will be enough. Restatement (Second) Contracts Section 79 (1981). Like many legal phrases, it has long outlived its original sense. At the time the phrase was coined, pepper was an expensive, imported luxury.

party has to promise something, even if that something is only to forbear doing something the party would otherwise have the right to do.[2]

Open source licenses clearly involve an offer: The licensor makes the software and states the terms on which it may be used (i.e., the open source license). They also clearly involve consideration, because every open source license has some requirements for exercising the license, ranging from the notice requirements of permissive licenses to the copyleft requirements of hereditary licenses. The difficult element is acceptance.

In traditional contracts, acceptance is indicated by a written signature. In the Internet era, we also indicate assent by clicking "I accept" or "I agree" or by using digital signatures. But open source licenses do not use these devices. Unlike a typical "click-wrap" license agreement, the GPL usually is attached to code simply by virtue of placing the appropriate notices in the code. The licensee does not click to accept, or indicate its assent by signing any document. In fact, Item 7 of the Open Source Definition does not allow open source licenses to include the requirement for downstream licensees to agree to a contract.[3]

The position that open source licenses are not contracts is, presumably, an attempt to sidestep this issue. When GPL2 was released in 1991, the law regarding online contracting was much less clear than it is today. In 1996, a Circuit Court of Appeals of the United States (the court one level below the U.S. Supreme Court) issued an opinion that formed the basis for enforceability of unsigned agreements.[4] Later cases reinforced this idea.[5] However, whether a licensee can avoid the terms of the agreement by challenging acceptance (sometimes called a *formation argument*, because the contract was not properly formed) often turns on whether the licensee should have been aware of the terms prior to accepting a copy of the software. In commercial transactions, the formation analysis will take into account whether the license terms were

---

[2]The classic example is paying someone for not smoking. See Restatement (Second) Contracts Section 71 (1981).

[3]www.opensource.org/docs/osd.

[4]*ProCD v. Zeidenberg,* 86 F.3d 1447 (7th Cir. 1996).

[5]The progeny of *ProCD* is voluminous and continually evolving. For a general discussion, see Ian Ballon, *E-Commerce and Internet Law* (Glasser Legalworks, 2003), Chapter 26.

described or presented prior to completion of the sale. In open source, of course, there is rarely any sale involved, but a similar analysis would be applied based on whether the licensee knew of the license terms prior to downloading the software. Some open source advocates are concerned that without a "click to accept" or other unambiguous indication of asset, the terms of the license might not be binding on the licensee.

Arguments Supporting Formation

There is much to suggest that the position taken by the Free Software Foundation (FSF) that licenses like the GPL are not contracts is an inaccurate statement of law. One of the main arguments advanced against the position is that under the law of some countries, there cannot be a license that is not a contract. Also, the license terms themselves suggest that the document is a contract. Uniform Commercial Code (UCC) warranty disclaimers in Section 11 apply only to contracts, because the warranties they disclaim arise only in contracts for the sale of goods. GPL2 Section 5's statement that "you indicate your acceptance of this License," if true, forms a contract, assuming that there has already been an offer and consideration. Moreover, if exercise of the license under GPL invokes promissory estoppel, the license will function substantially as a contract, whether it is one or not. (See the later discussion on promissory estoppel and "bare licenses.") But most important, the circumstances surrounding acceptance of the terms of GPL may be sufficient to constitute acceptance of the document as a contract in most cases. (For the legal rules that determine acceptance in the online context, see Chapter 13.)[6]

My view is that asking whether the GPL is a license or a contract is the wrong question; the document is not by nature a license *or* a contract regardless of the circumstances of its use; the document will describe the terms of a contract under circumstances when a contract is formed. Lawyers who counsel clients on how to write enforceable online contracts are accustomed to the notion that the contents of the license document

---

[6]See Uniform Commercial Code, Article 2, Section 1-204.

are not as important as how the license is implemented. If the proper mechanisms are employed to require acceptance by the user—such as clicking to accept prior to download and presenting users with terms to review and print—then a contract probably will be formed. If those mechanisms are insufficient to form a contract, no contract will be formed.

IMPLICATIONS OF ABSENCE OF CONTRACT FORMATION

This issue, though very controversial, has a significant effect on risk assessment in open source compliance work. The position that the GPL is a license and not a contract has two major corollaries.

First, the remedies available will be intellectual property infringement remedies but not contract remedies. In many disputes involving license agreements, the licensor brings claims under both contract and intellectual property theories. If a licensee exceeds the scope of a license—which might include failing to comply with a condition of the license—then the noncompliant activities can be viewed as unlicensed and therefore infringing. However, if the license is also a contract, the licensor may seek damages for breach of contract as well. If the GPL is a license and not a contract, no remedy for breach of contract is available.

In a sense this difference is illusory, because the remedies for copyright infringement tend to be broader than for breach of contract. Copyright is a property regime, and violation of property rights generally can be remedied by injunction. An injunction is an order by the court requiring a party to take action—or more often, to forgo taking action. An order to stop doing something sometimes is called a *prohibitory injunction*. Thus, if a plaintiff wins a copyright infringement action, the court may order the defendant to stop using the infringing material. Contract remedies, however, generally do not include injunction. They also generally do not include specific performance, which is when a court issues an order requiring a party to do something, which is sometimes called a *mandatory injunction*.

Generally, courts hesitate to issue any kind of injunction, and have some discretion whether to do so. Courts base the award of a preliminary injunction on four factors:

1. The likelihood of plaintiff's success on the merits
2. Irreparable harm in the absence of an injunction (i.e., the harm cannot adequately be compensated later by money damages)
3. The balance of hardships between the plaintiff and defendant
4. The public interest[7]

In a contract claim, injunctions are by far the exception and not the rule. Theoretically, contracts are economic bargains that a party has a right to breach if he or she is willing to pay the damages for it; this theory is sometimes called *efficient breach*.[8] Freedom to refuse to perform a contract is an important element of political freedom; the courts are not intended generally to order people to do things, other than pay money. To allow courts to do so would give them too much power and burden them with the running of society rather than simply the redress of wrongs.

Therefore, giving up contract remedies is no great sacrifice for a licensor. The same money damages are probably available via an infringement claim, and an injunction is more likely. But the one element that is not available under an infringement claim is specific performance. The only theoretical basis for an order to comply with the conditions of an open source license is contract. This is one reason why most lawyers assume that no licensee under a hereditary license will be ordered to lay open source code. First, generally courts are more likely to grant prohibitory injunctions than mandatory ones. Courts in general do not prefer to be in the position of monitoring performance of their orders. So, between the limitation on specific performance remedies and the disinclination toward positive injunction, an order to lay open source code is unlikely even if a contract exists. Second, if the licensor claims there is no contract, no contract remedy would be available, because a court is unlikely to enforce a contract whose existence the plaintiff has denied.

---

[7]See, e.g., *Metro-Goldwyn Mayer, Inc. v. 007 Safety Products, Inc.,* 183 F.3d 10, 15 n.2 (1st Cir. 1999).

[8]This idea was advanced in Charles Goetz and Robert Scott, "Liquidated Damages, Penalties, and the Just Compensation Principle: A Theory of Efficient Breach", 77 *Colum. L. Rev.* 554 (1977), but is often associated with law and economics theorist Richard Posner and the law and economics movement.

The second corollary is that the party with standing to sue will be the owner of the copyright, not the distributor of the software. In the United States, standing to sue for copyright infringement only exists for copyright owners or exclusive licensees.[9]

Finally, the question of whether GPL is a contract may bear on its revocability. There is a concept under law called a *bare license*, meaning one without consideration on the part of the licensee. This concept comes from real property, based on cases where a land owner grants a license or easement over land or property.[10] If you have ever seen a plaque on a walkway that says permission is granted to pass, but may be revoked at any time, that is an example of a bare license. A license is not, however, revocable at will if it is "coupled with an interest"—which may include the payment of royalties, or mere reliance on its terms.[11] This concept has been extended to intellectual property law, but case law on it is minimal and the references to "bare licenses" are largely oblique, so it is far from settled that this concept applies identically to real and intellectual property.[12] If the GPL is revocable at will, of course, that situation is an enormous issue for licensees. However, such a result seems extremely unlikely. A licensor cannot terminate a license if it is unfair or inequitable for him or her to do so and if he

---

[9]17 USC Section 501(b) says: "The legal or beneficial owner of an exclusive right under a copyright is entitled . . . to institute an action for any infringement of that particular right committed while he or she is the owner of it." Courts have held this statement to be exclusive under the doctrine of *expressio unius est exclusio alterius*. See, e.g., *Silvers v. Sony Pictures Entertainment, Inc.*, 402 F.3d 881 (9th Cir. 2005) (en banc).

[10]Rest. of Property, Servitudes Section 514.

[11]Rest. of Property, Servitudes Section 519(3).

[12]35 USC Section 261 states that patents have the attributes of personal property. However, some case law seems to assume that real property concepts also apply. See, e.g., *Weinar v. Rollform, Inc.*, 744 F.2d 797 (Fed. Cir. 1984); *Intellectual Prop. Dev., Inc. v. TCI Cablevision of Cal., Inc.*, 248 F.3d 1333, 1345 (Fed. Cir. 2001) (a bare license is "a covenant by the patent owner not to sue the licensee for making, using, or selling the patented invention"); *Spindelfabrik Suessen-Schurr Stahlecker & Grill GmbH v. Schubert & Salzer Maschinenfabrik Aktiengesellschaft*, 829 F.3d 1075, 1081 (Fed. Cir. 1987) (a bare license "is in essence nothing more than a promise by the licensor not to sue the licensee").

or she should have reasonably anticipated the licensee's reliance on it.[13] Particularly for a licensee who is a distributor, reliance on the grant of license ought to be easy to prove. The legal concept of reliance is sometimes called quasi-contract, detrimental reliance, or promissory estoppel, and the trend in U.S. law is to expand the applicability of promissory estoppel as time goes forward. This may be why the law on bare licenses is so sparse. The general trend in legal thought is to minimize the formalities necessary to create contracts or quasi-contract obligations.

INCENTIVES FOR FORMATION ARGUMENTS

The entire question of formation might be a red herring. The question of whether a validly binding contract has been formed is crucial to the licensee in the case of end user licensing, but not so much in open source. This is true is because, in the absence of a binding end user contract, the end user is better off. An end user who lawfully receives a copy of software has certain rights under background law: the right to create transitory copies as necessary to run the software (under 17 USC Section 1117(a)(1)) and the right to create backup copies (under 17 USC Section 1117(a)(2)). In addition, an end user not subject to a license agreement may avail him- or herself of the first-sale doctrine (17 USC Section 109), engage in reverse engineering to the extent it is fair use allowed by law (as described in *Sega v. Accolade*[14]), and avoid warranty disclaimers and limitations of liability that can only be disclaimed by contract (see UCC Section 2-316). The end user, therefore, has significant incentive to avoid the license agreement.

This is not so in open source. As GPL2 says:

> 5. You are not required to accept this License, since you have not signed it. However, nothing else grants you permission to modify or distribute the Program or its derivative works. These actions are prohibited by law if you do not accept this License. Therefore, by modifying or distributing the Program (or any work based on the Program), you indicate your acceptance of this License to do so, and all its terms and conditions for copying, distributing or modifying the Program or works based on it.

---

[13]Rest. of Property, Servitudes Section 519(4) cmts. e–g.
[14]977 F.2d 1510 (9th Cir. 1992).

Thus, unless the licensee merely wishes to act as an end user, it has no incentive to avoid the license. It would be treacherous for a licensee to argue that the license terms are not binding.

It is not coincidental that the cases like *ProCD* and its progeny that address contract formation are brought almost exclusively by end users. To be more specific, they are brought by end users rather than distributors and by licensees rather than licensors, because end users are the very persons who have the most incentive to avoid contract formation because of the exceptions to infringement in the Copyright Act.

When one legitimately acquires a copy of a copyrightable work, in the absence of a binding licensing contract, one has certain rights to use the work that do not constitute copyright infringement:

1. One has the right to do anything not reserved to the copyright owner by the copyright law (i.e., copying, distribution, preparation of derivative works, public performance and display).
2. With respect to computer software, one has the right to do three things that the Copyright Act says are not infringement:
   a. Make a backup copy.
   b. Run the software.[15]
   c. Engage in fair use.[16]
3. Case law allows certain other limited rights, such as copying for the purpose of reverse engineering to achieve interoperability.[17]

The activities allowed by these exceptions are nearly identical to the rights granted in an end user license: the right to use and create backup copies. Most end user licenses limit all other activities, including reverse engineering, and place additional restrictions and legal obligations on the user. Therefore, end users almost always improve their legal position by avoiding the contract. Distributors, or users that prepare derivative works, are in a different position. Absent the permissions of the GPL, a distributor has no right to distribute and a user has no right to modify. Therefore, a distributor or modifier who claims that the GPL is not enforceable is engaging in copyright infringement, absent some separate grant of license.

---

[15]17 USC Section 117.
[16]17 USC Section 107.
[17]See *Sega v. Accolade,* 977 F.2d 1510 (9th Cir 1992).

Because an end user who does not modify the code does not require the permissions of GPL, the portion of the GPL that end users have the most incentive to avoid are the limitations of liability and warranty disclaimers. However, an end user making this argument may find itself in a dilemma: Implied warranties may not adhere unless a contract is formed under UCC Article 2. Therefore, claiming there was no effective acceptance may mean there was no transaction under UCC Article 2 and thus no implied warranty.

In sum, licensees may have little incentive to avoid the GPL's terms. However, licensees are the only parties that have any basis for avoiding contract formation. Therefore, the question is not whether the GPL is a license or a contract. The question is who has an incentive to characterize it as failing the test for contract formation and who has the ability to avoid the result of formation.

Licensees would be unwise to place too much reliance on the assumption that contract remedies are not available under GPL. It is worth noting that in the first two U.S. federal court lawsuits in which the GPL was at issue, the suits pled breach of contract.[18] In other words, while the FSF may forgo its right to seek contract remedies, other licensors are unlikely to do so.

During the time the GPL has been in existence, there has been at least one major push to rewrite software contracting law to account for the development of the software industry. This attempt, originally undertaken as a modification to UCC Article 2 by the National Conference of Commissioners for Uniform State Laws and the American Law Institute (ALI), was eventually rejected by ALI's membership and taken over by the National Conference of Commisioners for Uniform State Laws and renamed the Uniform Computer Information Transactions Act (UCITA). It was largely unsuccessful in that it was adopted by only two states, Virginia and Maryland. However, the UCITA discussions occurred too early for open source issues to be a central theme.[19] There is a current project

---

[18]*Progressive Software Corp. v. MySQL AB,* 195 F. Supp. 2d 328 (D. Mass. 2002); *MontaVista Software, Inc. v. Lineo, Inc.,* No. 2:02 CV-0309J (D. Utah filed July 23, 2002).

[19]The law was in development for years and finalized in 1999.

in the works by the ALI on the Principles of the Law of Software Contracts,[20] which is being formulated as a set of legal principles rather than
a restatement of law. These discussions are still under way as of this writing and will be in progress for some time to come. However, issues
regarding open source licenses—most particularly whether open source
licenses should be enforceable contracts and whether they should require
disclaimers of the UCC implied warranties such as merchantability and
fitness for a particular purpose[21]— are in the forefront of the
discussions.[22]

---

[20]www.ali.org/index.cfm?fuseaction=projects.proj_ip&projectid=9.
[21]UCC Article 2, Sections 314 and 315.
[22]The author, who is on the advisory committee for this project, reports the
nature of the discussions from personal participation.

CHAPTER 16

Defining Distribution

S econd to the "derivative works" question (see Chapter 14), the most important unresolved legal question in open source licensing is the question of what constitutes distribution. Recall that under U.S. law distribution is what triggers the hereditary requirements of the General Public License (GPL). Thus, using and modifying a program are allowed under the GPL without restriction, but when distribution occurs, the requirement to provide source code and license under GPL terms adheres.

Distribution, though one of the enumerated rights of copyright under U.S. law, is not defined in the Copyright Act (Title 17) (the Act). Title 17 grants a copyright owner the exclusive right "to distribute copies . . . of the copyrighted work to the public by sale or other transfer of ownership, or by rental, lease, or lending."[1] Note that the distribution right is limited to the distribution of copies and distribution to the public. Courts generally look to the 1976 House Report[2] on the Act, its primary legislative history, to interpret the Act. While distribution is not defined in the Act, "publication" is defined. The 1976 House report states that "any form of dissemination in which a material object does not change hands—performances or displays on television, for example—is not publication."[3] This is in contrast to the public performance right—a separate right of copyright—which can include broadcast transmission.[4] Courts have equated

---

[1] 17 USC Section 106(3).
[2] H.R. Rep. No. 94-1476.
[3] See http://copyright.gov/circs/circ1.html.
[4] See *Agee v. Paramount*, 59 F.3d at 325.

distribution with publication.[5] The Act does state that "offering to distribute copies . . . to a group of persons for purposes of further distribution, public performance, or public display, constitutes publication."[6]

In the United States, therefore, distribution means providing an actual copy to another person. Under law, corporations are considered legal persons. Therefore, in the corporate context, distribution means providing the copy to someone other than an employee of the company, because employees of the company are agents of the company and thus not other persons. But there are a number of situations in which companies give copies to persons other than their employees yet do not consider the situation distribution in the commercial sense.

- **Independent contractors: individuals.** Companies often engage individuals as independent contractors rather than employees. Start-up companies in particular do this to avoid the regulatory overhead costs associated with employees. The function of the contractor in such cases is nearly identical to that of an employee; however, because the contractor is not an employee, providing a copy of software to that person, either for use or modification, could be considered distribution.
- **Independent contractors: consultants.** Companies often hire small consulting firms to develop or test software. These developers are not agents of the company; therefore, providing a copy to them is clearly providing a copy outside the company.
- **Independent contractors: outsourcing.** Larger companies often outsource entire business areas, such as software development or information technology support. Outsourcers tend to be large companies, and therefore providing a copy to them is clearly providing a copy outside the company. Moreover, many outsourcers are outside the United States, a fact that complicates the question by making it unclear what body of law will define distribution for the purposes of triggering the copyleft requirement.
- **Subsidiaries and affiliates.** For various reasons, companies often create affiliate structures to conduct business. These reasons may include

---

[5]*Harper & Row Publs., Inc. v. Nation Enters.*, 471 U.S. 539, 552 (1985).
[6]17 USC Section 101.

tax planning, the need to do business in other countries through local entities, or creating entities to engage in a particular line of business. For example, a company may use a copy of the Linux kernel, which it has modified for its own purposes, to run an online service. It may provide this modified software to a subsidiary or affiliate in Europe or China to offer its service there. For tax, regulatory, or other reasons, it may be important to locate the servers for the businesses in Europe or China in those territories. If the recipient entity is a wholly owned subsidiary, the company has a good argument that, due to unity of ownership, the copy has only been given to the company itself, and therefore no distribution has taken place. This argument is also reasonably strong for a majority-owned affiliate. But if the recipient is a minority-owned affiliate, the company faces a serious concern over whether distribution has taken place. This scenario is quite common, particularly for operating entities in territories, such as China, that have restrictions on foreign-owned assets for businesses operating within its borders.

- **Mergers and acquisitions.** U.S. law can be quirky and counter-intuitive on the subject of assignments by operation of law in connection with mergers and acquisitions. An assignment of a contract (or a license) occurs when one party to the contract transfers its rights to another. Therefore, for instance, if a corporation enters into an agreement with another party, it may be able to transfer that agreement to another corporation—depending on what the agreement has to say about it. Contracts generally are considered assignable under U.S. law,[7] but intellectual property licenses are subject to quite different rules. Generally, nonexclusive copyright and patent licenses are not assignable.[8] Therefore, if a corporation takes a

---

[7] Other than special kinds of contracts, where assignment would change the basic nature of the contract, like contracts for personal services or requirements contracts. See Restatement (Second) Contracts, Section 317 (1981).

[8] For patent, see *PPG Indus. Inv. v. Guardian Indus. Corp.*, 597 F.2d 1090 (6th Cir. 1979). For copyright, although the law is conflicting, see e.g., *SQL Solutions, Inc. v. Oracle Corp.*, 1991 U.S. Dist. LEXIS 21097 (N.D. Cal. 1991). This is an unpublished decision and arguably contrary to the California Supreme Court's view in *Trubowich v. Riverbank Canning Co.*, 182 P.2d 182 (Cal. 1947).

nonexclusive license to a patent, it could not transfer that license to another corporation unless the license agreement expressly allows that. To make matters even more complicated, some courts have held that an acquisition is an "assignment by operation of law." Therefore, even if the licensee is the same corporation before and after the acquisition (called the *surviving entity*), the license may not be exercisable after the transaction. An average shrink-wrap license usually contains an express restriction against assignment by operation of law. The effect of this rubric on the transferability of open source licenses via merger is discussed in Chapter 17. However, this rule of law also may have an effect on the definition of distribution. If a change of control is an assignment by operation of law, it also may constitute providing a copy to another entity and thus a distribution triggering copyleft obligations.

The other key issue related to distribution is whether software transmissions or remote use—sometimes called the application service provider (ASP) or software-as-a-service (SAAS) model—constitute distribution. If they do, then the GPL's copyleft requirements could apply to SAAS use as well. However, the law in the United States is clear that distribution requires actual delivery of a copy, in whatever form. The result may be different in other jurisdictions, however. Some commentators suggest that the law in Germany may include making copies available rather than actually transferring them.[9] If so, GPL could cover these activities.

---

[9] This was suggested in GPL3 discussions, including by Till Jaeger, an attorney in private practice who has worked with Harald Welte and gpl-violations.org, and has represented Free Software Foundation Europe. Note this formulation in the German Free Software License at http://www.dipp.nrw.de/d-fsl/lizenzen/en/D-FSL-1_0_en.txt.

CHAPTER 17

Open Source in Mergers and Acquisitions and Other Transactions*

The treatment of open source in mergers and acquisitions (M&As) and other transactions has grown with the popularity of open source and with the adoption of open source by commercial technology developers. When open source was relatively unknown and considered within the purview of hobbyists, most agreements relating to technology licensing or development sought primarily to exclude open source. However, as open source has become more popular, and particularly more popular in commercial technology development, the treatment of open source in commercial agreements and mergers and acquisitions has necessarily become more sophisticated.

In the 1990s, when contracts relating to routine technology development and licensing generally contained nothing about open source, representations like the following were common in a merger, acquisition, or investment agreement:

> The Company Intellectual Property[1] contains no software source code that is covered by a so-called "open source" license. For purposes of

---

*An earlier version of this chapter appeared in "Open Source in M&A and Other Transactions," *Oregon Intellectual Property Newsletter* (December 2006).
[1]This term would have a typical definition, including the intellectual property components of the assets being acquired, or of the assets of the company being acquired.

this paragraph, "open source" is any software that is made generally publicly available in source code form.

This kind of representation demonstrates a few of the problems that arose in negotiating agreements when awareness of open source was minimal. For instance, the definition of open source in the language above is too broad. Many kinds of software are, of course, available in source code form regardless of the type of license agreement applied to them, because not all software is compiled. Thus, the preceding definition captures all uncompiled or scripted languages such as PERL, Hypertext Markup Language (HTML), or uncompiled forms of BASIC. Open source, instead, is more sensibly applied to software that can be distributed only in a compiled or binary form but is voluntarily made available in source code form.

When attorneys became more familiar with concepts of open source, representations tended to be rewritten in this way:

> The Company Intellectual Property contains no software source code that is covered by a so-called "open source" license. For purposes of this paragraph, "open source" is any software that is made generally publicly available under any license approved by the Open Source Initiative.

This definition is too narrow. Even before the organization changed its criteria for approval of licenses in 2006, the Open Source Initiative did not approve all licenses that are generally thought to be open source. Many variations of permissive licenses (such as Berkeley Software Distribution (BSD), MIT, and Apache version 1.1) are not on the official list of approved licenses but generally are understood to be open source and to fit the open source definition.

Of course, representations like this were unqualified statements that the target assets contained no open source software, and by the 2000s most people realized that was rarely true. At that point, such representations sought to compel disclosure of open source rather than simply excluding it. This was accomplished by a trivial variation such as:

> Except as set forth in the Disclosure Schedule, the Company Intellectual Property contains no software source code that is covered by a so-called "open source" license. For purposes of this paragraph, "open source" is any software that is made generally publicly available under licensed approved by the Open Source Initiative.

Such a representation was designed to cause the target company to disclose all the open source it was using in its business. Although this was a step in the right direction, it was not very nuanced. Such a broad representation requested more information than the acquirer cared to know and not enough. Such a representation—depending of course on the definition of Company Intellectual Property—sought disclosure either of all open source used in the business or all open source contained in the company's products. Generally it was drafted to capture of the former, and broader, category. The failure to make this distinction generally grew from an assumption, now generally thought to be erroneous, that the primary liability and risk associated with open source was the possibility that it infringed third-party rights. If this were the case, it would be just as important to know all open source used in a business as it would be to know all open source contained in a company's products.

However, over time it became clear that the primary risks of open source were focused on compliance with open source licenses rather than concerns about third-party intellectual property infringement. Thus, the representation asked for information that might not be very useful—namely a list of open source that was used in the business but not incorporated into products. This form of representation would compel a disclosure of the use of common open source tools, such as the Apache Web server. It is probably fair to say that no merger, acquisition, or investment was ever sidelined or revalued based on an organization's use of such open source code. At the same time, a representation like this does not compel disclosure of important information necessary to analyze the compliance of the target company with its inbound open source licenses. It compels the disclosure of a list of open source code but no information about how it is used.

This approach gave way to a more sophisticated one that tried to distinguish two things:

1. It was understood that open source simply used in a business was of less concern than open source embedded in products.
2. It was understood that open source provided under permissive licenses was of less concern than open source provided under hereditary ones.

Although custom and practice in this area are still developing, an open source representation that might be found in a merger, acquisition, or investment agreement today that takes a more sophisticated approach to the topic might read:

"Copyleft Software" means any software subject to a Copyleft License.

"Open Source Software" means any software subject to an Open Source License.

"Open Source License" means any license meeting the Open Source Definition (as promulgated by the Open Source Initiative) or the Free Software Definition (as promulgated by the Free Software Foundation), or any substantially similar license. For avoidance of doubt, Open Source Licenses include without limitation Copyleft Licenses.

"Copyleft License" means any license that requires, as a condition of use, modification or distribution of Copyleft Software, that such Copyleft Software, or modifications or derivative works thereof: (i) be made available or distributed in source code form, or (ii) be licensed for the purpose of preparing derivative works or distribution at no fee. Copyleft licenses include without limitation the GNU General Public License, the GNU Lesser General Public License, the Mozilla Public License, the Common Development and Distribution License, the Eclipse Public License, and, to the extent applied to software, all Creative Commons "sharealike" licenses.

Open Source and Copyleft Software. Target represents and warrants that all use and distribution of Open Source Software is in full compliance with all Open Source Licenses applicable thereto, including without limitation all copyright notice and attribution requirements. The Disclosure Schedule lists all Open Source Software used by Target in its Products (defined above), including without limitation in development or testing thereof, and describes (1) the manner in which any Copyleft Software is used, (2) whether (and, if so, how) the Copyleft Software has been modified by or for Target, (3) whether the Copyleft Software is distributed by or for Target, and (4) how such Copyleft Software is integrated with or interacts with other portions of the Products.

Note that this type of representation distinguishes between software covered by hereditary and by permissive licenses and compels disclosure of integration information necessary to analyze compliance issues for hereditary licenses.

OPEN SOURCE IN LICENSING AND COMMERCIAL TRANSACTIONS

The preceding discussion focuses on management of compliance risk regarding the use of open source code. Provisions in transactional agreements that seek to manage infringement risk look largely the same in mergers, acquisitions and investments as they do in commercial transactions.

However, license and development agreements also require provisions particular to open source that go beyond representations and warranties. The primary example is the language necessary to integrate open source software that is provided under hereditary licenses with that provided under permissive licenses or commercial terms. For instance, if a company (Licensor) is licensing a product that contains both open source and proprietary components, the Licensor must ensure that its commercial binary license agreement does not unintentionally violate the inbound hereditary licenses that apply to open source components of the product. Permissive code can, of course, be relicensed under proprietary terms. However, relicensing hereditary code under a binary license agreement generally will violate the terms of the hereditary license.

To avoid this problem, any commercial end user license covering a product that contains some components covered by hereditary agreements should contain a provision such as the next one (with Licensee, Software, and Agreement defined in a customary fashion):

> Notwithstanding the foregoing [include a reference to the license grant], Licensee acknowledges that certain components of the Software may be covered by so-called "open source" software licenses ("Open Source Components"), which means any software licenses approved as open source licenses by the Open Source Initiative or any substantially similar licenses, including without limitation any license that, as a condition of distribution of the software licensed under such license, requires that the distributor make the software available in source code format. Licensor shall provide a list of Open Source Components for a particular version of the Software upon Licensee's request. To the extent required by the licenses covering Open Source Components, the terms of such licenses will apply in lieu of the terms of this Agreement, and Licensor hereby represents and warrants that the licenses granted to such Open Source Components will be no less broad than the license granted in Section [____]. To the extent the terms of the licenses applicable to Open

Source Components prohibit any of the restrictions in this Agreement with respect to such Open Source Component, such restrictions will not apply to such Open Source Component.

At this point, the licensor needs to make a choice about whether other provisions of its commercial end user license agreement will cover any of the open source components. A typical end user license agreement contains many provisions other than the license. For instance, most enterprise license agreements contain provisions such as performance warranties (warranties that the software will perform according to specifications), maintenance and support obligations, intellectual property infringement indemnities, and the like. Hereditary open source license agreements permit a redistributor to make additional warranties and covenants about the software covered by the hereditary license. It is a business strategy decision, however, whether to cover open source software under these commercial terms.

Most commercial end users will demand that all software included in a product, whether open source or not, be subject to performance warranties. Sometimes licensors will be successful in excluding open source code from intellectual property warranties and indemnities, but many are not. While the licensor can make a convincing case that it cannot control whether open source code violates third-party rights, licensees who are paying commercial fees for license to a product generally take the position that it is the licensor's decision to include open source in the product and therefore the licensor's burden to bear liability for possible infringements, the theory being that the licensor is in the better position to take a reserve against expenses associated with intellectual property infringement than the licensee and that the license fees for the product should be used to fund that reserve. There is no clear industry custom here; some licensors bear risk for open source components and some do not. However, those that do generally have not suffered great losses—at least with respect to infringement risk—because there have been relatively few cases regarding infringement of third-party intellectual property rights by open source software.

DEVELOPMENT AGREEMENTS

The popularity of open source has bred a new kind of development agreement: one in which the material developed is primarily covered by open source licenses, instead of the customary work-made-for-hire arrangement that is typical with development in a proprietary environment. When developers are hired to modify software code that is covered by hereditary license agreements, the deliverables that they provide consist primarily of third-party code whose rights cannot be assigned to the customer. It may be meaningful to assign the rights in the modifications to the customer; however, developers increasingly take the position that modifications they make to open source code should be shared with the community. In this way they are solving a perennial problem that developers face when doing sequential development projects: the ability to reuse past work in future engagements. While many consulting agreements in the proprietary context contain provisions that allow for the delivery of third-party code, these provisions generally have been considered exceptions rather than the thrust of the development.

When development takes place in an open source context, the terms of the development agreement often are adjusted to suit this new context. Thus, the intellectual property ownership provisions in an open source development contract might look like this:

> **Deliverables.** All copyrightable material, software, documentation, and other works of authorship embodied in materials delivered to Customer hereunder ("Deliverables") will be licensed by Developer to Customer under the terms of the GNU General Public License version 2.0 or any later version.

Or alternatively:

> **Deliverables.** All software prepared, conceived, or reduced to practice by Developer in the course of performing this Agreement ("Foreground Software") will be the property of Customer, and Developer hereby assigns to Customer all right, title and interest therein. Customer shall make such Foreground Software generally available under the GNU General Public License version 2.0 or any later version. Customer acknowledges that all copyrightable material, software, documentation, and other works of authorship embodied in materials delivered to Customer hereunder, other than the Foreground Software ("Deliverables") are licensed to customers by third parties under the GNU General Public License version 2.0 or any later version.

The missing piece here is what happens to patent rights. Generally developers who insist on this type of arrangement do not wish patents to be filed. Therefore, the developer (or in the second case, the customer) often will promise not to file any patent applications claiming the foreground software. Interestingly, for open source licenses that contain express patent license provisions for contributors, the customer will prefer the developer to own the rights to the software and contribute the software developed for the customer to the applicable open source project. In this case, the customer may not be in the position of granting patent licenses.

CHAPTER 18

GPL Version 3.0

WHAT IS THE EFFECT OF THE RELEASE OF GPL3?

Version 3 of the GNU General Public License (GPL3) was released on June 29, 2007. Because this version was released shortly before this book went to press, what follows is a brief description of the changes in version 3. Industry reaction to the release of this version, its rate of adoption, and the interpretation of its key provisions have yet to be seen, and may be uncertain for some time. GPL3 today is like a news story: easier to describe than to analyze in context. Only with time will the kind of analysis that has been applied to GPL version 2 (GPL2) emerge. This chapter answers the most frequent questions about GPL3, mindful that many interpretive and practical questions currently remain unanswered.

GPL2 was released in 1991. At the time of its release, free software was relatively unknown, except to the immediate free software community. Between 1991 and 2007, the technology industry slowly grew to accept GPL2, driven mostly by the popularity of the Linux operating system. However, that acceptance was hard fought. The corporate world perceived the license as difficult to understand, vague, and therefore risky to use. However, over the years, corporate users grew comfortable, primarily because of the development of industry practice that helped provide an interpretation of the license. Also, the Free Software Foundation (FSF) published extensive explanatory material about the license in the form of frequently asked questions (FAQs).[1]

Over that time, there was some criticism of GPL2 from all sides. Industry constituents criticized its lack of clarity on the scope of works it covered, lawyers criticized its ambiguous drafting style, and the free software community believed it contained loopholes, most particularly the so-called ASP (application service provider) problem. Meanwhile, however, GPL2 was wildly successful by any reasonable measure, becoming the most widely used license in the world.[2] Therefore, while there was much pressure to revise and improve the license, there was also an entrenched world community using it, so changing it was at least a momentous process and at worst a serious disruption of the free software model.

The process of revising the license was long and controversial, and took place within a quasi-legislative process. The FSF released a first discussion draft on January 16, 2006. Comment committees were organized representing free software projects, distributors, users, and hackers.[3] Comments were accepted from the public at large and filtered through the committees, who made recommendations. The second discussion draft was released on July 27, 2006, and a third discussion draft released on March 28, 2007. The long period between the two drafts was the

---

[1]However, as explained in Chapter 14, this explanation was of uncertain value as legal evidence of meaning. Therefore, the comfort of the industry came slowly, based primarily on the safety-in-numbers quality of industry practice.

[2]This fact, though true, is misleading in a way. Before open source, almost no license was used by more than one licensor, so comparing GPL's penetration to that of proprietary licenses is like comparing the use of a standardized product to that of many unstandardized ones. Implicit in much of the philosophy of the free software movement is the assumption that standardization in licensing is good, a tenet that is not often discussed. For more on this, see the discussion in Chapter 14 regarding whether the rules concerning interpretation of licenses needs to change in light of open source licensing.

[3]Bruce Byfield, "The GPLv3 Process: Public Consultation and Private Drafting," Linux.com, August 25, 2006, www.linux.com/article.pl?sid=06/08/18/1539226. In practice the committees were populated with persons who represented overlapping interests.

result of controversy surrounding the patent provisions of the second draft and the intervening announcement of the Microsoft/Novell deal, to be described. After a last-call draft released on May 31, 2007, the final release was made on June 29, 2007. With each draft the FSF released a rationale document describing the reasoning behind the revisions included.

During the GPL3 process, there were two significant disruptive events. First, Linus Torvalds and the Linux kernel maintainers publicly announced that they disagreed with some of the provisions of the discussion drafts, most notably the so-called Digital Rights Management (DRM) provisions and the patent provisions.[4] The second event was the announcement of the Microsoft/Novell patent deal.

Adoption of GPL3

Most instantiations of the GPL allow any code released under a particular version also to be used under any later version of the license. Now that GPL3 has been released, many projects licensed under GPL2 may be available under either version, but some projects will migrate to GPL3 (or better said, GPL3 or any later version). For those projects that do not migrate, licensees will have the option to take the code under either GPL2 or GPL3. However, if that licensee distributes modified code, any downstream licensees must use the version selected by the licensee. (See Exhibit 18.1.)

For projects that do migrate to GPL3, the code available on the date of migration will no longer be available under GPL2. However, if a licensee is already using code under GPL2, that license will not be extinguished. Therefore, some licensees could fork the licensing path, continuing to exercise their rights under GPL2. However, if a licensee has taken code under GPL2, any updated versions of the project released after the date of migration will not be available except under GPL3.

One of the looming issues surrounding GPL3 is that it is not compatible with GPL2. Therefore, a code base that links GPL2 and GPL3 code is not a logical possibility. Many in the open source community are concerned

---

[4]www.lwn.net/Articles/200422.

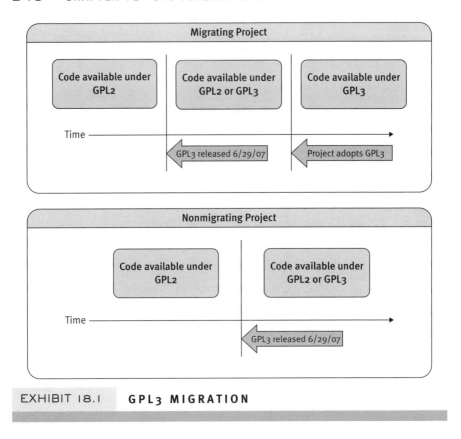

EXHIBIT 18.1   GPL3 MIGRATION

that this will be a problem, particularly for Linux distributions. The FSF clearly considers the two licenses incompatible:

> When we say that GPLv2 and GPLv3 are incompatible, it means there is no legal way to combine code under GPLv2 with code under GPLv3 in a single program.[5]

POLITICS AND CONTEXT

The GPL3 drafting and comment process flushed out deep divisions in the free software community. These divisions had been in existence prior to the process but had not aired quite so publicly prior to 2006. Divisions

---

[5]Richard Stallman, "Why Upgrade to GPL Version 3," communication distributed to the comment committee distribution list on May 31, 2007.

came to a head after the release of the second discussion draft. IBM voiced complaints about the breadth of the patent licenses—a significant dissent because IBM had long been a staunch supporter of Linux. The Linux kernel maintainers (including Linus Torvalds) then posted a public critique of GPL3 that objected to the DRM, patent, and license compatibility provisions. They said:

> Since GPL has served us so well for so long, and since it is the foundation of our developer contract which has helped propel Linux to the successes it enjoys today, we are extremely reluctant to contemplate tampering with that license except as bug fixes to correct exposed problems or updates [to] counter imminent dangers. So far, in the whole history of GPLv2 . . . we have not found any bugs serious enough to warrant such correction.

This posting was moderate in tone; not so Torvalds' own comments on Groklaw (a web site devoted to legal issues relating to open source), which were so vehement it prompted the moderator to comment, "I'm sorry, Linus, but I had to remove your comment because you violated our comment policy by swearing so much." Torvalds vented his disagreement with the philosophy of the FSF, which he characterized as basing GPL3 decisions on "fear and loathing."

While this was a clear statement that GPL3 would not be adopted for Linux, such adoption may never have been likely in the first place. As far back as 2001, Torvalds had anticipated that GPL3 would not be consistent with his goals:

> I don't trust the FSF. I like the GPL a lot—although not necessarily as a legal piece of paper, but more as an intent. Which explains why, if you've looked at the Linux COPYING file, you may have noticed the explicit comment about "only _this_ particular version of the GPL covers the kernel by default." That's because I agree with the GPL as-is, but I do not agree with the FSF on many other matters. . . . The FSF has long been discussing and is drafting the "next generation" GPL, and they generally suggest that people using the GPL should say "v2 or at your choice any later version." . . . The "v2 only" issue might change some day, but only after all documented copyright holders agree on it, and only after we've seen what the FSF suggests. From what I've seen so far from the FSF drafts, we're not likely to change our v2-only stance, but there might of course be legal reasons why we'd have to do something

like it (i.e. somebody challenging the GPLv2 in court, and part of it to be found unenforceable or similar would obviously mean that we'd have to reconsider the license).[6]

The rift was now public and bitter. FSF sensibly invited the kernel maintainers to join the comment process rather than post public criticism, but they did not do so. Behind the scenes, followers of the GPL3 process began to use the phrase "dead on arrival" to describe the new license. However, the process continued.

In November 2006, the Microsoft/Novell bombshell hit. While the details of the deal were not made public at the time, they were made available on a confidential basis to the Software Freedom Law Center,[7] and the documents (in redacted form) were later filed as part of Novell's 10-K Securities and Exchange Commission filing in May 2007. The central plank of the deal was that Novell's customers received a covenant not to sue directly from Microsoft covering the use of Novell products, including Linux.[8] Novell distributes a popular Linux distribution called SuSE Linux Enterprise. Knowing that the open source software community fears patent infringement lawsuits, a broad covenant not to sue by a major patent holder in favor of a major Linux distribution might seem like a net positive. After all, other companies, such as IBM and Hewlett Packard, had announced "patent donations"—in truth covenants not to sue—in the past. However, the move was universally seen as a tactical ploy by Microsoft and Novell against other Linux distributors, such as Red Hat.

The FSF then went back to the drawing board. In discussion draft 3, it acceded to the wishes of IBM and other corporate constituents to limit the scope of the patent license. It also included the "Microsoft" and "Novell" paragraphs.

---

[6]www.atnf.csiro.au/people/rgooch/linux/docs/licensing.txt.

[7]Tom Sanders, "Novell Opens Legal Books to GPL Pundits,"vunet.com, www.vnunet.com/vnunet/news/2168151/novells-opens-microsoft.

[8]See Novell's FAQ on the deal: www.novell.com/linux/microsoft/faq_opensource.html. Microsoft's customers received a similar covenant not to sue from Novell. A redacted version of the agreement was also released in Novell's 10-K filing dated May 25, 2007.

The other significant development in the process was the attempt to make the GPL compatible with other licenses, including Affero GPL. Doing this flushed out a deep divide in the free software community, between those who felt the ASP loophole should be closed and those who felt it should not—or that doing so would endanger adoption of GPL3. In addition, the license compatibility provisions were criticized as making the license too complex and notification of the applicable license terms too confusing, which, it was feared, would cause users and distributors without political motivation to use GPL3 to put the license on their "black lists," resulting in limited adoption of GPL3 by projects trying to avoid the fate of blacklisted code.

"Derivative Works" Problem

Under GPL2, assessing the scope of code covered by GPL2 involved a pastiche of language in the agreement and outside commentary. (See Chapter 14 for further explanation.) GPL3 treats the subject quite differently by defining a new term, "Corresponding Source," and removing some of the conflicting glosses on "work based on the Program" that were in GPL2. The term "Corresponding Source" now defines what must be distributed to effectuate the license. Many of the concepts here relating to linking and so forth were essentially taken from the GPL2 FAQ.[9] This definition explicitly includes

> definition files associated with source files for the work, and the source code for shared libraries and dynamically linked subprograms that the work is specifically designed to require, such as by intimate data communication or control flow between those subprograms and other parts of the work.

This streamlining will help those trying to sort out GPL compliance issues in applications, but because the Linux kernel migration to GPL3 is not contemplated currently, it may not affect the most frequent and thorny issue here: analysis of binary loadable kernel modules. For more discussion, see Chapter 14.

---

[9]www.gnu.org/licenses/gpl-faq.html.

However, the ambiguities are not gone, and the license still refers back to copyright concepts for its scope. Section 5 says:

> A compilation of a covered work with other separate and independent works, which are not by their nature extensions of the covered work, and which are not combined with it such as to form a larger program, in or on a volume of a storage or distribution medium, is called an "aggregate" if the compilation and its resulting copyright are not used to limit the access or legal rights of the compilation's users beyond what the individual works permit. Inclusion of a covered work in an aggregate does not cause this License to apply to the other parts of the aggregate.

"PROPAGATION" AND "CONVEYING"

Under GPL2, the threshold for application of copyleft requirements was characterized as "distribution" and thought to be roughly consistent with the definition of this term under U.S. copyright law. GPL3 has defined a new term, "conveying," that includes distribution. The movement from "distribution" to "conveying" is expressly intended to allow for differences in international copyright laws. To emphasize this point, The FSF purposely chose a word that was not one of the enumerated rights of U.S. copyright. GPL3 has clarified the distribution issue, stating in the definitions that "[m]ere interaction with a user through a computer network, with no transfer of a copy, is not conveying."

PATENTS

The patent terms of GPL3 represent a significant change from GPL2. GPL2 did not contain an express license, although many posited that a patent license, the contours of which were unclear, was implied. GPL3 now contains an express patent license.

The patent terms of the second discussion draft drew broad criticism, largely centering on whether "mere distributors" would be required to grant patent licenses. Many companies redistribute GPL code but do not contribute to the code base. These companies were worried about being required to grant licenses that would affect their ability to enforce their patent portfolios by, for instance, allowing GPL code to be distributed on servers they run but not actively engaging in development. The FSF, however, is strongly anti-patent and favors broad licenses. Both constituencies active in the drafting process eventually acknowledged that broader licenses might discourage adoption of GPL3. After the initial flurry of criticism on discussion draft 2, the positions of the FSF and big patent holders were coming closer. But the announcement of the Novell/Microsoft deal derailed this. The final text of GPL3 has new patent terms that are clearly directed at that deal.

Licensors under GPL3 grant a license in their "essential patent claims." This term employs an indefinite, forward-looking capture period and extends to patents "owned or controlled" by the contributor, "whether already acquired or hereafter acquired." The language "owned or controlled" is a customary way of expressing this notion in patent licensing. However, it includes "the right to grant patent sublicenses in a manner consistent with the requirements of this License," which ordinarily would not be considered control in conventional patent license drafting. There is no patent license termination provision in GPL3, although many other hereditary licenses contain them. Such a provision was in earlier discussion drafts, but deleted. However, this language was added as part of the "No Further Restrictions" provision in Section 10.

> You may not impose any further restrictions on the exercise of the rights granted or affirmed under this License. For example, you may not impose a license fee, royalty, or other charge for exercise of rights granted under this License, and you may not initiate litigation (including a cross-claim or counterclaim in a lawsuit) alleging that any patent claim is infringed by making, using, selling, offering for sale, or importing the Program or any portion of it.

The scope of the patent license in GPL3 is similar to that of other hereditary licenses, but not identical. The most important limitation is that essential claims "do not include claims that would be infringed only as a consequence of further modification of the contributor version." However, essential claims in GPL3 include claims invoked by the portions of the program not contributed by the contributor. Other hereditary licenses limit the claims to those covered by the contribution of the contributor and combinations of the contribution with the remainder of the work.

Three paragraphs in the patent section of GPL3 are of particular note and are highly controversial. The first addresses broad cross-licenses that are typical among larger industry players, particularly licenses that are not sublicensable (as most are not).

From Section 11:

If you convey a covered work, knowingly relying on a patent license, and the Corresponding Source of the work is not available for anyone to copy, free of charge and under the terms of this License, through a publicly available network server or other readily accessible means, then you must either (1) cause the Corresponding Source to be so available, or (2) arrange to deprive yourself of the benefit of the patent license for this particular work, or (3) arrange, in a manner consistent with the requirements of this License, to extend the patent license to down-stream recipients. "Knowingly relying" means you have actual knowledge that, but for the patent license, your conveying the covered work in a country, or your recipient's use of the covered work in a country, would infringe one or more identifiable patents in that country that you have reason to believe are valid.

Criticism of this paragraph includes the difficulty of assessing knowledge within corporate organizations, the administrative burden of determining whether any patents included in a broad cross-license would be related to the code, and the necessity to make a legal decision as to whether a patent would be infringed. Also, commentators questioned whether option (2) would be likely to be undertaken in any instance. Theoretically, causing the corresponding source to be generally available under option (1) would allow the free software community to more easily engineer around patent infringement claims.

Two paragraphs addressed the Microsoft/Novell deal:

So-called Microsoft paragraph:

If, pursuant to or in connection with a single transaction or arrangement, you convey, or propagate by procuring conveyance of, a covered work, and grant a patent license to some of the parties receiving the covered work authorizing them to use, propagate, modify or convey a specific copy of the covered work, then the patent license you grant is automatically extended to all recipients of the covered work and works based on it.

Questions will arise as to how this automatic patent license can bind a party that is not operating under this license. In the arrangement between Microsoft and Novell, Microsoft was not a distributor of Linux, much less a contributor, and is not a licensee, and so would not be bound by the terms of GPL.

So-called Novell paragraph:

A patent license is "discriminatory" if it does not include within the scope of its coverage, prohibits the exercise of, or is conditioned on the non-exercise of one or more of the rights that are specifically granted under this License. You may not convey a covered work if you are a party to an arrangement with a third party that is in the business of distributing software, under which you make payment to the third party based on the extent of your activity of conveying the work, and under which the third party grants, to any of the parties who would receive the covered work from you, a discriminatory patent license (a) in connection with copies of the covered work conveyed by you (or copies made from those copies), or (b) primarily for and in connection with specific products or compilations that contain the covered work, unless you entered into that arrangement, or that patent license was granted, prior to 28 March 2007.

This provision is an attempt to prevent a party actually engaging in distribution under GPL from entering into limited patent licenses such as the one Novell entered into with Microsoft. Note the date grandfathering in the Novell deal. This was the date of the first discussion draft of GPL3 that included language addressed at the deal.

DIGITAL MILLENNIUM COPYRIGHT ACT PROVISIONS

Between the release of GPL2 in 1991 and the release of GPL3, several controversial pieces of legislation were enacted that troubled advocates of free software. In the United States, this legislation consisted primarily of the Digital Millennium Copyright Act (DMCA). The DMCA implements the terms of two World Intellectual Property Organization (WIPO) treaties that the United States had entered into in the 1990s. This act had many elements,[10] but the one of concern was the one that placed civil

---

[10]It is easy to confuse them because they are all referred to shorthand as DMCA. The act also provides for a safe harbor for online service providers, which is quite a different provision.

and criminal penalties on reverse engineering for the purpose of circum-
venting copyright protection. The law was criticized because it was viewed
as undermining the fair use defense under copyright law. Before DMCA,
cases such as *Sega v. Accolade*[11] had held that some copying of copyrightable material was noninfringing if done to achieve interoperability. The
circumvention prohibitions of the DMCA were enacted in anticipation of
the entertainment industry implementing electronic controls on the use
of content such as music or audiovisual records, sometimes known as
Digital Rights Management (DRM) technology. However, the DMCA
was soon used in attempts to prevent reverse engineering, outside of the
scope of DRM.[12]

Popular criticism of these provisions of the DMCA mostly centered
around objections that DRM would prevent making free copies of music.
However, such criticisms, based as they were on the anti-property view
that the ability to make free copies of music was a good policy objective,
were not taken very seriously in the business world. Although the free
software community seems generally to concur in this view,[13] that was not
the most important issue for free software with the DMCA. Open source
programs designed to hack DRM protections are fairly common, and some
in the free software community objected that the DMCA effectively crimi-
nalized the distribution of this software. But the most cogent objection was
that the DMCA, even though it was codified as part of the copyright law,
was not clearly limited to copyrightable subject matter and provided an
independent right of action—separate from copyright infringement—for
the kind of activities that normally would be controlled by copyright law.

This, in a nutshell, was the motivation for the DRM provisions in
GPL3. In the first draft of GPL3, these were coyly entitled "Digital Restrictions Management" and caused great concern that they meant that no GPL
code could be used to implement DRM functionality. Such a restriction
would have been contrary to the Open Source Definition's plank regarding
nondiscrimination as to fields of endeavor. It also would have effectively

---

[11]977 F.2d 1510 (9th Cir 1992).

[12]See *Chamberlain v. Skylink*, 381 F.3d 1178 (Fed. Cir. 2004), and *Lexmark Int'l,
Inc. v. Static Control Components, Inc.*, 387 F.3d 522 (6th Cir. 2004).

[13]Richard Stallman, for one. See the page on anti-DRM protests and materials
at www.billxu.com/friend/rms/zeuux.rms.anti.drm.html.

caused a refusal to use GPL3 code in any mainstream media device—it being anticipated that most such devices will implement DRM in the near future, if they do not already. In subsequent drafts, the provision was scaled back (or clarified, depending on one's views of the original meaning) to simply not allow a licensor who released code under GPL3 to use a DMCA action to prevent the full exercise of rights under the license. In this respect, the DRM provision is similar to the patent license and the provisions to address the use of disabling codes (discussed later in this chapter), disallowing actions such as patent infringement suits or code obfuscation that might interfere with the exercise of the license grant.

"Java Problem"

Under GPL2, questions arose as to whether the GPL's reach extended to additional code such as programming language standard objects or classes. This issue is sometimes characterized as the "Java problem," because Java code is necessarily linked to standard Java libraries provided under proprietary terms. If we assume that the GPL requires all linked code also to be covered by GPL, then it would be logically impossible for any Java program to be covered by GPL, because the Java Virtual Machine (the Java interpreter) and its standard classes are proprietary code. GPL3 attempts to clarify that standard libraries need not be covered by GPL even if they interact with GPL code. This clarification means that the "safe harbor" line that existed between Linux as an operating system and applications running on top of Linux has been extended up the software stack. Inevitably, those modifying code will try to push the envelope of what constitutes a "system library," claiming that their own interfaces to proprietary code fit this definition and therefore allowing them to segregate and keep proprietary code that interfaces through such an interface.

Disabling and Obfuscation

Some companies distribute products under GPL with technical limitations on the ability to access or modify source code.[14] GPL3 contains provisions expressly restricting this. Although earlier discussion drafts of

---

[14]This is sometimes called the *Tivo problem*. I make no claims about Tivo or its practices; this is simply a shorthand phrase common in the free software world.

GPL3 contained more extensive terms, such terms in the final version are focused on consumer products. Section 6 defines a "User Product" as (1) a consumer product; or (2) anything designed or sold for incorporation into a dwelling. Note the focus on the product rather than the recipient.[15] Section 6 contains provisions requiring the distribution of information or tools necessary to access and modify the source code. This section is still controversial; some think it may interfere with legitimate security and cryptography restrictions. Indeed, an earlier version of this provision was one with which the Linux kernel maintainers took public issue. Some makers of integrated systems have a legitimate interest in preventing modifications that will make warranty work difficult or interfere with proper operation of the device or related services. Militating against this is the interest of the licensee in having the right to exercise all the rights under GPL without the licensor giving with one hand and taking away with the other, by granting rights to modify that cannot be exercised effectively.

ASP PROBLEM

Some companies make extensive use of open source software but do not distribute it. Some in the free software community have seen this as a "loophole."

This so-called loophole was "closed" in a variant of the GPL promulgated by Affero, Inc., effectively equating online access to software with distribution, triggering application of the copyleft requirements even when a copy was not actually provided to the user. The Affero GPL (version 1) contains this provision:

> d) If the Program as you received it is intended to interact with users through a computer network and if, in the version you received, any user interacting with the Program was given the opportunity to request transmission to that user of the Program's complete source code, you must not remove that facility from your modified version of the Program or work based on the Program, and must offer an equivalent opportunity

---

[15]The open source definition disallows making distinctions between users; www.opensource.org/docs/definition.php.

for all users interacting with your Program through a computer network to request immediate transmission by HTTP of the complete source code of your modified version or other derivative work.[16]

Before the first discussion draft of GPL3 was released, there was wide speculation that GPL3 would include such a change. Instead, the FSF offered a variation of GPL3 that made this change in a section called "Additional Permissions," which addressed license compatibility (see the next section). In the end, however, the FSF retreated from this approach, citing "irreconcilable views from different parts of our community" as to whether the loophole needed to be closed.[17] The final version of GPL3 in Section 13 allows linking of code to other code licensed under Affero GPL version 3—but the combined work will be subject to Affero GPL. Version 3 of the Affero license is currently in the drafting and comment stage; this license will be stewarded by the FSF going forward.[18]

LICENSE COMPATIBILITY

One of the main goals of GPL3 was to ensure compatibility[19] with other licenses, in other words, to allow code received under licenses to be relicensed under GPL. Of course, relicensing can occur only when more restrictions, not fewer ones, are created. (Anything else would cause the diligence problem discussed in Chapter 4.) We also know that Section 6 of the GPL (Section 7 of GPL3) has an explicit prohibition against adding restrictions to the license. A new section of GPL3 focuses on license compatibility and allows a licensor using GPL to add incremental license terms that may be required by other inbound licenses. (For a discussion of the controversy regarding capability between Apache 2.0 and GPL2, see Chapter 4.)

Earlier discussion drafts contained an extensive menu of additional permissions. This section was drastically reduced after discussion drafts 1 and 2 were heavily criticized. The main lines of criticism concerned the added

---

[16]www.affero.org/oagpl.html.

[17]See the Rationale Document accessible at http://gplv3.fsf.org/gpl-draft-2007-03-28.html.

[18]See http://gplv3.fsf.org/agplv3-dd1-guide.html.

[19]For the meaning of "compatibility," see Chapter 4.

complexity that so many available combinations implied and the worry that those altering the license would not sufficiently notify licensees of which combination was being used. In an atmosphere of backlash against license proliferation, the FSF bowed to the criticism and simplified this section.

The variations allowed by this section are now relatively trivial compared to their original scope: They are limited to, for instance, warranty disclaimers, notice provisions, preventing misattribution, and disallowing the use of names or trademarks.[20]

---

[20]See Section 7 of GPL3.

CHAPTER 19

LGPL Version 3.0

New Approach for LGPL

GNU Lesser General Public License Version 3.0 (LGPL3)[1] was released June 29, 2007, to accompany the release of GNU General Public License version 3 (GPL3). The LGPL is now an amendment to GPL3 rather than a standalone document. This is a step in the right direction, as LGPL generally was considered and treated as a variant of GPL in the past. Because LGPL3 is a variation of GPL3, the document is very short, and most of the terms applicable to LGPL code are in GPL3.

Adoption of LGPL3

The rules for availability of code under LGPL3 are the same as for GPL3. Most instantiations of the LGPL allow any code released under a particular version also to be used under any later version of the license. Now that LGPL3 has been released, many projects licensed under LGPL2 may be available under either version, but some projects will migrate to LGPL3 (or better said, LGPL3 or any later version). For those projects that do not migrate, licensees will have the option to take the code under either LGPL2 or LGPL3. However, if that licensee distributes modified code, any downstream licensees must use the version selected by the licensee.

---

[1]Available at www.gnu.org/licenses/lgpl-3.0.html.

POLITICS AND CONTEXT

The LGPL3 drafting and comment process was largely overshadowed by the GPL3 process and therefore received relatively little attention. The Free Software Foundation (FSF) has always considered LGPL an undesirable necessity, having posted and retained on its web site an article entitled "Why You Shouldn't Use the Library GPL for Your Next Library."[2] Nevertheless, the LGPL remains a very popular license, particularly for library code, and the FSF recognizes the need for the compromise it represents.

DEFINITIONS

Most readers will find the layered definitions in LGPL3 confusing. Here are the most important terms (all in Section 0) and how they interrelate:

- "The Library" is the work covered by the LGPL (whether it is implemented as a library or not).
- An "Application" is a program that uses the library.
- A "Combined Work" is the program created by linking an Application with the Library.
- The "Minimal Corresponding Source" for a Combined Work means the source code for the Combined Work, *excluding* source code for the Application. (This essentially means the source code for the Library.)
- The "Corresponding Application Code" means the object code for the Application, including any data and utility programs needed for reproducing the Combined Work. (Presumably this includes build instructions.)

Exhibit 19.1 provides a simple illustration.

COMPLIANCE

The LGPL no longer explicitly restricts Combined Works to those using the Library via dynamic linking (though tighter integration may not be compliant). Note that Section 4.d.1 of LGPL3 requires a "suitable shared library mechanism for linking"—which includes dynamic linking but is not necessarily limited to it.

---

[2]www.gnu.org/licenses/why-not-lgpl.html. The reference to "Library GPL" has been superseded by "Lesser GPL," but the article has not changed.

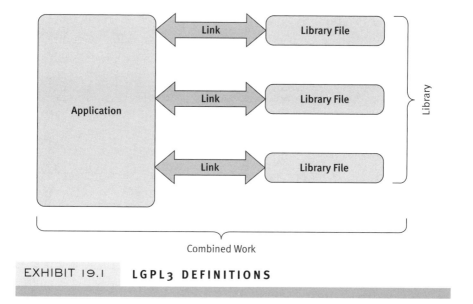

EXHIBIT 19.1   **LGPL3 DEFINITIONS**

The rules of compliance for LGPL3 have not greatly changed from LGPL2:

- You may license Applications (assuming you otherwise have the right to do so) under proprietary terms, as long as you license the Library under LGPL. (See Section 4.)
- Notice requirements apply that have not changed greatly from LGPL2. Note that the requirement to provide copies of GPL3 stems from the fact that LGPL3 is now simply a variant of that license.
- If you modify the Library, you must license the modifications under the LGPL.
- LGPL code can always be relicensed under GPL (but not vice versa).

Several new glosses have replaced the rules in LGPL3 about not restricting the combined work in ways that defeat the permissions of the license (which in version 2 largely took the form of a restriction on prohibition of reverse engineering for applications using the Library):

- Applications licensed under other terms can contain header files for the Library (Section 3). This is probably obvious, and in many languages there is no other way to use a library source file.
- If you modify the Library, and "a facility or function or data" is supplied by the Application supplied in binary form, you must "make a

good faith effort to ensure that . . . the facility still operates and performs whatever part of its purpose remains meaningful." This language is vague, but essentially means you must provide whatever information or source code is necessary to allow the licensee to exercise the rights under the LGPL to modify the Library, along with sufficient rights to use that information or source code. See the definition of "Installation Information" (in Section 6 of GPL3 on User Products) and Section 4.e for more details.

- You must permit the licensee to recombine the Application with modified versions of the Library (Section 4.d.0). In other words, your proprietary Application's license terms cannot prohibit this.

DRAWBACKS

Unfortunately, one of the most troublesome items in LGPL has been retained: the 10-line limitation on macros and inline functions (Section 3). Many engineers have commented that a 10-line limitation is both inconsistent with contemporary programming practices and impossible to police, given the workings of modern development environments. The language of the LGPL also still seems skewed toward the technical requirements of certain programming languages, such as C and Java.

Open Source Development Agreement

This form is an example of a simple consulting agreement for the open source context. It is drafted for the developer. It is provided here primarily for the provisions in Section 4.1 regarding license.

AGREEMENT FOR CONSULTING BY_____

This Agreement ("Agreement") is made and entered into as of the _____ day of _____, 200__ by and between _____ ("Consultant") a corporation organized under the laws of [_____] with offices at _____, and the party indicated in Exhibit A ("Customer"). In consideration of the mutual promises contained herein, the parties agree as follows:

1. STATEMENTS OF WORK

1.1. Statements of Work

From time to time, Customer and Consultant may agree on certain services to be performed under this Agreement, and in that case, shall prepare a statement of work in substantially the form set forth in Exhibit A ("Statement of Work"). Each Statement of Work, upon execution by both of the parties hereto, will be incorporated into this Agreement. Consultant shall perform for Customer the services ("Services") described in each Statement of Work. Customer shall perform the tasks designated as the responsibility of

Customer, if any, set forth in the statement of Work. Where Services are to be performed upon Customer's premises, Customer shall provide the following as reasonably required by Consultant at Customer's premises: office space, telephone, and high-speed Internet connections.

1.2. Lost Time

If the Statement of Work indicates any responsibilities on the part of Customer, Consultant's obligations related thereto will be subject to the complete and timely performance by Customer of Customer's responsibilities. The remainder of this Section will only apply to Services performed by Consultant pursuant to a Statement of Work on a fixed-fee basis. Any delays or additional costs incurred by Consultant during the course of a fixed-fee engagement as a result of Customer's failure to provide timely and properly the cooperation described in this Agreement ("Lost Time") shall be the responsibility of Client and payment for all Lost Time shall be made to Consultant at Consultant's then-current rates. Any payments for Lost Time will be in addition to any fixed-fee for Services. For purposes of this Agreement, "Lost Time" will include without limitation: (i) any time Consultant stands idle as a result of any failure of Customer to perform Customer's responsibilities as set forth in the applicable Statement of Work; and (ii) any time and materials expended by Consultant in an attempt to correct discrepancies in Services that are demonstrated by Consultant to the reasonable satisfaction of Customer to have been the result of an error or discrepancy in materials, technology, or information provided by Customer rather than errors of Consultant.

1.3. Acceptance Testing

This Section will only apply to Services performed by Consultant pursuant to a Statement of Work on a fixed-fee basis. For purposes of this Section, a "Milestone" is a task described in the Statement of Work to be performed by Consultant, and "Deliverable" is an item or materials to be delivered to Customer as described in the Statement of Work. Consultant will notify Customer when it believes it has completed a Milestone and will deliver to Customer the associated Deliverable. Customer will evaluate the Deliverable. Customer agrees that when it has made a finding as to whether Consultant has completed a Deliverable in accordance with the applicable specifications provided to Consultant by

Customer, it will promptly provide a written acceptance or rejection to Consultant. In the event Customer has not provided a written notice of rejection within 10 days after delivery of the Deliverable, the Deliverable will be deemed accepted. Any notice of rejection shall set forth in reasonable detail the basis for Customer's rejection. Upon receipt of a written notice of rejection, Consultant shall make commercially reasonable efforts to submit a revised deliverable within 30 days, and the Deliverable shall again be subject to the acceptance procedure described above.

2. COMPENSATION

2.1. Services

Customer shall pay Consultant for performing the Services as shown in Exhibit A.

2.2. Status Reports

Consultant shall from time to time during the term of this Agreement keep Customer advised as to Consultant's progress in performing the Services hereunder. Consultant shall, as requested by Customer, prepare written reports with respect thereto; provided however, that if the Services are performed on a time and materials basis, the time for preparing such reports will be deemed time spent performing the Services.

2.3. Expenses

Customer shall also reimburse Consultant for the reasonable actual travel and living expenses of its personnel engaged in the performance of Services at locations other than Consultant facilities, together with other reasonable out-of-pocket expenses incurred in connection with performance of the Services. Consultant shall adhere to any travel policy reasonably promulgated by Customer.

2.4. Payments

Consultant shall invoice Customer for all amounts on or after the due date. Payment terms will be net 30 days. Any amounts due Consultant under this Agreement not received by the date due will be subject to a service charge of 1% per month, or the maximum charge permitted by law, whichever is less.

3. CONFIDENTIALITY

3.1. Definition

"Confidential Information" means any Customer proprietary information, technical data, trade secrets or know-how, including, but not limited to, research, product plans, products, services, customers, customer lists, markets, software, developments, inventions, processes, formulas, technology, designs, drawings, engineering, hardware configuration information, marketing, finances, or other business information disclosed by Customer either directly or indirectly in writing, orally, or by drawings or inspection of parts or equipment.

3.2. Non-Use and Non-Disclosure

Consultant shall not, during or subsequent to the term of this Agreement, use Customer's Confidential Information for any purpose whatsoever other than the performance of the Services on behalf of Customer or disclose Customer's Confidential Information to any third party. It is understood that said Confidential Information will remain the sole property of Customer. Consultant further shall take all reasonable precautions to prevent any unauthorized disclosure of such Confidential Information including, but not limited to, having each employee of Consultant, if any, with access to any Confidential Information, execute a nondisclosure agreement containing provisions in Customer's favor identical to this Section 3. Confidential Information does not include information that: (i) is known to Consultant at the time of disclosure to Consultant by Customer as evidenced by written records of Consultant; (ii) has become publicly known and made generally available through no wrongful act of Consultant; or (iii) has been rightfully received by Consultant from a third party who is authorized to make such disclosure. Without Customer's prior written approval, Consultant shall not directly or indirectly disclose to anyone the existence of this Agreement or the fact that Consultant has this arrangement with Customer.

3.3. Return of Materials

Upon the termination of this Agreement, or upon Customer's earlier request, Consultant shall deliver to Customer all of Customer's property or Confidential Information that Consultant may have in Consultant's possession or control.

4. INTELLECTUAL PROPERTY

4.1. Deliverables

"Deliverables" means all copyrightable material, software, documentation, and other works of authorship embodied in materials delivered to Customer hereunder. Consultant will [provide the Deliverables to Customer under the terms of the open source license agreements described in Exhibit B.] [Consultant shall contribute the Software to the _____ project for release under the _____ license, version _____. To the extent that such project does not include the Software (or any portion thereof) in a public release under such license, in such a manner that Customer is able to license the Software under such terms, Consultant hereby grants to Customer, under all of Consultant's rights in and to the Software, a perpetual, irrevocable, worldwide, non-exclusive, sublicenseable license to use, copy, prepare derivative works of, publicly perform and display the Software and derivative works thereof.] Consultant shall not prosecute any patent application with respect to the Software. Consultant shall not assign to any third party the right to pursue any patent application related to the Software.

4.2. Third-Party Materials

For all materials designated as "Third–Party Materials" on Exhibit B, the parties acknowledge that such materials will be necessary for Customer to use the Deliverables, and Customer will be solely responsible for obtaining necessary licenses to the Third–Party Materials. Consultant may provide copies of the Third–Party Materials as a courtesy; however, the licenses to such materials will be as specified in Exhibit B.

4.3. Intellectual Property Claims

Each party shall, at its own expense, defend or at its option settle any claim brought against the other party on the issue of infringement of any copyright or trade secret of any third party by (in the case of Consultant) the Deliverables or (in the case of Customer) any materials provided by Customer hereunder, ("Indemnified Materials"), provided that the other party provides such party with (i) prompt written notice of such claim, (ii) control over the defense and settlement of such claim, and (iii) proper and full information and assistance to settle and/or defend any such claim. The foregoing provisions of this Section 4.3 state the entire liability and obligation of each party, and the exclusive remedy of each party, with respect to any actual or alleged infringement of any intellectual property right or breach of any intellectual property non-infringement warranty.

4.4. Warranty and Disclaimer

Consultant hereby warrants that (a) the Deliverables will not contain any virus, trap door, worm, or any other device that is injurious or damaging to software or hardware used in conjunction with the Deliverables; and (b) except as may be otherwise indicated in the applicable Statement of Work, the Deliverables are the original work of authorship of Consultant, or Consultant otherwise has the right to provide the Deliverables under the terms of this Agreement; provided, however, that the sole remedy for breach of the warranty in this subsection (b) is Consultant's indemnity obligation under Section 4.3. EXCEPT FOR THE WARRANTIES EXPLICITLY SET FORTH IN THIS AGREEMENT, NEITHER PARTY MAKES ANY REPRESENTATIONS OR WARRANTIES OF ANY KIND, WHETHER ORAL OR WRITTEN, WHETHER EXPRESS, IMPLIED, OR ARISING BY STATUTE, CUSTOM, COURSE OF DEALING OR TRADE USAGE, WITH RESPECT TO THE SUBJECT MATTER HEREOF, IN CONNECTION WITH THIS AGREEMENT. EACH PARTY SPECIFICALLY DISCLAIMS ANY AND ALL IMPLIED WARRANTIES OR CONDITIONS OF TITLE, MERCHANTABILITY, FITNESS FOR A PARTICULAR PURPOSE, AND NON-INFRINGEMENT.

5. TERM AND TERMINATION

5.1. Term

This Agreement will commence on the date first written above and will continue until final completion of the Services or termination as provided below.

5.2. Termination

Customer may terminate this Agreement or any Statement of Work without cause upon giving 10 business days prior written notice thereof to Consultant. If Customer terminates this Agreement under the prior sentence, Customer shall pay to Consultant the fees for any Services performed before the effective date of termination on a time and materials basis. If the fees for the applicable Statement of Work are to be paid on a milestone basis, such fees will not exceed the amount associated with the next uncompleted milestone. Any such notice must be addressed to Consultant at the address shown below or such other address as either party may notify the other of and will be deemed given upon delivery if personally delivered, or 48 hours after deposited in the United States mail, postage prepaid, registered or certified mail, return receipt requested. Customer may terminate this Agreement immediately and without prior notice if Consultant refuses to or is unable to perform the Services or is in breach of any material provision of this Agreement.

5.3. Survival

Upon such termination all rights and duties of the parties toward each other will cease except: (a) Customer shall pay, within 30 days after the effective date of termination, all amounts owing to Consultant for Services completed prior to the termination date and related expenses, if any, in accordance with the provisions of Section 2; and (b) Sections 3, 4, and 6 will survive termination of this Agreement.

6. MISCELLANEOUS

6.1. Non-Assignment/Binding Agreement

The parties acknowledge that the unique nature of Consultant's services are substantial consideration for the parties' entering into this Agreement. Neither this Agreement nor any rights under this Agreement may be assigned or otherwise transferred by Consultant, in whole or in part, whether voluntarily or by operation of law, without the prior written consent of Customer, which consent will not be unreasonably withheld. Subject to the foregoing, this Agreement will be binding upon and will inure to the benefit of the parties and their respective successors and assigns. Any assignment in violation of the foregoing will be null and void.

6.2. Notices

Any notice required or permitted under the terms of this Agreement or required by law must be in writing and must be (a) delivered in person, (b) sent by first class registered mail, or air mail, as appropriate, or (c) sent by overnight air courier, in each case properly posted and fully prepaid to the appropriate address set forth in the preamble to this Agreement. Either party may change its address for notice by notice to the other party given in accordance with this Section. Notices will be considered to have been given at the time of actual delivery in person, three business days after deposit in the mail as set forth above, or one (1) day after delivery to an overnight air courier service.

6.3. Waiver

Any waiver of the provisions of this Agreement or of a party's rights or remedies under this Agreement must be in writing to be effective. Failure, neglect, or delay by a party to enforce the provisions of this Agreement or its rights or remedies at any time, will not be construed as a waiver of such party's rights under this Agreement and will not in any way affect the validity of the whole or any part of this Agreement or prejudice such party's right to take subsequent action. No exercise or enforcement by either party of any right or remedy under this Agreement will preclude the enforcement by such party of any other right or remedy under this Agreement or that such party is entitled by law to enforce.

6.4. Severability

If any term, condition, or provision in this Agreement is found to be invalid, unlawful or unenforceable to any extent, the parties shall endeavor in good faith to agree to such amendments that will preserve, as far as possible, the intentions expressed in this Agreement. If the parties fail to agree on such an amendment, such invalid term, condition or provision will be severed from the remaining terms, conditions and provisions, which will continue to be valid and enforceable to the fullest extent permitted by law.

6.5. Integration

This Agreement (and all Statements of Work) contains the entire agreement of the parties with respect to the subject matter of this Agreement and supersedes all previous communications, representations, understandings and agreements, either oral or written, between the parties with respect to said subject matter. No terms, provisions or conditions of any purchase order, acknowledgment or other business form that either party may use in connection with the transactions contemplated by this Agreement will have any effect on the rights, duties or obligations of the parties under, or otherwise modify, this Agreement, regardless of any failure of a receiving party to object to such terms, provisions or conditions. This Agreement may not be amended, except by a writing signed by both parties.

6.6. Counterparts

This Agreement may be executed in counterparts, each of which so executed will be deemed to be an original and such counterparts together will constitute one and the same agreement.

6.7. Governing Law

This Agreement will be interpreted and construed in accordance with the laws of the State of [California] and the United States of America, without regard to conflict of law principles. All disputes arising out of this Agreement will be subject to the exclusive jurisdiction of the state and federal courts located in [San Francisco County, California], and each party hereby consents to the personal jurisdiction thereof.

6.8. Independent Contractors

It is the express intention of the parties that Consultant is an independent contractor. Nothing in this Agreement will in any way be construed to constitute Consultant as an agent, employee or representative of Customer, but Consultant shall perform the Services hereunder as an independent contractor. Consultant shall furnish (or reimburse Customer for) all tools and materials necessary to accomplish this contract, and will incur all expenses associated with performance, except as expressly provided on the applicable Statement of Work. Consultant acknowledges and agrees that Consultant is obligated to report as income all compensation received by Consultant pursuant to this Agreement, and Consultant acknowledges its obligation to pay all self-employment and other taxes thereon. Consultant further shall indemnify and hold harmless Customer and its directors, officers, and employees from and against all taxes, losses, damages, liabilities, costs and expenses, including attorney's fees and other legal expenses, arising directly or indirectly from (i) any negligent, reckless or intentionally wrongful act of Consultant or Consultant's assistants, employees or agents, (ii) a determination by a court or agency that the Consultant is not an independent contractor, or (iii) any breach by the Consultant or Consultant's assistants, employee or agents of any of the covenants contained in this Agreement.

6.9. Attorney's Fees

In any court action at law or equity which is brought by one of the parties to enforce or interpret the provisions of this Agreement, the prevailing party will be entitled to reasonable attorney's fees, in addition to any other relief to which that party may be entitled.

6.10. Non-Solicitation

Customer acknowledges and agrees that the employees and contractors of Consultant who perform the Services are a valuable asset to Consultant and are difficult to replace. Accordingly, Customer agrees that, for the term of this Agreement and for a period of 12 months thereafter, it will not offer employment as an employee, independent contractor, or Consultant to any Consultant employee or Consultant. In the event Customer breaches the provisions of this Section 6.10, the parties agree that it would be difficult to determine the amount of actual damages to Consultant that would result from such breach. The parties further agree that in the event Customer breaches the provisions of this Section 6.10, Customer shall pay Consultant liquidated damages of $50,000 for each such breach, which is the parties' good faith estimate of the amount of damages to Consultant from such breach.

6.11. Limitation of Remedies and Damages

THE LIABILITY OF CONSULTANT ARISING HEREUNDER WILL BE LIMITED TO FEES PAID BY CUSTOMER HEREUNDER. CONSULTANT SHALL NOT BE LIABLE FOR ANY CONSEQUENTIAL,

INCIDENTAL, OR INDIRECT DAMAGES, INCLUDING WITH-OUT LIMITATION DAMAGES FOR LOSS OF BUSINESS PROFITS AND/OR BUSINESS INTERRUPTION, WHETHER FORESEEABLE OR NOT, AND WHETHER ARISING IN CONTRACT, TORT, OR NEGLIGENCE, EVEN IF A REPRESENTATIVE OF CONSULTANT HAS BEEN ADVISED OF THE POSSIBILITY OF SUCH DAMAGES. THESE LIMITATIONS SHALL APPLY NOTWITHSTANDING ANY FAILURE OF ESSENTIAL PURPOSE OF ANY LIMITED REMEDY.

"CUSTOMER"   "CONSULTANT"

By:_____   By:_____

Print Name:_____   Print Name:_____

Title:_____   Title:_____

EXHIBIT A   STATEMENT OF WORK

Alternative 1 Sample Statement of Work with Milestone Schedule

Customer: [Fill in name and address]

Services to be performed by Consultant:

Deliverables and Milestone Schedule. Consultant shall perform the tasks set forth below (each a **"Milestone"**) in accordance with the following schedule indicating each deliverable item of work product (**"Deliverable"**), and the associated due date and payment.

Milestone Schedule

Deliverable/ Milestone	Due Date	Responsible Party (Customer or Consultant)	Payment

Alternative 2 Sample Statement of Work for Time and Materials Work

Customer: [Fill in name and address]

Services to be performed by Consultant:

Compensation of Consultant:

(a) Rate of pay: per

(b) Total payment limitation:

(c) Advance payment:

(d) Expenses authorized for reimbursement by Consultant:

(e) Other:

(f) Expected duration of project:

Consultant may revise these rates from time to time but shall give Consultant 30 days prior written notice of any such revision.

EXHIBIT B	LICENSES FOR DELIVERABLES

[Include a list of modules and licenses, or:]

All Deliverables will be provided under the **[GNU General Public License version 2, or any later version].**

Glossary

Apache. The Apache web server is one of the more successful open source projects.

Apache Foundation. The Apache Foundation is a not-for-profit organization that administers many projects including the development of the Apache web server, and stewards the Apache Software License.

BSD-style License. A permissive license containing broad grant of rights, notice provisions, and disclaimers. The OSI-approved version of the BSD license is on the OSI web site. Many licenses that constitute trivial variations of the original BSD license are referred to as BSD type licenses.

Bundle of Rights. The copyright law is typically referred to as a "bundle of rights"—specifically to reproduce, distribute, prepare derivative works, publicly perform, and publicly display.

C. The programming language developed at AT&T Bell Laboratories in connection with the development of the UNIX operating system.

Cathedral and the Bazaar, The. The seminal article written by Eric Raymond that describes the theory of the open source development model. In it, he compares the development of a proprietary software product—a cathedral designed by a single source and whose development takes place in a hierarchical fashion—and the open source software product—developed by many contributors whose suggestions compete in a "bazaar" of software development ideas.

Contribution Agreement. The agreement used by an open source project to convey rights from contributors to the project and its licensees. The model for such agreements is generally thought to be the Apache Contribution Agreement. Some projects (such as the FSF) use assignments of rights instead of licenses.

Copyleft. The conditions of the GPL, triggered by distribution, requiring the provision of source code and relicensing on GPL terms.

Copyright. The intellectual property paradigm that protects works of authorship fixed in tangible media. The United States copyright law is set forth in Title 17 of the United States Code.

CPL. The Common Public License. This license, which was approved by the Open Source Initiative, was the second corporate style hereditary license. Written by IBM to succeed the IBM Public License, its terms are similar to that of GPL, translated to a conventional drafting style.

"Cuddle" (CDDL). A license drafted primarily by Sun Microsystems, based on the Mozilla Public License, and the last license (as of 2006) approved by the Open Source Initiative. This is a corporate style hereditary license in template form.

CVS. A software development version control system popular in open source development that allows multiple developers to contribute to a code base while managing versions of the software. Other examples are Subversion, Bazaar, SVK, and Open CVS.

Derivative Work. A "derivative work" is defined in United States copyright law as "a work based upon one or more pre-existing works, such as a translation, musical arrangement, dramatization, fictionalization, motion picture version, sound recording, art reproduction, abridgment, condensation, or any other form in which a work may be recast, transformed, or adapted." Contrast a "collective work" which is a "work, such as a periodical issue, anthology, or encyclopedia, in which a number of contributions, constituting separate and independent works in themselves, are assembled into a collective whole." See 17 USC Section 101.

Distribute. Distribution is one of the enumerated rights under copyright law. See Chapter 16.

Dual Licensing. A method of software distribution that includes distribution under an open source license, usually GPL or another hereditary license, and commercial terms. The commercial terms generally include the ability to avoid the copyleft provisions of GPL—in other words, the ability to distribute copies without making source code available—and customary commercial representations, warranties, indemnities and maintenance and support terms. Dual licensing has become a very popular business model, practiced by companies such as MySQL, Sleepycat, and Trolltech. The software that is made available under the commercial licensing channel is not always identical to that available under the open source licensing channel. When it is, this is occasionally called a "pure" dual-licensing model.

Dynamic Link. A method of combining binary objects at runtime. Most software today is written in many different modules, which interface with each other through modular in standard interfaces. When creating the whole executable program that is capable of being run by the computer, the development environment needs to resolve the references from one object to another. A programmer building the program can elect that these references be resolved, and the applicable modules loaded into memory, either at the time the program is run, or when the particular module is needed. The latter is called the dynamic link. A dynamic link will be loaded into computer memory when it is requested by the program, and erased from memory when it is no longer needed. Contrast a static link.

Executable. An executable is a program that can be executed by a computer. In the Microsoft Windows operating system, executables are denoted by the file suffix ".exe"

Electronic Frontier Foundation. The Electronic Frontier Foundation is a nonprofit advocacy organization that seeks to promote the public interest in a wide variety of subjects relating to information technology. Its web site is available at http://www .eff.org/. The EFF has taken public stands and been involved in legislative and litigation matters relating to topics such as DRM, copyright term extension, and software patents.

Fair Use.   The doctrine set forth in 17 USC 107. This statute is a codification of prior case law. It contains certain defenses to copyright infringement. The exercise of a right that would ordinarily be copyright infringement is not considered unlawful if it constitutes "fair use." The calculation of whether a particular use is fair use depends on a balancing test based on four nonexclusive factors: the purpose and character of the use (including whether the use is commercial), the nature of the copyrighted work, the portion of the work used in relation to the copyrighted work as a whole, and the effect of use upon the potential market for the copyrighted work.

Free Software.   The term free software refers generally to software licensed under terms that require that the source be made freely available. There is some lack of clarity whether this term refers only to GPL software, or also to software licensed under other hereditary licenses.

Free Software Foundation.   A nonprofit organization that grew from the GNU project. The FSF stewards the general public license and engages in public advocacy regarding various issues related to software development, such as DRM, software patents, and copyright extension.

"Google Problem."   The so-called "loophole" identified by certain advocates of free software that allows companies to make changes to free software (such as Linux) and to use the modified software to make services publicly available, without being subject to the copyleft requirements of the GPL. Because no copy is distributed, the copyleft requirements of the GPL are not triggered. Despite some expectation that version 3 of GPL would close this loophole, it did not.

GPL.   The GNU General Public License (http://www.gnu.org/copyleft/gpl.html). The original free software license, stewarded by the Free Software Foundation. Version 2 was published in 1991.

Java.   A high-level programming language with syntax similar to C, written by Sun Microsystems. Java programs are executed on the Java Virtual Machine, a layer that runs in user space and causes Java programs to run on a particular operating system. Java is intended to be a "write-once-run-many" language similar to Perl. The Java Virtual Machine for many years was not open source but freeware, available free of charge in binary form. It was often confused with open source software because it is a programming language.

"Java Problem."   The question of whether standard library routines, such as the Java classes necessary to run programs on the Java platform, are subject to the copyleft requirements of GPL because they link or are otherwise integrated with programs covered by GPL. GPL version 3 addresses this issue explicitly, whereas GPL version 2 was long thought to be subject to FSF's interpretation that standard library routines need not be subject to copyleft requirements. The problem was a serious one because generally the standard library routines at issue were not owned by the same authors as the programs.

LAMP Stack.   This term refers to the use of Linux (as operating system), Apache (as web server), MySQL (as database), and PHP (as programming language). Sometimes Perl is referred to instead of PHP. All of these are open source products. The term "stack" refers to the fact that these products sit in a stack atop each other in the virtual sense; Linux is the lowest level functionality, and PHP the highest.

LGPL. The GNU Lesser (or Library) General Public License. A variation on the GPL that expressly allows the code covered by it to be used as a dynamically linked library by other code, without requiring the other code to be covered by GPL.

"Liberty or Death." The provision in GPL that provides that if a distributor cannot distribute the program free of patent encumbrances, it cannot distribute the program at all. See paragraph 7 of GPL version 2.

Linux. An operating system for small computers that was originally coded to meet the specifications of UNIX. Written originally by Linus Torvalds, it is the "killer app" of the open-source movement. The development of Linux now contains significant contributions from corporate contributors like IBM and Hewlett-Packard. It is stewarded by Linus Torvalds, and licensed under GPL version 2.

Moglen, Eben. The General Counsel of the free software foundation and a professor of law at Columbia University School of Law.

Mozilla or MPL. The first corporate style hereditary license, based on the Netscape Public License, and drafted primarily to cover the open source version of the browser originally authored by Netscape. Because it is not a template license, the MPL has been criticized by certain members of the open-source community. However, all of the corporate style hereditary licenses are heavily based on MPL.

Non-Free. Any software that is not free software.

Non-Literal Infringement. A doctrine of copyright infringement on which the law is conflicting and unclear. Copyright covers only expression and not ideas. However, certain courts have held that it is possible to infringe copyright without literally copying. The case law on this topic with respect to software is sparse, and the seminal cases on it, arising in the entertainment context, are difficult to apply to computer software scenarios.

Non-Viral. A term used to describe software licensed under permissive or nonhereditary licenses.

Object Oriented Programming (OOP). A type of computer software programming that allows the programmer to define complex data objects that may include algorithms or methods. OOP languages include Java, C++, and similar languages. The rise of OOP has led to some complexity in determining whether the interface between software modules contains merely data, or code that may be subject to copyright.

Open Source. A development model and a kind of licensing agreement. The development model refers to a model under which many contributors from the community may contribute to a single code base. The licensing model refers to software licensed under hereditary or nonhereditary agreements that makes source code freely available.

Open Source Development Laboratories (OSDL). A not-for profit entity supported by a consortium of IT companies that promotes the development and deployment of Linux-based operating systems in the enterprise. It is most famously the current sponsor of Linus Torvalds.

Open Source Initiative (OSI). The nonprofit organization that maintains the open-source certification mark and approves licenses as open source licenses. Note that the open source definition is broader than the free software definition; thus the open-source approves licenses that are both hereditary and nonhereditary.

Patent. The right to exclude third parties from exercising certain rights in technology. A patent is a non-enabling right, in the sense that its owner can only exclude third parties from practicing the right, and owning a patent does not allow the owner to exercise any right. The patent law in the United States is set forth in Title 35.

Patent Peace. A "patent peace" provision is a provision in a license that terminates a patent license if the licensee sues or threatens to sue the licensor or others for patent infringement.

Perens, Bruce. Author of the Open Source Definition and co-founder of the Open Source Initiative. See his web page at www.perens.com.

Process. A single program operating on a computer's operating system. Most modern interactive operating systems are capable of multiprocessing, or operating multiple programs at once that are activated by the user as needed.

Proprietary Software. The term used in the free software community for software that is licensed in binary form under commercial licensing terms. This is a misnomer, causing some to believe that open source software is not proprietary. However, both open source and proprietary software are subject to the proprietary rights of copyright.

Raymond, Eric. Author of "The Cathedral and the Bazaar" and co-founder of the Open Source Initiative.

Red Hat. A distributor of the Linux operating system and related software. Red Hat is a public company and arguably the most successful open source company.

Software Freedom Law Center. A nonprofit organization founded by Richard Stallman whose stated mission is to provide legal representation and other law-related services to protect and advance free and open source software. See its web site at www.softwarefreedom.org.

Source Code. The form in which software programs are written. Most software is written in a human-readable form called source code. That form is then processed through a batch computer program called a compiler, linker, or builder, which produces an executable program. The result is called binary or object code.

Stallman, Richard. Founder of the GNU project and author of the GPL. See his web site at http://www.stallman.org/.

Static Link. A method of combining binary objects at compile time. Most software today is written in many different modules, which interface with each other through modular in standard interfaces. When creating the whole executable program that is capable of being run by the computer, the development environment needs to resolve the references from one object to another. A programmer building the program can elect that these references be resolved, and the applicable modules loaded into memory, either at the time the program is first run, or when the particular module is needed. The former is called a static link. Statically linked code forms a single executable at the time the program is run, and remains in memory for the entire time the program is in operation. Contrast a dynamic link.

Steward. The author or manager of an open source license. A steward is responsible for revising the license from time to time as needed, and informally, for dealing with the community regarding its concerns about the license.

Title 17.   The codification of United States copyright law, 17 U.S.C.

Title 35.   The codification of United States patent law, 35 U.S.C.

"Tivo Problem."   The practice of distributing code covered by GPL with technical mechanisms to prevent access or modification of the code. See the chapter of this book on GPL3.

Torvalds, Linus.   The author of Linux. Torvalds wrote the first version of Linux as a teenager in Helsinki. Though still part of the open-source movement, he has also been part of various commercial business initiatives.

Trade Secret.   In the United States, a trade secret is information that is kept confidential and derives commercial value from its confidentiality. Open source software is, by definition, not trade secret. Software distributed in binary form is generally provided under commercial licensing terms that designate the source code for the software as a trade secret.

Trademark.   The trademark is a logo, business name, or brand that designates the source or origin of a product or service. When applied to services, it is called a service mark. In the United States, ownership of trademark vests when the entity applies the mark to a product or service used in commerce. The registration system in the United States is considered evidence of trademark ownership, but does not create any ownership interest in the trademark. Other countries do not follow this rule, and allow certain ownership rights to be vested as a result of registration. Although every open source project has a trademark associated with it, the parties that promulgate those projects do not always maintain control of their mark. For instance, the trademark Linux is arguably diluted to the point where its rights can no longer be enforced.

UNIX.   The large system operating system written in the 1970s for mainframe computers such as the IBM 370. UNIX was considered the first modern operating system. It was notable in that it was written in a programming language (C). Originally written by AT&T Bell Labs, it was licensed under extremely permissive terms as a result of the consent decree that applied to AT&T during the 1970s and 1980s due to antitrust enforcement. Later, when the decree was lifted, AT&T privatized UNIX, resulting in many variations, most of which were not compatible, and all of which were licensed in binary form only. It is generally thought that the free software movement is a reaction to this phenomenon.

Use.   Software licenses often grant the right to "use" although there is no such right under copyright law. There is such a right under patent law in the United States; however, the right to use is generally not thought to refer to this. In copyright licenses, the right to use generally means the right to load and execute a program on a computer. However, the word is sometimes used generically with a broader meaning.

Viral.   The pejorative term applied to hereditary licenses.

WIPO.   The World Intellectual Property Organization. WIPO is a specialized agency of the United Nations devoted to protection of intellectual property around the world. One WIPO treaty contains requirements similar to those of the DMCA prohibiting circumventions of technical measures such as DRM.

Index